Get the eBook FREE!

(PDF, ePub, Kindle, and liveBook all included)

We believe that once you buy a book from us, you should be able to read it in any format we have available. To get electronic versions of this book at no additional cost to you, purchase and then register this book at the Manning website.

Go to https://www.manning.com/freebook and follow the instructions to complete your pBook registration.

That's it!
Thanks from Manning!

Deep Learning for Search

Deep Learning for Search

TOMMASO TEOFILI

FOREWORD BY CHRIS MATTMANN

MANNING
SHELTER ISLAND

Manning Publications Co.   Development editor: Frances Lefkowitz
20 Baldwin Road   Review editor: Ivan Martinović
PO Box 761   Production editor: Tiffany Taylor
Shelter Island, NY 11964   Copy editor: Tiffany Taylor
                                  Proofreader: Katie Tennant
                                  Typesetter: Dottie Marsico
                              Cover designer: Marija Tudor

ISBN 9781617294792
Printed in the United States of America

To Mattia, Giacomo, and Michela

"Happiness is only real when shared."

—Christopher McCandless

brief contents

contents

foreword

It's hard to quantify how commonplace terms like *neural networks* and *deep learning* have become, and, more directly, how these technologies are impacting our lives. From automating routine jobs, to replicating difficult decisions, to helping cars drive themselves (and human beings) to their destinations, the power of neural networks and deep learning as techniques for revolutionizing computing is only in its nascence.

That's why this book is so material and important. Not only are neural networks, AI, and deep learning automating routine jobs and decisions and making them easier, but they are also making search easier. Formerly, the state of the art in information retrieval and search involved complex linear algebra, including matrix multiplication to represent the matching of user queries to documents. Today, instead of using algebraic and linear models, the state of the art involves—as an example—the application of neural networks to discern word similarity between documents after learning how to summarize the documents into words using separate networks. And that is only one area in the search process where AI and deep learning are being used.

Tommaso Teofili, in *Deep Learning for Search*, takes a practical approach toward showing you the state of the art in using neural networks, AI, and deep learning in the development of search engines. The book is filled with examples and walks the reader through the architecture of today's search engines—while also giving you enough background to understand how and where deep learning fits, and how it makes search better. From building your first network to find similar words in a query expansion, to learning word embeddings to help with search ranking, to searching across languages and images, Tommaso shows you where AI and deep learning can supercharge your code and search capability.

The book is written by a true pioneer of open source. Tommaso is a former chair of the Apache Lucene project—the de facto search indexing engine that powers Elasticsearch and Apache Solr—and he has also contributed greatly to language understanding and translation on Apache OpenNLP. More recently, he is the proposed chair for the Apache Joshua (incubating) project for statistical machine translation.

I know that you will learn a great deal from this book, and I commend it for finding a middle ground in common sense, explanations of complex theory, and real code that you can play with using the latest deep learning and search technologies.

Enjoy. I know I did!

—CHRIS MATTMANN
ASSOCIATE CHIEF TECHNOLOGY
AND INNOVATION OFFICER, NASA JPL

preface

The field of natural language processing bewitched me as soon as I came to know about it nearly 10 years ago, while studying for my master's degree. The promise that computers could help us understand the (already, even then) vast amount of textual documents in existence sounded like magic. I still remember how exciting it was to see my first NLP programs extract even vaguely correct and useful information from a few text documents.

About the same time, at work, I was asked to do some consulting for a customer on their new open source search architecture. My colleague, who was an expert in the field, was busy on another project, so I was given a copy of *Lucene in Action*,[1] which I studied for a couple of weeks; then I was sent out on the consulting job. A couple of years after I worked on that Lucene/Solr-based project, the new search engine went live (and, as far as I know, it's still used). I can't tell you how many times the search engine algorithms needed to be adjusted because of this or that query or this or that fragment of indexed text, but we made it work. I could see users' queries, and I could see the data that was there to be retrieved, but a minimal difference in spelling or omitting a certain word could cause very relevant information to not show up in the search results. So while I was very proud of my work, I kept wondering how I could have done better to avoid the many manual interventions the product managers asked me to perform in order to provide the best possible user experience.

Right after this, I quite by chance found myself involved in machine learning thanks to Andrew Ng's first machine learning online class (which originated the Coursera MOOC series). I was so fascinated with the concepts behind the neural networks shown in the class that I decided to try to implement a small library for neural

---

[1] Michael McCandless, Erik Hatcher, and Otis Gospodnetić (Manning, 2010), http://www.manning.com/books/lucene-in-action-second-edition.

networks in Java myself, just for fun (http://svn.apache.org/repos/asf/labs/yay/). I started hunting for other online courses like Andrej Karpathy's course on convolutional neural networks for visual recognition and Richard Socher's course on deep neural networks for natural language processing. Since then, I have kept working on search engines, natural language processing, and deep learning, mostly in open source.

A couple of years ago (!), Manning reached out to me to review a book on NLP, and I was naive enough to write at the bottom of my review that I would be interested in writing a book on search engines and neural networks. When Manning came back to me, expressing interest, I was kind of surprised, and wondered, do I *really* want to write a book on that? I realized that, yes, I was interested.

While deep learning has revolutionized computer vision and natural language processing, there's still a lot to uncover for its applications in search. I'm sure we can't (yet?) rely on deep learning to automatically set up and tune search engines on our behalf, but it can help a lot in making the search engine user's experience smoother. With deep learning, we can do things in search engines that we can't do with other existing techniques so far, and we can use deep learning to enhance the techniques we already use in search engines. The journey toward making search engines more effective through deep neural networks has just started. I hope you enjoy it.

acknowledgments

First and foremost I would like to thank my lovely wife Michela for encouraging and supporting me throughout this long journey: thanks for the love, energy, and dedication during long days, nights, and weekends of writing!

Thanks go to Giacomo and Mattia for helping me choose the coolest cover illustration possible and for all the playing and laughs while I was trying to write.

I would like to thank my father for his pride and his confidence in me.

Big thanks go to my friend Federico for his tireless effort in reviewing all the book material (book, code, images, and so on) and for the enjoyable discussions and ideas shared. More huge thanks go to my friends and colleagues Antonio, Francesco, and Simone for their support, laughs, and advice. Thanks also go to my fellow Apache OpenNLP (http://opennlp.apache.org) friends Suneel, Joern, and Koji for providing feedback, advice, and ideas that helped shape the book.

I thank Chris Mattmann for writing such an inspiring foreword.

My thanks also go to Frances Lefkowitz, my development editor, for her patience and guidance throughout the writing process, including our discussions about Steph, KD, and the Warriors. And I thank the others at Manning who made this book possible, including publisher Marjan Bace and everyone on the editorial and production teams who worked behind the scenes. In addition, I thank the technical peer reviewers led by Ivan Martinović —Abhinav Upadhyay, Al Krinker, Alberto Simões, Álvaro Falquina, Andrew Wyllie, Antonio Magnaghi, Chris Morgan, Giuliano Bertoti, Greg Zanotti, Jeroen Benckhuijsen, Krief David, Lucian Enache, Martin Beer, Michael Wall, Michal Paszkiewicz, Mirko Kämpf, Pauli Sutelainen, Simona Ruso, Srdan Dukic, and Ursin Stauss—and the forum contributors. On the technical side, thanks go to Michiel Trimpe, who served as the book's technical editor; and Karsten Strøbaek, who served as the book's technical proofreader.

Finally I'd like to thank the Apache Lucene and Deeplearning4j communities for providing such excellent tools and for supporting users in a friendly manner.

about this book

Deep Learning for Search is a practical book about how to use (deep) neural networks to help build effective search engines. This book examines several components of a search engine, providing insights on how they work and guidance on how neural networks can be used in each context. Emphasis is given to practical, example-driven explanations of search and deep learning techniques, most of which are accompanied by code. At the same time, references to relevant research papers are provided where applicable to encourage you to read more and deepen your knowledge on specific topics. Neural network and search-specific topics are explained throughout the book as you read about them.

After reading this book, you'll have a solid understanding of the main challenges related to search engines, how they are commonly addressed, and what deep learning can do to help. You'll gain a solid understanding of several different deep learning techniques and where they fit in the context of search. You'll get to know the Lucene and Deeplearning4j libraries well. In addition, you'll develop a practical attitude toward testing the effectiveness of neural networks (rather than viewing them as magic) and measuring their costs and benefits.

Who should read this book

This book is intended for readers with an intermediate programming background. It will be best if you're proficient in Java programming, with an interest or active involvement in developing search engines. You should read this book if you would like to make your search engine more effective at giving relevant results and therefore more useful for end users.

Even if you don't have a search background, basic concepts about search engines are introduced during the course of the book as each specific aspect of search is touched on. Similarly, you aren't expected to already know about machine or deep learning. This book will introduce all the required machine learning and deep learning basics, together with practical tips regarding the application of deep learning to search engines in production scenarios.

You should be ready to get your hands on the code and extend existing open source libraries to implement deep learning algorithms to solve search problems.

Roadmap

This book is divided into three parts:

- Part 1 introduces the basic concepts of search, machine learning, and deep learning. Chapter 1 introduces the rationale for applying deep learning techniques to search problems by touching on problems with respect to most common approaches to information retrieval. Chapter 2 gives a first example of how to use a neural network model to improve the effectiveness of a search engine by generating synonyms from the data.
- Part 2 deals with common search engine tasks that can be better addressed with the help of deep neural networks. Chapter 3 introduces the use of recurrent neural networks for generating queries that are alternatives to the ones entered by users. Chapter 4 addresses the task of providing better suggestions while the user is typing the query, with the help of deep neural networks. Chapter 5 focuses on ranking models: in particular, how to provide more-relevant search results using word embeddings. Chapter 6 deals with the use of document embeddings both in ranking functions and in the context of content recommendation.
- Part 3 takes up more-complex scenarios like deep learning–powered machine translation and image search. Chapter 7 guides you through giving your search engine multilanguage capabilities through neural network–based approaches. Chapter 8 deals with searching a collection of images based on their contents, empowered by deep learning models. Chapter 9 discusses production-related topics like fine-tuning deep learning models and dealing with constantly incoming streams of data.

The complexity of the topics and concepts addressed grows over the course of the book. If you're new to deep learning, search, or both, I highly recommend reading chapters 1 and 2 first. Otherwise, feel free to jump around and pick chapters based on your needs and interests.

About the code

In this book, code snippets are preferred over fully detailed code listings, in order to provide quick, easy insight into what the code is doing and how. The full source code can be found on the book's page on the Manning website: www.manning.com/books/deep-learning-for-search. The software will also be kept up to date on the book's official GitHub page (https://github.com/dl4s), including both the Java source code in the book (using Apache Lucene and Deeplearning4j: https://github .com/dl4s/dl4s) and a Python version of the same algorithms (https://github.com/ dl4s/pydl4s).

The code examples use the Java programming language and the two open source (Apache licensed) libraries Apache Lucene (http://lucene.apache.org) and Deep-learning4j (http://deeplearning4j.org). Lucene is one of the most widely used librar-ies for building search engines, and Deeplearning4j is, at the time of writing, the best choice for a native Java library for deep learning. Together, they will allow you to eas-ily, quickly, and smoothly test and experiment with search and deep learning.

In addition, many researchers working on deep learning–related projects nowa-days use Python (with frameworks like TensorFlow, Keras, PyTorch, and so on). There-fore, a Python repository hosting TensorFlow (https://tensorflow.org) versions of the algorithms detailed in the book is also provided.

In the book, source code is formatted in a `fixed-width font like this` to sepa-rate it from ordinary text. In many cases, the original source code has been reformat-ted; we've added line breaks and reworked indentation to accommodate the available page space in the book. In rare cases, even this was not enough, and listings include line-continuation markers (➥). Additionally, comments in the source code have often been removed from the listings when the code is described in the text. Code annota-tions accompany many of the listings, highlighting important concepts.

liveBook discussion forum

Purchase of *Deep Learning for Search* includes free access to a private web forum run by Manning Publications where you can make comments about the book, ask technical questions, and receive help from the author and from other users. To access the forum, go to https://livebook.manning.com/#!/book/deep-learning-for-search/ discussion. You can learn more about Manning's forums and the rules of conduct at https://livebook.manning.com/#!/discussion.

Manning's commitment to our readers is to provide a venue where a meaningful dialogue between individual readers and between readers and the author can take place. It is not a commitment to any specific amount of participation on the part of the author, whose contribution to the forum remains voluntary (and unpaid). We sug-gest you try asking the author some challenging questions lest his interest stray! The forum and the archives of previous discussions will be accessible from the publisher's website as long as the book is in print.

about the author

TOMMASO TEOFILI is a software engineer with a passion for open source and machine learning. As a member of the Apache Software Foundation, he contributes to a number of open source projects, ranging from topics like information retrieval (such as Lucene and Solr) to natural language processing and machine translation (including OpenNLP, Joshua, and UIMA).

He currently works at Adobe, developing search and indexing infrastructure components, and researching the areas of natural language processing, information retrieval, and deep learning. He has presented search and machine learning talks at conferences including BerlinBuzzwords, International Conference on Computational Science, ApacheCon, EclipseCon, and others. You can find him on Twitter at @tteofili.

about the cover illustration

The figure on the cover of *Deep Learning for Search* is captioned "Habit of a Lady of China." The illustration is taken from Thomas Jefferys' *A Collection of the Dresses of Different Nations, Ancient and Modern* (four volumes), London, published between 1757 and 1772. The title page states that these are hand-colored copperplate engravings, heightened with gum arabic.

Thomas Jefferys (1719–1771) was called "Geographer to King George III." He was an English cartographer who was the leading map supplier of his day. He engraved and printed maps for government and other official bodies and produced a wide range of commercial maps and atlases, especially of North America. His work as a map maker sparked an interest in local dress customs of the lands he surveyed and mapped, which are brilliantly displayed in this collection. Fascination with faraway lands and travel for pleasure were relatively new phenomena in the late eighteenth century, and collections such as this one were popular, introducing both the tourist as well as the armchair traveler to the inhabitants of other countries.

The diversity of the drawings in Jefferys' volumes speaks vividly of the uniqueness and individuality of the world's nations some 200 years ago. Dress codes have changed since then, and the diversity by region and country, so rich at the time, has faded away. It's now often hard to tell the inhabitants of one continent from another. Perhaps, viewing it optimistically, we've traded a cultural and visual diversity for a more varied personal life—or a more varied and interesting intellectual and technical life.

At a time when it's difficult to tell one computer book from another, Manning celebrates the inventiveness and initiative of the computer business with book covers based on the rich diversity of regional life of two centuries ago, brought back to life by Jefferys' pictures.

Part 1

Search meets deep learning

Setting up search engines to effectively react to users' needs isn't an easy task. Traditionally, many manual tweaks and adjustments had to be made to a search engine's internals to get it to work decently on a real collection of data. On the other hand, deep neural networks are very good at learning useful information about vast amounts of data. In this first part of the book, we'll start looking into how a search engine can be used in conjunction with a neural network to get around some common limitations and provide users with a better search experience.

Neural search

This chapter covers

- A gentle introduction to search fundamentals
- Important problems in search
- Why neural networks can help search engines be more effective

Suppose you want to learn something about the latest research breakthroughs in artificial intelligence. What will you do to find information? How much time and work does it take to get the facts you're looking for? If you're in a (huge) library, you can ask the librarian what books are available on the topic, and they will probably point you to a few they know about. Ideally, the librarian will suggest particular chapters to browse in each book.

That sounds easy enough. But the librarian generally comes from a different context than you do, meaning you and the librarian may have different opinions about what's significant. The library could have books in various languages, or the librarian might speak a different language. Their information about the topic could be outdated, given that *latest* is a fairly relative point in time, and you don't know when the librarian last read anything about artificial intelligence, or if the library regularly receives publications in the field. Additionally, the librarian may not understand your inquiry properly. The librarian may think you're talking about intelligence from the psychology perspective,[1] requiring a few iterations back and forth before you understand one another and get to the pieces of information you need.

Then, after all this, you might discover the library doesn't have the book you need; or the information may be spread among several books, and you have to read them all. Exhausting!

Unless you're a librarian yourself, this is what often happens nowadays when you search for something on the internet. Although we can think of the internet as a single huge library, there are many different librarians out there to help you find the information you need: search engines. Some search engines are experts in certain topics; others know only a subset of a library, or only a single book.

Now imagine that someone, let's call him Robbie, who already knows about both the library and its visitors, can help you communicate with the librarian in order to better find what you're looking for. That will help you get your answers more quickly. Robbie can help the librarian understand a visitor's inquiry by providing additional context, for example. Robbie knows what the visitor usually reads about, so he skips all the books about psychology. Also, having read a lot of the books in the library, Robbie has better insight into what's important in the field of artificial intelligence. It would be extremely helpful to have advisors like Robbie to help search engines work better and faster, and help users get more useful information.

This book is about using techniques from a machine learning field called *deep learning* (DL) to build models and algorithms that can influence the behavior of search engines, to make them more effective. Deep learning algorithms will play the role of Robbie, helping the search engine to provide a better search experience and to deliver more precise answers to end users.

One important thing to note is that DL isn't the same as *artificial intelligence* (AI). As you can see in figure 1.1, AI is a huge research field; machine learning is only part of it, and DL, in turn, is a sub-area of machine learning. Basically, DL studies how to make machines "learn" using the deep neural network computing model.

1.1 *Neural networks and deep learning*

The goal of this book is to enable you to use deep learning in the context of search engines, to improve the search experience and results. Even if you're not going to build the next Google search, you should be able to learn enough to use DL techniques within small or medium-sized search engines to provide a better experience to users. Neural search should help you automate work that you'd otherwise have to perform manually. For example, you'll learn how to automate extraction of synonyms from search engine data, avoiding manual editing of synonym files (chapter 2). This saves time while improving search effectiveness, regardless of the specific use case or

---

[1] This happened to me in real life.

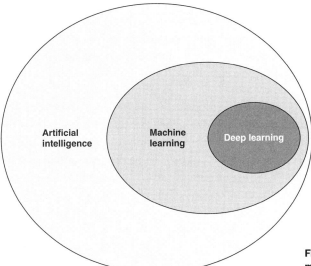

Figure 1.1 Artificial intelligence, machine learning, and deep learning

domain. The same is true for having good related-content suggestions (chapter 6). In many cases, users are satisfied with a combination of plain search together with the ability to navigate related content. We'll also cover some more-specific use cases, such as searching content in multiple languages (chapter 7) and searching for images (chapter 8).

The only requirement for the techniques we'll discuss is that they have enough data to feed into neural networks. But it's difficult to define the boundaries of "enough data" in a generic way. Let's instead summarize the minimum number of documents (text, images, and so on) that are generally needed for each of the problems addressed in the book: see table 1.1.

Table 1.1 Per-task requirements for neural search techniques

Task	Minimum number of docs (range)	Chapter
Learning word representations	1,000–10,000	2, 5
Text generation	10,000–100,000	3, 4
Learning document representations	1,000–10,000	6
Machine translation	10,000–100,000	7
Learning image representations	10,000–100,000	8

Note that table 1.1 isn't meant to be strictly adhered to; these are numbers drawn from experience. For example, even if a search engine counts fewer than 10,000 documents, you can still try to implement the neural machine translation techniques from chapter 7; but you should take into account that it may be harder to get high-quality results (for example, perfect translations).

As you read the book, you'll learn a lot about DL as well as all the required search fundamentals to implement these DL principles in a search engine. So if you're a search engineer or a programmer willing to learn neural search, this book is for you.

You aren't expected to know what DL is or how it works, at this point. You'll get to know more as we look at some specific algorithms one by one, when they become useful for solving particular types of search problems. For now, I'll start you off with some basic definitions. Deep learning is a field of machine learning where computers are capable of learning to represent and recognize things incrementally, by using deep neural networks. Deep *artificial neural networks* are a computational paradigm originally inspired by the way the brain is organized into graphs of neurons (although the brain is much more complex than an artificial neural network). Usually, information flows into neurons in an *input layer*, then through a network of hidden neurons (forming one or more *hidden layers*), and then out through neurons in an *output layer*. Neural networks can also be thought of as black boxes: smart functions that can transform inputs into outputs, based on what each network has been trained for. A common neural network has at least one input layer, one hidden layer, and one output layer. When a network has more than one hidden layer, we call the network *deep*. In figure 1.2, you can see a deep neural network with two hidden layers.

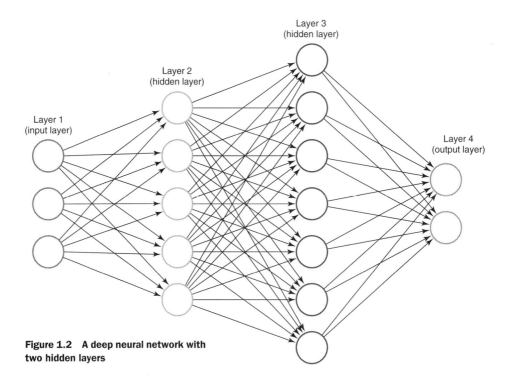

Figure 1.2   A deep neural network with two hidden layers

Before going into more detail about neural networks, let's take a step back. I said deep learning is a subfield of machine learning, which is part of the broader area of artificial intelligence. But what is machine learning?

1.2 What is machine learning?

An overview of basic machine learning concepts is useful here before diving into DL and search specifics. Many of the concepts that apply to learning with artificial neural networks, such as *supervised* and *unsupervised* learning, *training*, and *predicting*, come from machine learning. Let's quickly go over some basic machine learning concepts that we'll be using in DL (applied to search) during the course of this book.

Machine learning (ML) is an automated approach to solving problems based on algorithms that can learn optimal solutions from previous experience. In many cases, this experience comes in the form of pairs made from what has been previously observed together with what you want the algorithm to infer from it. For example, an ML algorithm can be fed text pairs, where the input is some text and the output is a category that can be used to classify similar texts. Imagine you're back in the library, but this time as the librarian; you've bought thousands of books, and you want to organize them on bookshelves so people can easily find them. To that end, you want to categorize them so that books belonging to the same category are placed close to each other on the same bookshelf (which perhaps has a small tag indicating the category). If you can spend a few hours categorizing the books manually, you'll have built the experience your ML algorithm needs. Afterward, you can train an ML algorithm based on your wise judgment, and it will do the categorization of the remaining books on your behalf.

This type of training, where you specify the desired output corresponding to each input, is called *supervised learning*. Each pair made of an input and its corresponding target output is called a *training sample*. Table 1.2 shows some of the categorizations a librarian might make manually, to help create a supervised learning algorithm.

Table 1.2 Example data for book categorization

Title	Text	Categories
Taming Text	If you're reading this book, chances are you're a programmer…	NLP, search
Relevant Search	Getting a search engine to behave can be maddening …	Search, relevance
OAuth2 in Action	If you're a software developer on the web today …	Security, OAuth
The Lord of the Rings	…	Fantasy, novels
Lucene in Action	Lucene is a powerful Java search library that lets you …	Lucene, search

A supervised learning algorithm is fed data like the kind shown in the table during what's called a *training phase*. During the training phase, an ML algorithm crunches the training set (the set of training samples) and learns how to map, for example, input text to output categories. *What* an ML algorithm learns depends on the task it's used for; in the example case, it's being used for a *document categorization* task. *How* an ML algorithm learns depends on how the algorithm itself is built. There isn't only one algorithm to perform ML; there are various subfields of ML, and many different algorithms exist for each of them.

> **NOTE** DL is just one way of doing ML, by using neural networks. But a vast number of alternatives are available when it comes to deciding which kind of neural network is best suited for a certain task. In the course of this book, we'll mostly cover ML topics via DL. Occasionally, though, we'll quickly cover other types of ML algorithms, mostly for the sake of comparison and reasoning for real-world scenarios.

Once the training phase has completed, you'll usually end up with a *machine learning model.* You can think of this as the artifact that captures what the algorithm has learned during training. This artifact is then used to perform *predictions.* A prediction is performed when a model is given a new input without any attached desired output, and you ask the model to tell you the correct output, based on what it's been learning during the training phase. Note that you need to provide a lot of data for training (not hundreds, but at least tens of thousands of training samples) if you want to obtain good results when predicting outputs.

In the book categorization example, when given the following text, the model will extract categories such as "search" and "Lucene":

```
Lucene is a powerful Java search library that lets you easily add search to
    any application ...
```

These are the opening words from *Lucene in Action, 2nd edition.*

As I mentioned, the extracted categories can be used to place books belonging to the same category on the same bookshelf in a library. Are there other ways to accomplish this, without first providing a training set with book texts labeled by category? It would be helpful if you could find a way to measure the similarity between books so that you could place similar ones near to each other without caring too much about the exact naming of each book category. To do that without categories, you can use *unsupervised learning* techniques to cluster similar documents together. In unsupervised learning, as opposed to supervised learning, an ML algorithm looks at the data with no information about any expected output and extracts patterns and data representations during the *learning phase.* During *clustering,* each piece of input data—in this case, the text of a book—is transformed into a point that's placed on a graph. During the training phase, a clustering algorithm places points in clusters, assuming that nearby points are semantically similar. After training has completed, books belonging to the same clusters can be picked up and placed on bookshelves accordingly.

In this case, the output of unsupervised learning is the set of clusters with their assigned points. Just as before, such models can be used for predictions, such as, "What cluster does this new book/point belong to?"

ML can help solve a lot of different problems, including categorizing books and grouping similar texts together. Until the early 2000s, several different techniques were used to achieve decent results when trying to address these kinds of tasks. Then DL became mainstream, not just in research labs of universities, but also in industry. Many ML problems were better resolved with DL, so DL became better known and more frequently used. The success and wide use of DL has resulted in extracting more-accurate book categories and more-accurate clustering, and many other improvements.

1.3 *What deep learning can do for search*

When deep artificial neural networks are used to help solve search problems, this field is called neural search. In this book, you'll get to know how neural networks are composed, how they work, and how they can be used in practice, all in the context of search engines.

> **Neural search**
>
> The term *neural search* is a less academic form of the term *neural information retrieval*, which first appeared during a research workshop at the SIGIR 2016 conference (www.microsoft.com/en-us/research/event/neuir2016) focused on applying deep neural networks to the field of information retrieval.

You might be wondering why we need neural search: after all, we already have good search engines on the web, and we often manage to find what we need. So what's the value proposition of neural search?

Deep neural networks are good at the following:

- Providing a representation of textual data that captures word and document semantics, allowing a machine to say which words and documents are semantically similar.
- Generating text that's meaningful in a certain context: for example, useful for creating chatbots.
- Providing representations of images that pertain not to the pixels but rather to their composing objects. This allows us to build efficient face/object-recognition systems.
- Performing machine translation efficiently.
- Under certain assumptions, approximating *any* function.[2] There's theoretically no limit to the kinds of tasks deep neural networks can achieve.

---

[2] See Kurt Hornik, Maxwell Stinchcombe, and Halbert White, "Multilayer Feedforward Networks Are Universal Approximators," *Neural Networks* 2, no. 5 (1989): 359-366, http://mng.bz/Mxg8.

This might sound a bit abstract, so let's look at how these capabilities can be useful for you as a search engineer and/or a user. Think of the major struggle points when using search engines. Most likely you'll experience concerns like these:

- I didn't get good results: I found somewhat related documents, but not the one I was looking for.
- It took me too much time to find the information I was looking for (and then I gave up).
- I had to read through some of the provided results before getting a good understanding of the topic I wanted to learn about.
- I was looking for content in my native language, but I could find good search results only in English.
- I was looking for a certain image I had once seen on a website, but I couldn't find it again.

Such problems are common, and various solutions exist to mitigate each of them. But the exciting thing is that deep neural networks, if tailored properly, can help in all these cases.

With the help of DL algorithms, a search engine is able to

- Provide more-relevant results to its end users, increasing user satisfaction.
- Search through binary content like images the same way we search text. Think of this as being able to search for an image with the phrase "picture of a leopard hunting an impala" (and you're not Google).
- Serve content to users speaking different languages, allowing more users to access the data in the search system.
- Generally become more sensitive to the data it serves, which means less chance for queries that give no results.

If you've ever worked on designing, implementing, or configuring a search engine, you've surely faced the problem of obtaining a solution that adapts to your data. DL will help a lot in providing solutions to these problems that are accurately based on your data, not on fixed rules or algorithms.

The quality of search results is crucial for end users. There's one thing a search engine should do well: find out which of the possibly matching search results would be most useful for a specific user's information needs. Well-ranked search results allow users to find important results more easily and quickly; that's why we put a lot of emphasis on the topic of *relevant results*. In real life, this can make a huge difference. According to an article published in *Forbes*, "By providing better search results, Netflix estimates that it is avoiding canceled subscriptions that would reduce its revenue by $1B annually."[3] Deep neural networks can help by automatically tweaking the end user query under the hood based on past user queries or based on the search engine contents.

---

[3] Louis Columbus, "McKinsey's State of Machine Learning and AI, 2017," July 9, 2017, http://mng.bz/a7KX.

People today are used to working with web search engines to retrieve images. If you search for "pictures of angry lions" on Google, for instance, you'll get strongly relevant images. Before the advent of DL, such images had to be decorated with *metadata* (data about data) describing their contents before being put into the search engine. And that metadata usually had to be typed by a human. Deep neural networks can abstract a representation of an image that captures what's in there so that no human intervention is required to put an image description in the search engine.

For scenarios like web search (searching over all the websites on the internet), users can come from all over the world, so it's best if they can search in their native languages. Additionally, the search engine could pick user profiles and return results in their language even if they search in English; this is a common scenario for tech queries, because lots of content is produced in English. An interesting application of deep neural networks is called *neural machine translation*, a set of techniques that use deep neural networks to translate a piece of text from a source language into another target language.

Also exciting is the possibility of using deep neural networks to change the way search engines return relevant information to end users. Most commonly, a search engine will give a list of search results in response to a search query. DL techniques can be used to let the search engine return a single piece of text that should give all the information needed by a user.[4] This would save users from looking at each and every result to get all the knowledge they required. We could even aggregate all of these ideas and build a search engine serving both text and images seamlessly to users from all over the world, which, instead of returning search results, returns the single piece of text or image the user needs.

These applications are all examples of *neural search.* As you can imagine, they have the potential to revolutionize the way we work and use search engines today.

There are many possibilities for how computers can help people obtain the information they need. Neural networks have been discussed for the past few years, but only recently have they become so popular; that's because researchers have discovered how to make them much more effective than they used to be. In the early 2000s, for example, adding the help of more-powerful computers was a key advance. To take advantage of all the potential of deep neural networks, people interested in computer science—especially in the fields of natural language processing, computer vision, and informational retrieval—will need to know how such artificial neural networks work in practice.

This book is intended for people interested in building smart search engines with the help of DL. This doesn't necessarily mean you're going to build the next Google search. It could mean making use of what you learn here to design and implement an efficient, effective search engine for your company, or expanding your knowledge base to apply DL techniques in larger projects that may include web search engines.

---

4   Christina Lioma et al., "Deep Learning Relevance: Creating Relevant Information (As Opposed to Retrieving It)," June 27, 2016, https://arxiv.org/pdf/1606.07660.pdf.

The goal here is to enrich your skill set around search engines and DL, because these skills can be useful in numerous contexts. For example:

- Training a deep neural network to learn to recognize objects in images and use what the neural network has learned when searching for images
- Using neural networks to populate a "related content" bar in a search engine's search results list
- Training neural networks to learn to make the user query more specific (fewer but better search results) or broader (more search results, even if some may be less relevant)

1.4   A roadmap for learning deep learning

We'll run our neural search examples on top of open source software written in Java with the help of Apache Lucene (http://lucene.apache.org), an information retrieval library; and Deeplearning4j (http://deeplearning4j.org), a DL library. But we'll focus as much as possible on principles rather than implementation, in order to make sure the techniques explained in this book can be applied with different technologies and/or scenarios. At the time of writing, Deeplearning4j is a widely used framework for DL in the enterprise communities; it's part of the Eclipse Foundation. It also has good adoption because of integration with popular big data frameworks like Apache Spark. Full source code accompanying this book can be found at www.manning.com/ books/deep-learning-for-search and on GitHub at https://github.com/dl4s/dl4s. Other DL frameworks exist, though; for example, TensorFlow (from Google) is popular among the Python and research communities. Almost every day, new tools are invented, so I decided to focus on a relatively easy-to-use DL framework that can be easily integrated with Lucene, which is one of the most widely adopted search libraries for the JVM. If you're working with Python, you can find TensorFlow implementations of most of the DL code used in this book together with some instruction on GitHub at https://github.com/dl4s/pydl4s.

While planning this book, I decided to present chapters in a kind of ascending level of difficulty, so each chapter will teach a certain application of neural networks to a specific search problem, supported by well-known algorithms. We'll keep an eye on state-of-the-art DL algorithms, but we're also quietly conscious that we can't cover everything. The aim is to provide good baselines that can be easily extended if a new and better neural network-based algorithm comes out next week. Key things we'll improve with the help of deep neural networks are relevance, query understanding, image search, machine translation, and document recommendation. Don't worry if you don't know about any of these: I'll introduce such tasks as they exist without any DL technique and then show when and how DL can help.

In part 1 of this book, I'll present an overview of how neural networks can help to improve search engines in general. I'll do this first with an application where neural networks help the search engine build multiple versions of the same query by generating synonyms. In part 2 of the book, we'll mostly examine DL-based techniques to make search queries more expressive. This improved expressiveness will make the queries better fit user intent, and thus make the search engine return better (more relevant) results. Finally, in part 3 of the book, we'll work on more-complex things like searching over multiple languages and searching for images, and finally address performance aspects of neural search systems.

Along the way, we'll also pause to consider accuracy and how to measure the final results when we apply neural search. Without numbers constantly demonstrating what we think is good, we won't go far. We need to measure how good our systems are, with and without fancy neural nets.

In this chapter, we'll start with a look at the problems search engines try to solve and the most common techniques used to solve them. This survey will introduce you to the basics of how text is analyzed, ingested, and retrieved within a search engine, so you'll get to know how queries hit search results, as well as some fundamentals of solving the problem of returning relevant results first. We'll also uncover some weaknesses inherent in common search techniques, which sets up a discussion of what DL can be used for in the context of search. Then we'll look at which tasks DL can help to solve and what the practical implications are of its applications in the search field. This will help paint a realistic picture of what you can and can't expect from neural search in real-life scenarios.

1.5 *Retrieving useful information*

Let's start by learning how to retrieve search results that are relevant to users' needs. This will give you the search fundamentals you need to understand how deep neural networks can help build innovative search platforms.

First question: what is a search engine? It's a system, a program running on a computer, that people can use to retrieve information. The main value of a search engine is that whereas it ingests "data," it's expected to provide "information." This goal means the search engine should do its best to make sense of the data it gets in order to provide something that can be easily consumed by its users. As users, we rarely need lots of data about a certain topic; we're often looking for a specific piece of information and would be satisfied with just *one* answer, not hundreds or thousands of results to inspect.

When it comes to search engines, most people tend to think to Google, Bing, Baidu, and other large, popular search engines that provide access to huge amounts of information coming from a lot of diverse sources. But there are also many smaller search engines that focus on content from a specific domain or topic. These are often called *vertical search engines* because they work on a constrained set of document types or topics, rather than the entire set of content that is online nowadays. Vertical search engines play an important role, too, because they're often able to provide more-precise results about "their" data—because they've been tailored to that specific content. They often allow us to retrieve more-fine-grained results with higher accuracy (think of searching for an academic article on Google versus using Google Scholar).

(For now, we won't go into the details of what *accuracy* means; here, I'm talking about the general concept of the accuracy of an answer to an inquiry. But accuracy is also the name of a well-defined measure used to evaluate how good and precise an information retrieval system's results are.) We'll make no distinction at this point about the size of the data and user base, because all the concepts that follow apply to most of the existing search engines no matter how big or small.

Key responsibilities of a search engine usually involve the following:

- *Indexing*—Ingesting and storing data efficiently so that it can be retrieved quickly
- *Querying*—Providing retrieval functionality so that search can be performed by an end user
- *Ranking*—Presenting and ranking the results according to certain metrics to best satisfy users' information needs

A key point in practice is also *efficiency*. If it takes too much time to get the information you're looking for, it's likely you'll switch to another search engine next time.

But how does a search engine work with pages, books, and similar kinds of text? In the following sections, you'll get to know

- How big chunks of text are split into smaller pieces for the search engine to take a given query and quickly retrieve a document
- Basics of how to capture the importance and relevance of search results, for a particular query

Let's start with the fundamentals of information retrieval (indexing, querying, and ranking). Before diving into that, you need to understand how big streams of texts end up in a search engine; this is important, because it impacts the search engine's capabilities of searching fast and providing sensitive results.

1.5.1   *Text, tokens, terms, and search fundamentals*

Put yourself in the shoes of the librarian, who has just received an inquiry for books related to a certain topic. How would you be able to say that one book contains information about a certain topic? How would you know if a book even contains a certain word?

Extracting the categories a certain book belongs to (high-level topics like "AI" and "DL") is different from extracting all the words contained in the book. For example, categories make searching for a book about AI easier for a newbie, because no prior knowledge of AI-specific techniques or authors is required. A user will go to the search engine website and start browsing between the existing categories and look for something that's close enough to the topic of AI. On the other hand, for an AI expert, knowing whether a book contains the words *gradient descent* or *backpropagation* allows results to be found that contain finer-grained information about certain techniques or problems in the field of AI.

Humans generally have a hard time remembering all the words contained in a book, although we can easily tell a book's topic by reading a few paragraphs from the book or even from looking at the preface or foreword. Computers tend to behave the opposite way. They can easily store large amounts of text and "remember" all the words contained in millions of pages so that they can be used while searching; on the other hand, they aren't so good at extracting information that's implicit, scattered, or not directly formulated in a given piece of text, such as which category a book belongs to. For example, a book about neural networks may never mention "artificial intelligence" (although it would probably refer to ML). But it would still belong to the broad category of "books about artificial intelligence."

Let's first look at the task computers can do well already: extracting and storing text fragments (also known as *terms*) from streams of text. You can think of this process, called *text analysis*, as breaking down the text of a book into all of its constituent words. Imagine having a tape on which the contents of a book are written in a stream, and a machine (the text analysis algorithm) into which you insert such tape as input. You receive many pieces of such tape as output, and each of those output pieces contains a word or a sentence or a noun phrase (for example, "artificial intelligence"); you may realize that some of the words written on the input tape have been eaten by the machine and not outputted in any form.

Because the final units to be created by the text analysis algorithm might be words but also might be group of words or sentences, or even portions of words, we refer to these fragments as terms. You can think of a term as the fundamental unit that a search engine uses to store data and, consequently, retrieve it.

That's the basis of one of the most fundamental forms of search, *keyword search*: a user types a set of words and expects the search engine to return all the documents that contain some or all of the terms. This is how web search started decades ago. Although many search engines today are much smarter, many users keep composing queries based on the keywords they expect the search results to contain. This is what you'll learn now: how the text entered by a user into a search box makes the search engine return results. A *query* is what we call the text the user enters in order to search for something. Although a query is just text, it conveys and encodes what the user needs and how the user expresses this possibly general or abstract need (for example, "I want to learn about the latest and greatest research in the field of artificial intelligence") in a way that's concise but still descriptive (for example, "latest research in ai," as in figure 1.3).

If, as a user, you want to find documents that contain the word "search," how would the search engine return such documents? A not-so-smart way of doing that could be to go over each document's content from the beginning and scan it until the search engine finds a match. But it would be very expensive to perform such text scans for each query, especially with many large documents:

- Many documents may not contain the word "search"; therefore, it would be a waste of computation resources to scan through them.
- Even if a document contains the word "search," this word may occur toward the end of the document, requiring the search engine to "read" through all the preceding words before finding a match for "search."

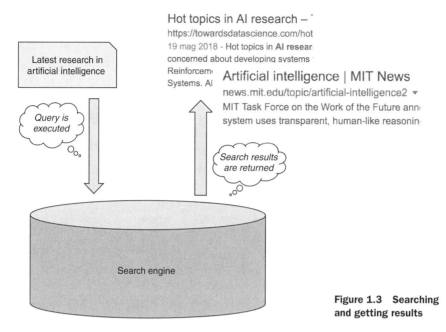

Figure 1.3   Searching and getting results

You have a *match* or a *hit* when one or more *terms* that are part of a query are found in a search result.

You need to find a way to compute this retrieval phase quickly. One fundamental method to accomplish that is to break down sentences like "I like search engines" into smaller units: in this case, ["I", "like", "search", "engines"]. This is a prerequisite for efficient storage mechanisms called *inverted indexes,* which we'll cover in the next section. A text analysis program is often organized as a pipeline: a chain of components, each of which takes the previous component's output as its input. Such pipelines are usually composed of building blocks of two types:

- *Tokenizers*—Components that break a stream of text into words, phrases, symbols, or other units called *tokens*
- *Token filters*—Components that accept a stream of tokens (from a tokenizer or another filter) and can modify, delete, or add new tokens

The output of such text analysis pipelines is a sequence of consecutive terms, as shown in figure 1.4.

You now know that text analysis is useful for performance reasons to build fast search engines. Another equally important aspect is that it controls how queries and the text to be put into the index match. Often, text analysis pipelines are used to filter

Figure 1.4   Getting the words of "I like search engines" using a simple text analysis pipeline

some tokens that aren't considered useful or needed for the search engine. For example, a common practice is to avoid storing common terms like articles or prepositions in the search engine, because those words exist in most text documents in languages like English, and you usually don't want a query to return everything in the search engine: that wouldn't give much value to the user. In such cases, you can create a token filter responsible for removing tokens like "the," "a," "an," "of," "in," and so on, while letting all the other tokens flow out as the tokenizer produces them. In this simplistic example,

- The tokenizer will split tokens every time it encounters a whitespace character.
- The token filter will remove tokens that match a certain blacklist (also known as a *stopword list*).

In real life, it's common, especially when setting up a search engine for the first time, to build several different text analysis algorithms and try them on the data you want to put into the search engine. This allows you to visualize how content will be handled by such algorithms, such as which tokens are generated, which ones eventually are filtered out, and so on. You've built this text analysis chain (also called an *analyzer*) and want to make sure it works as expected and filters articles, prepositions, and so forth. Let's try to pass a first piece of text to the simplistic analyzer and submit the sentence "the brown fox jumped over the lazy dog" to the pipeline; you expect articles to be removed. The generated output stream will look like figure 1.5.

Figure 1.5 The traversed token graph

The resulting token stream has "the" tokens removed, as expected; you can see that from the dotted arrows at the start of the graph and between the nodes "over" and "lazy." The numbers beside the tokens represent the starting and ending positions (in number of characters) of each token. The important bit of this example is that a query for "the" won't match, because the analyzer has removed all such tokens, and they won't end up being part of the search engine contents. In real life, text analysis pipelines are often more complex; you'll see some of them in the following chapters. Now that you've learned about text analysis, let's see how search engines store the text (and terms) to be queried by end users.

INDEXING

Although the search engine needs to split text into terms for the sake of fast retrieval, end users expect search results to be in the form of a single unit: a document. Think about search results from Google. If you search for "books," you'll receive a list of results, each composed of a title, a link, a text snippet of the result, and so on. Each of those results contains the term "books," but what's shown is a document that has lot more information and context than just the text snippet where the term matched. In practice, tokens resulting from text analysis are stored with a reference to the original piece of text they belong to.

This link between a term and a document makes it possible to

- Match a keyword or search term from a query
- Return the referenced original text as a search result

This whole process of analyzing streams of text and storing the resulting terms (along with their referenced documents) in the search engine is usually referred to as *indexing*.

The reason for such wording is that terms are stored in an *inverted index*: a data structure that maps a term into the text that originally contained it. Probably the easiest way to look at it is as the analytic index of an actual book, where each word entry points to the pages where it's mentioned; in the case of the search engine, the words are the terms and the pages are the original pieces of text.

From now on, we'll refer to the pieces of text to be indexed (pages, books) as *documents*. In order to visualize how documents end up after being indexed, let's assume you have the following two very similar documents:

- "the brown fox jumped over the lazy dog" (document 1)
- "a quick brown fox jumps over the lazy dog" (document 2)

Assuming you use the text analysis algorithm defined earlier (whitespace tokenization with stop words "a," "an," and "the"), table 1.3 shows a good approximation of an inverted index containing such documents.

As you can see, there's no entry for the term "the" because the stopword-based token filter has removed such tokens. In the table, you can find the dictionary of terms in the first column and a *posting list*—a set of document identifiers—associated with each term for each row. With inverted indexes, retrieval of documents that contain a given term is very fast: the search engine picks the inverted index, looks for an entry for the search term, and eventually

Table 1.3   Inverted index table

Term	Document IDs
brown	1, 2
fox	1, 2
jumped	1
over	1, 2
lazy	1, 2
dog	1, 2
quick	2
jumps	1

retrieves the documents contained in the posting list. With the example index, if you search for the term "quick," the inverted index will return document 2 by looking into the posting list corresponding to the term "quick." We've just gone through a quick example of indexing text into a search engine.

Let's think about the steps that go into indexing a book. A book is composed of pages, the core content, but it also has a title, an author, an editor, a publication year, and so on. You can't use the same text analysis pipeline for everything; you wouldn't want to remove "the" or "an" from a book title. A user knowing a book's title should be able to find it by exact matching it! If the text analysis chain removes "in" from the book title *Tika in Action*, a query for "Tika in action" won't find it. On the other hand, you may want to avoid keeping such tokens for the book contents so you have a text analysis pipeline that's more aggressive in filtering unwanted terms. If the text analysis chain removes "in" and "the" from the book title *Living in the Information Age*, it shouldn't be problematic: it's very unlikely that a user will search for "Living in the Information Age," but they may search for "information age." In this case, there's little or no loss of information, but you get the benefit of storing smaller texts and, more important, improving relevance (we'll talk about this in the next section). A common approach in real life is to have multiple inverted indexes that address indexing of different parts of a document, all within the same search engine.

SEARCHING

Now that we have some content indexed in the search engine, we'll look at searching. Historically, the first search engines allowed users to search with specific terms, also known as *keywords*, and, eventually, Boolean operators that let users determine which terms *must* match, *must not* match, or *can* match in the search results. Most commonly, a term in a query *should* match, but that isn't mandatory. If you want search results that must contain such a term, you must add the relevant operator: for example, using + in front of the term. A query like "deep +learning for search" requires results that contain both "deep" and "learning" and optionally contain "for" and "search." It's also common to allow users to specify that they need entire phrases to match, instead of single terms. That allows users to search for an exact sequence of words instead of single terms. The previous query could be rephrased as ""deep learning" for search," in order to return search results that must contain the sequence "deep learning" and optionally the terms "for" and "search."

It may sound surprising, but text analysis is also important during the search, or *retrieval*, phase. Suppose you want to search for this book, *Deep Learning for Search*, on top of the data you just indexed; assuming you have a web interface, you'd probably type a query like "deep learning for search." The challenge in this retrieval phase is to make it possible to retrieve the right book. The first thing that sits between a user and a classic search engine UI is a *query parser*.

A query parser is responsible for transforming the text of the search query entered by the user into a set of clauses that indicate which terms the search engine should look for and how to use them when looking for a match in the inverted indexes. In the previous query examples, the query parser would be responsible for making sense of the symbols + and ". Another widespread syntax allows you to put Boolean operators among query terms: "deep AND learning." In this case, the query parser will give a special meaning to the "AND" operator: terms to the left and right of it are mandatory. A query parser can be thought as a function that takes some text and outputs a set of constraints to apply to the underlying inverted index(es) in order to find results. Let's again pick an example query like "latest research in artificial intelligence." A smart query parser would create clauses that reflect the semantics of words; for example, instead of having two clauses for "artificial" and "intelligence," it should create only one clause for "artificial intelligence." In addition, probably the term "latest" isn't to be matched; you don't want results containing the word "latest"; you instead want to retrieve results that have been "created" recently. So a good query parser would transform the "latest" term into a clause that can be expressed, for example, like "created between today and 2 months ago" in natural language. The query engine would encode such a clause in a way that's more easily handled by a computer, such as `created < today() AND created > (today() - 60days)`; see figure 1.6.

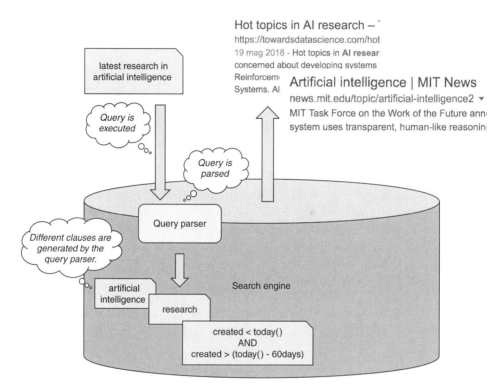

Figure 1.6   Query parsing

During indexing, a text analysis pipeline is used to split the input text into terms to be stored in the index; this is also called *index-time text analysis*. Similarly, text analysis can be applied during search on the query in order to break the query string into terms; this is therefore called *search-time text analysis*. A document is retrieved by the search engine when the search-time terms match a term in the inverted index referenced by that doc.

Figure 1.7 shows an index-time analysis on the left, which is used to split a document text into terms. These end up in the index, all referencing *doc 1*. The index-time analysis is composed of a whitespace tokenizer and two token filters: the former is used to remove unwanted stopwords (like "the"), and the latter is used to convert all the terms into lowercase (for example, "Fox" gets converted to "fox"). At upper right, the query "lazy foxes" is passed to the search-time analysis, which splits tokens using a whitespace tokenizer but filters using a lowercase filter and a *stemming* filter. A stemming filter transforms terms by reducing inflected or derived words to their root form; this means removing plural suffixes, *ing* form in verbs, and so on. In this case, "foxes" is transformed into "fox."

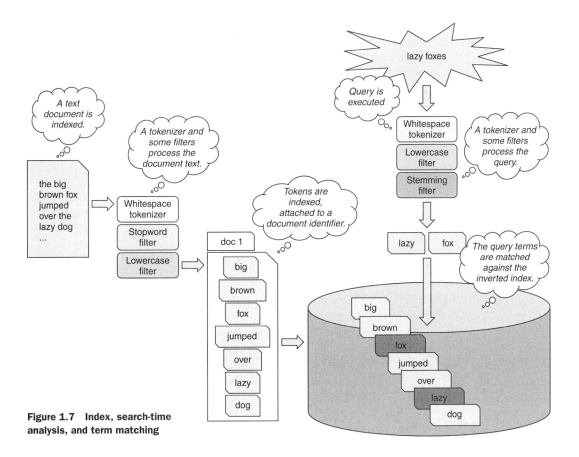

Figure 1.7   Index, search-time analysis, and term matching

A common way to verify that indexing and search text analysis pipelines work as expected is to follow these steps:

1 Take sample content.
2 Pass the content to the index-time text analysis chain.
3 Take a sample query.
4 Pass the query to the search-time text analysis chain.
5 Check whether the produced terms match.

For example, it's common to have stopword filters at indexing time, because performing the filtering then won't have any performance impact on the retrieval phase. But it may be possible to have other filters within either the indexing or search phases. With index- and search-time text analysis chains and query parsing in place, we can look at how the process of retrieving search results works.

You've learned one of the basic techniques at the core of every search engine: text analysis (tokenization and filtering) allows the system to break down text into the terms you expect users to type at query time and place them into a data structure called an inverted index, which allows efficient storage (space-wise) and retrieval (time-wise). As users, however, we don't want to look into all the search results, so we need search engine to tell us which ones are supposed to be the best. Now, you may be wondering, what does *the best* mean? Is there a measure of how good a piece of information is, given our queries? The answer is yes: we call such a measure *relevance*. Ranking search results in an accurate way is one of the most important tasks a search engine has to accomplish. In the next section, we'll have a brief look at how to address the problem of relevance.

1.5.2   *Relevance first*

You now know how search engines retrieve a document, given a query. In this section, you'll learn how search engines rank the search results so that the most important results are returned first. This will give you a solid understanding of how common search engines work.

Relevance is a key concept in search; it's a measure of how important a document is with respect to a certain search query. As humans, it's often easy for us to tell why certain documents are more relevant than others with respect to a query. So, in theory, we could try to extract a set of rules to represent our knowledge about ranking the importance of a document. But in practice, such an exercise would probably fail:

- The amount of information we have doesn't allow us to extract a set of rules applicable to most of the documents.
- Documents in the search engine change a lot over time, and it's a huge effort to keep adjusting the rules accordingly.
- Documents in the search engine can belong to diverse domains (for example, in web search), and it's not possible to find a good set of rules that works for all types of information.

One of the central themes in the field of information retrieval is to define a model that doesn't require a search engineer to extract such rules. Such a *retrieval model* should capture the notion of relevance as accurately as possible. Given a set of search results, a retrieval model will *rank* each of them: the more relevant the result, the higher its score.

Most of the time, as a search engineer, you won't get perfect results by just choosing a retrieval model; relevance is a capricious beast! In real-life scenarios, you may have to continuously adjust your text analysis pipelines, as well as the retrieval model, and possibly make some fine-grained tuning to the search engine internals. But retrieval models help a lot by providing a solid baseline to obtain good relevance.

1.5.3   *Classic retrieval models*

Probably one of the most commonly used information retrieval models is the *vector space model* (VSM).[5] In this model, each document and query is represented as a vector. You can think of a vector as an arrow in a coordinate plane; each arrow in VSM can represent a query or a document. The closer two arrows are, the more similar they are (see figure 1.8); each arrow's direction is defined by the terms that compose the query/document.

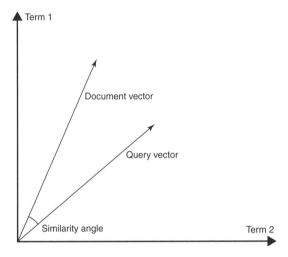

Figure 1.8   Similarities between document and query vectors according to VSM

In such a vector representation, each term is associated with a *weight*: a real number that tells how important that term is in that document/query with respect to the rest of the documents in the search engine. Such weights can be calculated in various ways. At this point, we won't go too deep into the details of how these weights are calculated; I'll mention that the most common algorithm is called *term frequency–inverse document frequency* (TF-IDF). The basic idea behind TF-IDF is that the more frequently a term appears in a single document (term frequency, or TF) the more important it is. At the same time, it states that the more common a term is among all the documents, the less important it is (*inverse document frequency*, or IDF). So in VSM, search results are ranked with respect to the query vector, so documents appear higher in the results list (get a higher rank/score) if they're closer to such query vector.

Whereas VSM is an information retrieval model based on linear algebra, over the years alternate approaches based on probabilistic relevance models have emerged. Instead of calculating how near a document and a query vector are, a probabilistic model ranks search results based on an estimate of the probability that a document is relevant to a certain query. One of the most common ranking functions for such

---

[5] See G. Salton, A. Wong, and C. S. Yang, "A vector space model for automatic indexing," *Communications of the ACM* 18, no. 11 (1975): 613-620, http://mng.bz/gNxG.

models is *Okapi BM25*. We won't dive into its details, but it has shown good results, especially on texts that aren't very long.

1.5.4   *Precision and recall*

We'll look into how neural search can help address relevance in future chapters, but first we need to be able to measure relevance! A standard way of measuring how well an information retrieval system is doing is to calculate its precision and recall. *Precision* is the fraction of retrieved documents that are relevant. If a system has high precision, users will mostly find results they're looking for at the top of the list of search results. *Recall* is the fraction of relevant documents that are retrieved. If a system has a good recall, users will find all results relevant for them in the search results, although they might not all be among the top results.

As you may have noticed, measuring precision and recall requires someone to judge how relevant search results are. In small-scale scenarios, that's an addressable task; but the effort required makes it hardly doable for huge collections of documents. An option to measure the effectiveness of search engines is to use publicly available datasets for information retrieval, like the ones from the National Institute of Standards and Technology (NIST) Text REtrieval Conference (also known as TREC[6]), which contain lots of ranked queries to be used for testing precision and recall.

In this section, you've learned some basics of classic information retrieval models like VSM and probabilistic models. We're now going to examine common issues that affect search engines. The rest of the book will discuss how to fix them with the help of DL.

1.6   *Unsolved problems*

We've had a closer look at how a search engine works, in particular how it strives to retrieve information relevant to the end user's needs. But let's take a step back and try to see the problem from the perspective of how, as users, we use search engines every day. We'll examine some of the problems that remain unresolved in many search scenarios, in order to better understand which issues we can hope to solve with the help of DL.

Filling a knowledge gap, as opposed to retrieving information, is a slightly more complex topic. Let's again take the example of going to a library, because you want to know more about interesting recent research in the field of AI. As soon as you meet the librarian, you have a problem: how do you get the librarian to accurately understand what you need and what would be useful to you?

Although this sounds simple, the usefulness of a piece of information is hardly objective, but instead is rather subjective and based on context and opinion. You may assume that a librarian has enough knowledge and experience that what you receive is good. In real life, you would probably talk to the librarian to introduce yourself and

---

[6]   See http://trec.nist.gov/data.html.

share information about your background and why you need something; that would allow the librarian to use such context in order to

- Exclude some books before even trying to search
- Discard some books after having found them
- Explicitly search in one or more areas that have a closer relation to your context (for example, coming from academia versus industry sources)

You'll be able to give feedback on the books given to you by the librarian afterward, although sometimes you can express concerns based on past experiences (for example, you don't like books written by a certain author, so you advise the librarian to explicitly not consider them). Both context and opinion can vary considerably and consequently influence the relevance of information over time and among different people. How does a librarian cope with this mismatch?

You as a user may not know the librarian, or at least not well enough to understand their context. The librarian's background and opinions are important because they influence the results you get. Therefore, the better you understand the librarian, the faster you'll get your information. So you need to know your librarian in order to get good results!

What if the librarian gives you a book about "deep learning techniques" in response to your first inquiry about "artificial intelligence"? If you don't know the subject, you need to make a second inquiry about "an introduction to what deep learning is" and whether there's a good book about it in the library. This process can repeat a number of times; the key thing to understand is that information is flowing incrementally—you don't upload stuff into your brain the way characters do in *The Matrix*. Instead, if you want to know something about AI, you may realize you need to know a bit about DL first, and, for that, you discover you need to read about calculus and linear algebra, and so on. In other words, you don't know all of what you need when you first ask.

To sum up, the process of getting the information you're looking for from the librarian has some flaws, caused by these situations:

- The librarian doesn't know you.
- You don't know the librarian.
- You may need a few iterations in order to get everything you need.

It's important to identify these issues, because we want to use deep neural networks to help us build better search engines that can be more easily used—and we'd like DL to help fix those problems. Understanding these issues is the first step toward resolving them.

1.7 *Opening the search engine black box*

Now let's try to understand how much of what the search engine is doing users can see. A crucial issue in creating effective search queries is which query language you use. Some years ago, you would enter one or more keywords in a search box to perform a query. Today, technology has evolved to the point that you can type queries in natural language. Some search engines index documents in multiple languages (for example, for web search) and allow subsequent querying. If you search for the same thing but express it with slightly different queries in a search engine like Google, you'll observe surprisingly different results.

Let's run a little experiment to see how search results change when the same request is expressed using different queries. If you were talking to a human and asking the same question in different ways, you'd expect to always get the same kind of answer. For example, if you ask someone, "What are the 'latest *breakthroughs* in artificial intelligence,' in your opinion?" you'll get an answer based on their opinion. If you ask that same person, "What are the 'latest *advancements* in artificial intelligence,' in your opinion?" you'll likely get exactly the same answer, or one that's semantically equivalent.

Today, this often isn't the case with search engines. Table 1.4 shows the results of searching for "latest breakthroughs in artificial intelligence" and some variants on Google.

Table 1.4   Comparing similar queries

Query	First result title
Latest breakthroughs in artificial intelligence	Academic papers for "latest breakthroughs in artificial intelligence" (Google Scholar)
Latest advancements in artificial intelligence	Google advancements artificial intelligence push with 2 top hires
Latest advancements on artificial intelligence	Images related to "latest advancements on artificial intelligence" (Google Images)
Latest breakthroughs in AI	Artificial Intelligence News—ScienceDaily
Più recenti sviluppi di ricerca sull'intelligenza artificiale	Intelligenza Artificiale (Wikipedia)

Although the first result of the first query isn't surprising, changing the term "breakthroughs" to one of its synonyms ("advancements") produces a different result, which seems to suggest that the search engine has a different understanding of the information needed: you weren't looking into how Google is improving AI! The third query gives a surprising result: images! We have no real explanation for this. Changing "artificial intelligence" to its acronym, "AI," leads to a different, but still relevant, result. And when you use the Italian translation of the original query, you get a completely different result with respect to the query in English: a Wikipedia page about artificial intelligence. That seems generic, given the fact that, for example, Google Scholar indexes research papers in different languages.

Search engine rankings can vary significantly, much like user opinions; although a search engineer could optimize a ranking to respond to a set of given queries, it's difficult to adjust it for possibly tens or hundreds of similar queries. So in real life, we don't manually adjust the rankings of search results; doing so would be nearly impossible and unlikely to result in a generally good ranking.

Often, performing search is a trial-and-error process: you issue an initial query and get too many results; you issue a second query and still get too many; and a third query may return trivial results you're not interested in. Expressing an informational need using a search query isn't a trivial task. You often end up performing a bunch of queries just to get a high-level understanding of what you think the search engine can do with them. It's like trying to look into a black box: you see almost nothing but try to make assumptions about what happens inside.

In most cases, users don't have the chance to understand what the search engine is doing. Even worse, things change a lot depending on the way the user expresses their request.

Now that you understand how a search engine generally works and you've learned about some important problems that haven't been completely solved yet in the search field, it's time to meet DL and discover how it can help to solve or at least mitigate such issues. We'll start with a high-level overview of the capabilities of deep neural networks.

1.8 Deep learning to the rescue

So far, we've explored information retrieval themes that are necessary to prepare you for the journey through neural search. You'll now start learning about DL, which can help create smarter search engines. This section will introduce you to basic DL concepts.

In the past, a key difficulty in *computer vision* (a field of computer science that deals with processing and understanding visual data like pictures or videos), when working with images, was that it was nearly impossible to obtain an image representation containing information about the enclosed objects and visual structures. How can you make a computer tell whether an image represents a running lion, a refrigerator, a group of monkeys, and so on? DL helped to solve this problem with the creation of a special type of deep neural network that could learn image representations incrementally, one abstraction at a time, as exemplified in figure 1.9.

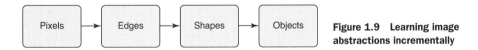

Figure 1.9 Learning image abstractions incrementally

As mentioned earlier in this chapter, DL is a subfield of ML that focuses on learning deep representations of text, images, or data in general by learning successive abstractions of increasingly meaningful representations. It does that by using deep neural networks (figure 1.10 shows a deep neural network with three hidden layers). Remember that a neural network is considered *deep* when it has at least two hidden layers.

At each step (or layer of the network), such deep neural networks are able to capture increasingly more complex structures in the data. It isn't by chance that

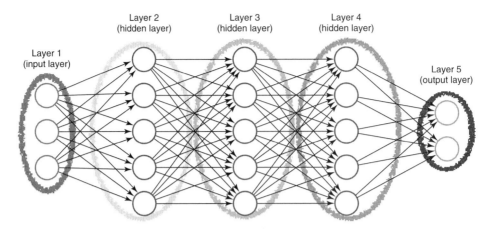

Figure 1.10   A deep feed-forward neural network with three hidden layers

computer vision is one of the fields that fostered the development and research of representation-learning algorithms for images.

Researchers have discovered that it makes sense to use such deep networks especially on data that is highly compositional.[7] This means they can help immensely when you can think of something as being formed by smaller parts of similar constituents. Images and text are good examples of compositional data, because they can be divided into smaller units incrementally (for example, text → paragraphs → sentences → words). But (deep) neural networks aren't useful only to learn representations; they can be used to perform a lot of different ML tasks. I mentioned that the document-categorization task can be solved via ML methods.

Although there are many different ways a neural network can be architected, neural networks are commonly composed of the following:

- A set of neurons
- A set of connections between all or some of the neurons
- A weight (a real number) for each directed connection between two neurons
- One or more functions that map how each neuron receives and *propagates* signals toward its outgoing connections
- Optionally, a set of layers that group sets of neurons having similar connectivity in the neural network

In figure 1.10, we can identify 20 neurons organized in a set of 5 layers. Each neuron within each layer is connected with all the neurons in the layers nearby (both the previous and the following layers), except for the first and last layers. Conventionally, information starts flowing within the network from left to right. The first layer that receives

---

[7] See, for example, H. Mhaskar, Q. Liao, and T. Poggio, "When and Why Are Deep Networks Better Than Shallow Ones?" *Proceedings of the AAAI-17: Thirty-First AAAI Conference on Artificial Intelligence* (Center for Brain, Minds & Machines), http://mng.bz/0Wrv.

the inputs is called the *input layer*, and the last layer, called the *output layer*, outputs the results of the neural network. The layers in between are called *hidden layers*.

Imagine that you could apply the same approach to text to learn representations of documents that capture increasingly higher abstractions within a document. DL-based techniques exist for such tasks, and over time these algorithms are becoming smarter: you can use them to extract word, sentence, paragraph, and document representations that can capture surprisingly interesting semantics.

When using a neural network algorithm to learn word representations within a set of text documents, closely related words lie near each other in the vector space. Think about creating a point on a two-dimensional plot for each word contained in a piece of text, and see how similar or closely related words lie close to one another, as in figure 1.11. That can be achieved by using a neural network algorithm called *word2vec* to learn such vector representations for words (also called *word vectors*). Notice that the words "Information" and "Retrieval" lie close to each other. Similarly, "word2vec" and "Skip-gram," terms that both relate to (shallow) neural network algorithms used to extract word vectors, are near each other.

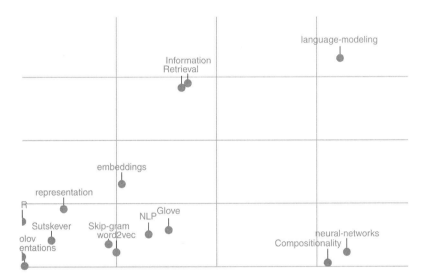

Figure 1.11 Word vectors derived from the text of research articles on word2vec

One of the key ideas of neural search is to use such representations to improve the effectiveness of search engines. It would be nice to have a retrieval model that relies on word and document vectors (also called *embeddings*) with these capabilities, so we could calculate and use document and word similarities efficiently by looking at the *nearest neighbors*. Figure 1.12 shows a deep neural network used to create word representations of the words contained in indexed documents, which are then put back into the search engine; they can be used to adjust the order of search results.

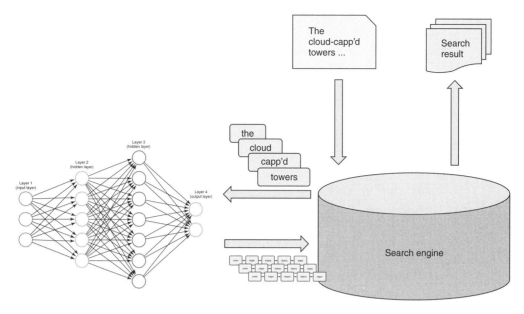

Figure 1.12   A neural search application: using word representations generated by a deep neural network to provide more-relevant results

The previous section analyzed the importance of context when compared to the complexity of expressing and understanding information needs via text queries. Good semantic representations of text are often built by using the context in which a word, sentence, or document appears, in order to infer the most appropriate representation. Let's look at the previous example to briefly see how DL algorithms can help get better results with relevance. Consider the two queries "latest breakthroughs in artificial intelligence" and "latest breakthroughs in AI" from table 1.4, assuming we're using the VSM. In such models, the similarity between queries and documents can vary a lot based on the text analysis chain. But this problem doesn't affect vector representations of text generated with recent algorithms based on neural networks. Although "artificial intelligence" and "AI" might lie far apart in VSM, they

Deep learning vs. deep neural networks

We need to make an important distinction. Deep learning is mostly about learning representations of words, text, documents, and images by using deep neural networks. Deep neural networks, however, have a wider adoption: they're used, for example, in language modeling, machine translation, and many other tasks. In this book, I'll make it clear when we're using deep neural nets to learn representations and when we're using them for other purposes. In addition to learning representations, deep neural networks can help solve a number of information retrieval tasks.

will likely be placed close together when they're plotted using word representations generated by neural nets. With such a simple change, we can boost the relevance of the search engine via more semantically grounded representations of words.

Before diving deeper into neural search applications, let's look at how search engines and neural networks can work together.

1.9 *Index, please meet neuron*

An artificial neural network can learn to predict outputs based on a training set with labeled data (supervised learning, where each input is provided with information about the expected output), or it can perform unsupervised learning (no information about the correct output for each input is given) in order to extract patterns and/or learn representations. A search engine's typical workflow involves indexing and searching content; notably, such tasks can happen in parallel. Although this may sound like a technicality at this point, the way you integrate a search engine with a neural network is important in principle because it impacts the neural search design's effectiveness and performance. You may have a super-accurate system, but if it's slow, no one will want to use it! In this book, you'll see several ways to integrate neural networks and search engines:

- *Train-then-index*—Train the network first on a collection of documents (texts, images), and then index the same data into the search engine and use the neural network in conjunction with the search engine at search time.
- *Index-then-train*—Index a collection of documents into the search engine first; then train the neural network with the indexed data (eventually retraining when data changes); and then use the neural network in conjunction with the search engine at search time.
- *Train-extract-index*—Train the network first on a collection of documents, and use the trained network to create useful resources that will be indexed along with the data. Search happens as usual with only the search engine.

You'll see each of these options in this book, being applied in the right context. For example, the train-then-index option will be used in chapter 3 for text generation, and the index-then-train option will be used in chapter 2 for synonym generation from the indexed data. The train-extract-index option makes sense when you use a neural network to learn something like a semantic representation of the data to be indexed; you'll use such representations at search time without requiring any interaction with the neural network. This is the case for the scenario outlined in chapter 8 for image search. The last chapter of the book also briefly looks at how to handle situations where the data isn't all available at first but rather arrives in a streaming fashion.

1.10 *Neural network training*

In order to use a neural net's powerful learning capabilities, you need to train it. Training a network like the one shown in the previous section via supervised learning means providing inputs to the network input layer, comparing the network (predicted) outputs with the known (target) outputs, and letting the network learn from the discrepancies between predicted and target outputs. Neural networks can easily represent many interesting mathematical functions; that's one of the reasons they can have very high accuracy. Such mathematical functions are governed by the connections' *weights* and neurons' *activation functions*. A neural network learning algorithm takes the discrepancies between desired and actual outputs and adjusts each layer's weights to reduce the output error in the future. If you feed enough data to the network, it will be able to achieve a very small error rate and therefore perform well. Activation functions have an impact on a neural network's ability to perform predictions and on how quickly it learns; the activation functions control when and how much the incoming signal to a neuron is propagated throughout to the output connections.

The most commonly used learning algorithm for neural networks is called *backpropagation*. Given desired and actual outputs, the algorithm *backpropagates* each neuron's *error* and consequently adjusts its internal state on each neuron's connections, one layer at a time, from output to input (backward); see figure 1.13. Each training example makes backpropagation "adjust" each neuron's state and connections to reduce the amount of error produced by the network for that pair of specific input and desired output. This is a high-level description of how a backpropagation algorithm works; we'll take a closer look in upcoming chapters, when you're more familiar with neural networks.

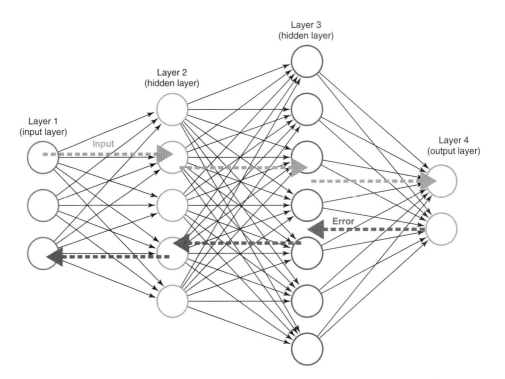

Figure 1.13   Forward step (feeding input) and backward step (backpropagating an error)

Now that you understand how neural nets learn, you need to decide how to plug in to the search engine. Search engines can receive data to be indexed continuously; because new content is added, existing content is updated or even deleted. Although it's relatively easy and quick to support this process in a search engine, many ML algorithms create *static* models that can't be adapted quickly as data changes. A typical development workflow for an ML task involves these steps:

1 Choosing and gathering data to be used as the training set
2 Keeping some portions of the training set apart for evaluation and tuning (test and cross-validation sets)
3 Training a few ML models according to algorithms (feed-forward neural networks, support vector machines, and so on) and hyperparameters (for example, the number of layers and the number of neurons in each layer for neural networks)
4 Evaluating and tuning the model over test and cross-validation sets
5 Choosing the best-performing model and using it to solve the desired task

As you can see, this process aims to generate a computational model to be used to solve a certain task or problem by using training data that is static; updates to the training sets (added or modified inputs and outputs) of such models often require the entire sequence of steps to be repeated. This conflicts with systems like search engines that deal with a constant stream of new data. For example, the search engine for an online newspaper will be updated with many different news items every day; you need to take this into account when architecting a neural search system. Neural networks are ML models: you may need to retrain the model or come up with solutions to allow your neural network to perform *online learning* (not require retraining).[8]

Think of the evolution across time of the meaning of certain English words. For example, the word "cell" today commonly refers to mobile phones or cells from the biological perspective; before mobile phones were invented, the word "cell" primarily referred to either biological cells or ... prisons! Some concepts are tightly bound to words only in specific time windows: political offices change every few years, so Barack Obama was President of the United States between 2009 and 2017, whereas the term "President of the United States" referred to John Fitzgerald Kennedy between 1961 and 1963. If you think about the books contained in a library archive, how many of them contain the phrase "President of the United States"? They will rarely relate to the same person, because of the different times at which they were written.

I mentioned that neural networks can be used to generate *word vectors* that capture word semantics so that words with similar meanings will have word vectors close to one another. What do you expect to happen to the word vector of "President of the USA"

---

[8] See, for example, Andrey Besedin et al., "Evolutive deep models for online learning on data streams with no storage" (Workshop on Large-scale Learning from Data Streams in Evolving Environments, 2017), http://mng.bz/K14O; and Doyen Sahoo et al., "Online Deep Learning: Learning Deep Neural Networks on the Fly," https://arxiv.org/pdf/1711.03705.pdf.

if you train the model over news articles from the 1960s and compare it with word vectors generated by a model trained on news articles from 2009? Will the word vector "Barack Obama" from the latter model be placed close to the word vector "President of the USA" from the former one? Probably not, unless you instruct the neural network how to deal with the evolution of words over time.[9] On the other hand, common search engines can easily deal with queries like "President of the USA" and return search results that contain such a phrase, regardless of when they were ingested into the inverted index.

1.11   *The promises of neural search*

Neural search is about integrating DL and deep neural networks into search at different stages. DL's ability to capture deep semantics lets us obtain relevant models and ranking functions that adapt well to underlying data. Deep neural networks can learn image representations that give surprisingly good results in image search. Simple similarity measures like cosine distance can be applied to DL-generated representations of data to capture semantically similar words, sentences, paragraphs, and so on; this has a number of applications, such as in the text analysis phase and in recommending similar documents. At the same time, deep neural networks can do more than "just" learn representations; they can learn to generate or translate text, and how to optimize search engine performance.

As you'll see throughout the book, a search system is made up of different components playing together. The most obvious parts are ingesting data into the search engine and searching for it. Neural networks can be used during indexing to enhance the data right before it enters the inverted index, or they can be used to broaden or specify the scope of a search query to provide a larger number of results or more-precise results. But neural networks can also be used to make smart suggestions to users to help them type queries or to translate their search queries under the hood and make a search engine work with multiple languages.

All this sounds awesome, but you can't throw neural networks at a search engine and expect it to become automagically perfect. Every decision has to be made in context; and neural networks have some limitations, including the cost of training, upgrading models, and more. But applying neural search to a search engine is a great way to make it better for users. It also makes for a fascinating journey for the search engineers, who get to explore the beauty of neural networks.

---

[9]   See, for example, Zijun Yao et al., "Dynamic Word Embeddings for Evolving Semantic Discovery" (International Conference on Web Search and Data Mining, 2018), https://arxiv.org/abs/1703.00607.

Summary

- Search is a hard problem: common approaches to information retrieval come with limitations and disadvantages, and both users and search engineers can have a difficult time making things work as expected.

- Text analysis is an important task in search, during both the indexing and search phases, because it prepares the data to be stored in inverted indexes and has a significant influence on the effectiveness of a search engine.

- Relevance is the fundamental measure of how well the search engine responds to users' information needs. Some information retrieval models can give a standardized measure of the importance of results with respect to queries, but there's no silver bullet. Context and opinions can vary significantly among users, and therefore measuring relevance needs to be a continuous focus for search engineers.

- Deep learning is a field of machine learning that uses deep neural networks to learn (deep) representations of content (text like words, sentences, and paragraphs, but also images) that can capture semantically relevant similarity measures.

- Neural search stands as a bridge between search and deep neural networks, with the goal of using deep learning to help improve different tasks related to search.

Generating synonyms

This chapter covers

- Why and how synonyms are used in search
- A brief introduction to Apache Lucene
- Fundamentals of feed-forward neural networks
- Using a word2vec algorithm
- Generating synonyms using word2vec

Chapter 1 gave you a high-level overview of the kinds of possibilities that open up when deep learning is applied to search problems. Those possibilities include using deep neural networks to search for images via a text query based on its content, generating text queries in natural language, and so on. You also learned about the basics of search engines and how they conduct searches from queries and deliver relevant results. You're now ready to start applying deep neural networks to solve search problems.

In this chapter, we'll begin with a shallow (not deep) neural network that can help you identify when two words are similar in semantics. This seemingly easy task is crucial for giving a search engine the ability to understand language.

In information retrieval, a common technique to improve the number of relevant results for a query is to use *synonyms*. Synonyms allow you to expand the number of potential ways a query or piece of indexed document is expressed. For example, you can express the sentence "I like living in Rome" as "I enjoy living in the Eternal City": the terms "living" and "enjoying" as well as "Rome" and "the Eternal City" are semantically similar, so the information conveyed by both sentences is mostly the same. Synonyms could help with the problem discussed in chapter 1, of a librarian and a student looking for a book understanding one another. That's because using synonyms allows people to express the same concept in different ways—and still retrieve the same search results!

In this chapter, we'll start working with synonyms using word2vec, one of the most common neural network–based algorithms for learning word representations. Learning about word2vec will give you a closer look at how neural networks work in practice. To do this, you'll first get an understanding of how *feed-forward* neural networks work. Feed-forward neural networks, one of the most basic types of neural networks, are the basic building blocks of deep learning. Next, you'll learn about two feed-forward neural network architectures: skip-gram and continuous-bag-of-words (CBOW). They make it possible to learn when two words are similar in meaning, and hence they're a good fit for understanding whether two given words are synonyms. You'll see how to apply them to improve search engine recall by helping the search engine avoid missing relevant search results.

Finally, you'll measure how much the search engine can be enhanced this way and what trade-offs you'll need to consider for production systems. Understanding these costs and benefits is important when deciding when and where to apply these techniques to real-life scenarios.

2.1 Introduction to synonym expansion

In the previous chapter, you saw how important it is to have good algorithms for performing text analysis: these algorithms specify the way text is broken into smaller fragments or terms. When it comes to executing a query, the terms generated at indexing time need to match those extracted from the query. This matching allows a document to be found and then appear in the search results.

One of the most frequent hurdles that prevent matching is the fact that people can express a concept in multiple different ways. For example, "going for a walk in the mountains" can be also expressed using the words "hiking" or "trekking." If the author of the text to be indexed uses "hike," but the user doing the search enters "trek," the user won't find the document. This is why you need to make the search engine aware of synonyms.

I'll explain how you can use a technique called *synonym expansion* to make it possible to express the same information need in several ways. Although synonym expansion is a popular technique, it has some limitations: in particular, the need to maintain a dictionary of synonyms that will likely change over time and that often isn't perfectly suited to the data to be indexed (such dictionaries are often obtained from publicly available data). You'll see how you can use algorithms like word2vec to learn word representations that help generate synonyms accurately based on the data that needs to be indexed.

By the end of the chapter, you'll have a search engine that can use a neural network to generate synonyms that can then be used to *decorate* the text to be indexed. To show how this works, we'll use an example in which a user sends the query "music is my aircraft" through the search engine user interface. (I'll explain why the user is using that particular query in a moment.) Figure 2.1 shows what you'll end up with.

Here are the major steps, as shown in the figure. In the search engine, the query is first processed by the text analysis pipeline. A *synonym filter* in the pipeline uses a neural network to generate synonyms. In the example, the neural network returns "airplane," "aeroplane," and "plane" as synonyms of "aircraft." The generated synonyms are then used together with the tokens from the user query to find matches in the inverted index. Finally, the search results are collected. That's the big picture. Don't worry: we'll now go through each step in detail.

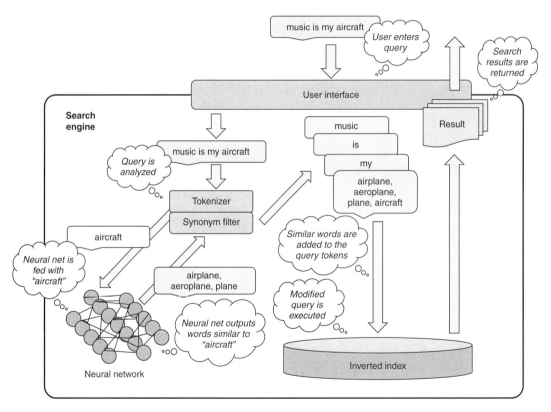

Figure 2.1   Synonym expansion at search time, with a neural network

2.1.1 Why synonyms?

Synonyms are words that differ in spelling and pronunciation, but that have the same or a very close meaning. For example, "aircraft" and "airplane" are both synonyms of the word "plane." In information retrieval, it's common to use synonyms to decorate text in order to increase the probability that an appropriate query will match. Yes, we're talking about probability here, because we can't anticipate all the possible ways of expressing an information need. This technique isn't a silver bullet that will let you *understand* all user queries, but it will reduce the number of queries that give too few or zero results.

Let's look at an example where synonyms can be useful. This has probably happened to you: you vaguely remember a short piece of a song, or you remember something about the meaning of a lyric, but not the exact wording from the song you have in mind. Suppose you liked a song whose chorus was along the lines of, "Music is my ... *something*." What was it? A car? A boat? A plane? Now imagine you have a system that collects song lyrics, and you want users to be able to search through it. If you have synonym expansion enabled in the search engine, searching for "music is my plane" will yield the phrase you're looking for: "music is my aeroplane"! In this case, using synonyms lets you find a relevant document (the song "Aeroplane" by Red Hot Chili Peppers) using a fragment and an incorrect word. Without synonym expansion, it wouldn't have been possible to retrieve this relevant response with queries like "music is my boat," "music is my plane," and "music is my car."

This is considered an improvement in recall. *Recall*, briefly mentioned in chapter 1, is a number between 0 and 1 equal to the number of documents that are retrieved and relevant, divided by the number of relevant documents. If none of the retrieved documents are relevant, recall is 0. And if all the retrieved documents are relevant, recall is 1.

The overall idea of synonym expansion is that when the search engine receives a stream of terms, it can enrich them by adding their synonyms, if they exist, at the same position. In the "Aeroplane" example, synonyms of the query terms have been expanded: they were silently decorated with the word "aeroplane" at the same position as "plane" in the stream of text; see figure 2.2.

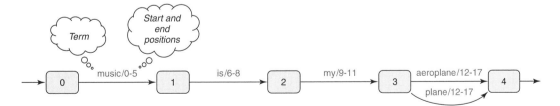

Figure 2.2 Synonym expansion graph

You can apply the same technique during indexing of the "Aeroplane" lyrics. Expanding synonyms at indexing time will make indexing slightly slower (because of the calls to word2vec), and the index will inevitably be bigger (because it will contain more terms to store). On the plus side, searching will be faster because the word2vec call won't happen during search. The decision of whether to do index-time or search-time synonym expansion may have a noticeable impact on the performance of the system as its size and load grow.

Now that you've seen why synonyms are useful in the context of search, let's look at how to implement synonym expansion, first by using common techniques and then by using word2vec. This will help you appreciate the advantages of using the latter rather than the former.

2.1.2   *Vocabulary-based synonym matching*

Let's start by seeing how to implement a search engine with synonym expansion enabled at indexing time. The simplest and most common approach for implementing synonyms is based on feeding the search engine a vocabulary that contains the mapping between all the words and their related synonyms. Such a vocabulary can look like a table, where each key is a word and the corresponding values are its synonyms:

```
aeroplane -> plane, airplane, aircraft
boat -> ship, vessel
car -> automobile
...
```

Imagine that you feed the lyrics of "Aeroplane" into the search engine for indexing, and you use synonym expansion with the previous vocabulary. Let's pick the chorus of the song—"music is my aeroplane"—and see how synonym expansion handles it. You have a simple text analysis pipeline composed of a tokenizer, which creates a token every time it encounters whitespace, resulting in creating a token for each of the words in the sentence. The index-time text analysis pipeline will thus create these tokens. Then you'll use a *token filter* for synonym expansion: for each received token, it will look at the vocabulary of synonyms and see if any of the keywords

Table 2.1   Posting list for the fragment "music is my aeroplane"

Term	Document(position)
aeroplane	1(12,17)
aircraft	1(12,17)
airplane	1(12,17)
is	1(6,8)
music	1(0,5)
my	1(9,11)
plane	1(12,17)

("aeroplane," "boat," "car") is equal to the token text. The posting list for the fragment "music is my aeroplane" (sorted in ascending alphabetical order) will look like table 2.1.

This particular posting list also records information about the position of the occurrence of a term in a specific document. This information helps you visualize the fact that the terms "plane," "airplane," and "aircraft," which weren't included in the original text fragment, were added to the index with the same position as information attached to the original term ("aeroplane").

You can record the *positions* of the terms in an inverted index in order to reconstruct the order in which a term appears in the text of a document. If you look at the inverted index table and pick the terms that have the lower positions in ascending order, you'll get "music is my aeroplane/aircraft/airplane/plane." The synonyms can be seamlessly replaced with one another, so, in the index, you can imagine having four different pieces of text: "music is my aeroplane," "music is my aircraft," "music is my airplane," and "music is my plane." It's important to emphasize that although you found four different forms in which the sentence can be indexed and searched, if any of them matches, only one document will be returned by a search engine: they all reference document 1 in the posting list.

Now that you understand how synonyms can be indexed into the search engine, you're ready to try things out and build your first Apache Lucene–based search engine that indexes lyrics, setting up proper text analysis with synonym expansion at indexing time.

> **NOTE** Going forward, I'll use *Lucene* and *Apache Lucene* interchangeably, but the proper trademarked name is Apache Lucene.

A quick look at Apache Lucene

I'll briefly introduce Lucene before diving into synonym expansion. This will allow you to focus more on the concepts rather than on the Lucene API and implementation details.

Obtaining Apache Lucene

You can download the latest release of Apache Lucene at https://lucene .apache.org/core/mirrors-core-latest-redir.html?. You can download either a binary package (.tgz or .zip) or the source release. The binary distribution is recommended if you just want to use Lucene within your own project; the .tgz/.zip package contains the JAR files of the Lucene components. Lucene is made of various artifacts: the only mandatory one is `lucene-core`, and the others are optional parts that you can use if needed. You can find the basics you need to know to get started with Lucene in the official documentation, available at https://lucene.apache.org/core/7_4_0/index .html. The source package is suitable for developers who want to look at the code or enhance it. (Patches for improvements, new features, bug fixes, documentation, and so on are always welcome at https://issues.apache.org/jira/browse/LUCENE.) If you use a build tool like Maven, Ant, or Gradle, you can include Lucene in your project, because all the components are released in public repositories like Maven Central (http://mng.bz/vN1x).

Apache Lucene is an open source search library written in Java, licensed under Apache License 2. In Lucene, the main entities to be indexed and searched are represented by `Documents`. A `Document`, depending on your use case, can represent anything: a page, a book, a paragraph, an image, and so on. Whatever it is, that's what you'll get in your search results. A Document is composed of a number of Fields, which can be used to capture different portions of the Document. For example, if your document is a web page, you can think of having a separate Field for the page title, the page contents, the page size, the creation time, and so on. The main reasons for the existence of fields are that you can do the following:

- Configure per-field text analysis pipelines
- Configure indexing options, such as whether to store in the posting list the term positions or the value of the original text each term refers to

A Lucene search engine can be accessed via a Directory: a list of files where the inverted indexes (and other data structures used, for example, to record positions) are persisted. A view on a Directory for reading an inverted index can be obtained by opening an IndexReader:

```
Path path = Paths.get("/home/lucene/luceneidx");   ◁──── Target path where the
                                                         inverted indexes are
                                                         stored on the filesystem
Directory directory = FSDirectory.open(path);   ◁──── Opens a Directory
                                                       on the target path
IndexReader reader = DirectoryReader.open(directory);   ◁──── Obtains a read-only
                                                               view of the search
                                                               engine via an
                                                               IndexReader
```

You can use an IndexReader to obtain useful statistics for an index, such as the number of documents currently indexed, or if there are any documents that have been deleted. You can also obtain statistics for a field or a particular term. And, if you know the *identifier* of the document you want to retrieve, you can get Documents from an IndexReader directly:

```
int identifier = 123;
Document document = reader.document(identifier);
```

An IndexReader is needed in order to search, because it lets you read an index. Therefore, you need an IndexReader to create an IndexSearcher. An IndexSearcher is the entry point for performing search and collecting results; the queries that will be performed via an IndexSearcher will run on the index data, exposed by the IndexReader.

Without getting too much into coding queries programmatically, you can run a user-entered query using a QueryParser. You need to specify (search-time) text analysis when searching. In Lucene, the text analysis task is performed by implementing the Analyzer API. An Analyzer can be made up of a Tokenizer and, optionally, TokenFilter components; or you can use out-of-the-box implementations, as in this example:

```
QueryParser parser = new QueryParser("title",      ◁──── Creates a query parser for the title
    new WhitespaceAnalyzer());                            field with a WhitespaceAnalyzer
Query query = parser.parse("+Deep +search");   ◁──── Parses the user-entered query
                                                      and obtains a Lucene Query
```

In this case, you tell the query parser to split tokens when it finds whitespace and run queries against the field named `title`. Suppose a user types in the query "+Deep +search." You pass it to the `QueryParser` and obtain a Lucene `Query` object. Now you can run the query:

```
IndexSearcher searcher = new IndexSearcher(reader);        ⟵ Performs the query against
TopDocs hits = searcher.search(query, 10);      ⟵             the IndexSearcher, returning
                                                             the first 10 documents

for (int i = 0; i < hits.scoreDocs.length; i++) {   ⟵  Iterates over the results

  ScoreDoc scoreDoc = hits.scoreDocs[i];     ⟵            Retrieves a ScoreDoc,
                                                          which holds the returned
  Document doc = reader.document(scoreDoc.doc);  ⟵        document identifier and its
                                                          score (given by the
  System.out.println(doc.get("title") + " : "            underlying retrieval model)
      + scoreDoc.score);     ⟵
}
```

Outputs the value of the title field of the returned document

Obtains a Document in which you can inspect fields using the document ID

If you run this, you'll get no results, because you haven't indexed anything yet! Let's fix this and examine how to index `Documents` with Lucene. First, you have to decide which fields to put into your documents and how their (index-time) text analysis pipelines should look. We'll use books for this example. Assume you want to remove some useless words from the books' contents while using a simpler text analysis pipeline for the title that doesn't remove anything.

Listing 2.1 Building per-field analyzers

Sets up a map where the keys are the names of fields and the values are the Analyzers to be used for the fields

Creates a stopword list of the tokens to remove from the books' contents while indexing

```
Map<String, Analyzer> perFieldAnalyzers = new HashMap<>();

CharArraySet stopWords = new CharArraySet(Arrays
    .asList("a", "an", "the"), true);    ⟵

perFieldAnalyzers.put("pages", new StopAnalyzer(
    stopWords));        ⟵

perFieldAnalyzers.put("title", new WhitespaceAnalyzer());  ⟵

Analyzer analyzer = new PerFieldAnalyzerWrapper(
    new EnglishAnalyzer(), perFieldAnalyzers);     ⟵
```

Uses a StopAnalyzer with the given stopwords for the pages field

Uses a WhitespaceAnalyzer for the title field

Creates a per-field Analyzer, which also requires a default analyzer (EnglishAnalyzer, in this case) for any other field that may be added to a Document

---

The inverted indexes for a Lucene-based search engine are written on disk in a `Directory` by an `IndexWriter` that will persist `Documents` according to an `IndexWriterConfig`. This config contains many options, but for you the most important bit is the required index-time analyzer. Once the `IndexWriter` is ready, you can create `Documents` and add `Fields`.

Listing 2.2   Adding documents to the Lucene index

Creates a configuration for indexing

Creates an IndexWriter to write Documents into a Directory, based on an IndexWriterConfig

```
IndexWriterConfig config = new IndexWriterConfig(analyzer);
IndexWriter writer = new IndexWriter(directory,
    config);

Document dl4s = new Document();
dl4s.add(new TextField("title", "DL for search",
    Field.Store.YES));
dl4s.add(new TextField("page", "Living in the information age ...",
    Field.Store.YES));

Document rs = new Document();
rs.add(new TextField("title", "Relevant search", Field.Store.YES));
rs.add(new TextField("page", "Getting a search engine to behave ...",
    Field.Store.YES));

writer.addDocument(dl4s);
writer.addDocument(rs);
```

Creates Document instances

Adds Fields, each of which has a name, a value, and an option to store the value with the terms

Adds Documents to the search engine

After you've added a few documents to the `IndexWriter`, you can persist them on the filesystem by issuing a `commit`. Until you do, new `IndexReaders` won't see the added documents:

```
writer.commit();    ⟵— Commits the changes
writer.close();     ⟵— Closes the IndexWriter (releases resources)
```

Run the search code again, and this is what you'll get:

```
Deep learning for search : 0.040937614
```

The code finds a match for the query "+Deep +search" and prints its title and score.

Now that you've been introduced to Lucene, let's get back to the topic of synonym expansion.

SETTING UP A LUCENE INDEX WITH SYNONYM EXPANSION

You'll first define the algorithms to use for text analysis at indexing and search time. Then, you'll add some lyrics to an inverted index. In many cases, it's a good practice to use the same tokenizer at both indexing and search time, so the text is split according to the same algorithm. This makes it easier for queries to match fragments of documents. You'll start simple and set up the following:

- A search-time `Analyzer` that uses a tokenizer that splits tokens when it encounters a whitespace character (also called a *whitespace tokenizer*)
- An index-time `Analyzer` that uses the whitespace tokenizer and a synonym filter

The reason for this is that you don't need synonym expansion at both query time and index time. For two synonyms to match, it's sufficient to do expansion once.

Assuming you have the two synonyms "aeroplane" and "plane," the following listing will build a text analysis chain that can take a term from an original token (for example, "plane") and generate another term for its synonym (for example, "aeroplane"). Both the original and the new term will be generated.

Listing 2.3   Configuring synonym expansion

```
SynonymMap.Builder builder = new SynonymMap.Builder();
builder.add(new CharsRef("aeroplane"), new CharsRef("plane"), true);   ◁─── Programmatically
final SynonymMap map = builder.build();                                      defines synonyms

Analyzer indexTimeAnalyzer = new Analyzer() {   ◁───
  @Override                                             Creates a custom
  protected TokenStreamComponents createComponents(     Analyzer, for indexing
      String fieldName) {
    Tokenizer tokenizer = new WhitespaceTokenizer();
    SynonymGraphFilter synFilter = new
        SynonymGraphFilter(tokenizer, map, true);   ◁───
    return new TokenStreamComponents(tokenizer, synFilter);   Creates a synonym filter
  }                                                            that receives terms from
};                                                             the whitespace
                                                               tokenizer and expands
Analyzer searchTimeAnalyzer = new WhitespaceAnalyzer();   ◁─   synonyms according to a
                                                               map word, ignoring case
                        Whitespace analyzer
                           for search time
```

This simplistic example creates a synonym vocabulary with just one entry. Normally, you'll have more entries, or you'll read them from an external file so you don't have to write the code for each synonym.

You're just about ready to put some song lyrics into the index using the `index-TimeAnalyzer`. Before doing that, let's look at how song lyrics are structured. Each song has an author, a title, a publication year, lyrics text, and so on. As I said earlier, it's important to examine the data to be indexed, to see what kind of data you have and possibly come up with reasoned text analysis chains that you expect to work well on that data. Here's an example:

```
author: Red Hot Chili Peppers
title: Aeroplane
year: 1995
album: One Hot Minute
text: I like pleasure spiked with pain and music is my aeroplane ...
```

Can you keep track of such a structure in a search engine? Would doing so be useful?

In most cases, it's handy to keep a lightweight document structure, because each part of it conveys different semantics, and therefore different requirements in the way it's hit by search. For example, the year will always be a numeric value; it makes no sense to use a whitespace tokenizer on it, because it's unlikely that any whitespace will appear in that field. For all the other fields, you can probably use the `Analyzer` you defined earlier for indexing. Putting it all together, you'll have multiple inverted indexes (one for each attribute) that address indexing of different parts of a document, all within the same search engine; see figure 2.3.

With Lucene, you can define a field for each of the attributes in the example (`author`, `title`, `year`, `album`, `text`). You specify that you want a separate `Analyzer` for the `year` field that doesn't touch the value; for all the other values, it will use the previously defined `indexTime-Analyzer` with synonym expansion enabled.

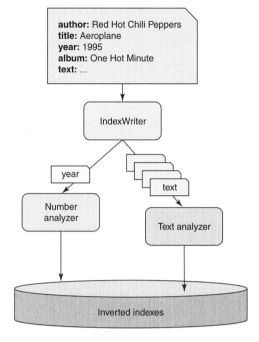

Figure 2.3 Splitting portions of the text depending on the type of data

---

Listing 2.4 Separate analysis chains for indexing and search

```
Directory directory = FSDirectory.open(Paths.get(          Opens a Directory for indexing
    "/path/to/index"));

Map<String, Analyzer> perFieldAnalyzers =                  Creates a map whose keys are the
    new HashMap<>();                                       names of the fields and the values
                                                           in the corresponding analysis
perFieldAnalyzers.put("year",                              chain to be used
    new KeywordAnalyzer());

Analyzer analyzer = new PerFieldAnalyzerWrapper(
    indexTimeAnalyzer, perFieldAnalyzers);                 Sets up a different analyzer
                                                           (keyword; doesn't touch
IndexWriterConfig config = new IndexWriterConfig(          the value) for the year
    analyzer);

IndexWriter writer = new IndexWriter(                      Creates a wrapping
    directory, config);                                    analyzer that can work
                                                           with per-field analyzers
                        Builds all the above in a
Creates an IndexWriter   configuration object
to be used for indexing
```

This mechanism allows indexing to be flexible in the way content is analyzed before being written into the inverted indexes; it's common to play with different Analyzers for different portions of Documents and to change them several times before finding the best combination for a data corpus. Even then, in the real world, it's likely that such configurations will need adjustments over time. For instance, you may only index English songs and then, at some later point, begin to add songs in Chinese. In this case, you'll have to adjust the analyzers to work with both languages (for example, you can't expect a whitespace tokenizer to work well on Chinese, Japanese, and Korean [CJK] languages, where words often aren't separated by a space).

Let's put your first document into the Lucene index.

Listing 2.5 Indexing documents

Creates a document for the song "Aeroplane"

Adds all the fields from the song lyrics

```
Document aeroplaneDoc = new Document();
aeroplaneDoc.add(new Field("title", "Aeroplane", type));
aeroplaneDoc.add(new Field("author", "Red Hot Chili Peppers", type));
aeroplaneDoc.add(new Field("year", "1995", type));
aeroplaneDoc.add(new Field("album", "One Hot Minute", type));
aeroplaneDoc.add(new Field("text",
    "I like pleasure spiked with pain and music is my aeroplane ...", type));

writer.addDocument(aeroplaneDoc);
writer.commit();
```

Adds the document

Persists the updated inverted index to the filesystem, making the changes durable (and searchable)

You create a document composed of multiple fields, one per song attribute, and then add it to the writer.

In order to search, you open the Directory (again) and obtain a view on the index, an IndexReader, on which you can search via an IndexSearcher. To make sure synonym expansion works as expected, enter a query with the word "plane"; you'll expect the "Aeroplane" song to be retrieved.

Listing 2.6 Searching for the word "plane"

```
IndexReader reader = DirectoryReader.open(directory);

IndexSearcher searcher = new IndexSearcher(reader);

QueryParser parser = new QueryParser("text",
    searchTimeAnalyzer);

Query query = parser.parse("plane");

TopDocs hits = searcher.search(query, 10);
```

Opens a view on the index

Instantiates a searcher

Creates a query parser that uses the search-time analyzer with the user-entered query to produce search terms

Transforms a user-entered query (as a String) into a proper Lucene query object using the QueryParser

Searches, and obtains the first 10 results

```
for (int i = 0; i < hits.scoreDocs.length; i++) {      Iterates over the results
    ScoreDoc scoreDoc = hits.scoreDocs[i];
    Document doc = searcher.doc(scoreDoc.doc);      Obtains the search result
    System.out.println(doc.get("title") + " by "
        + doc.get("author"));          Outputs the title and author
}                                      of the returned song
```

As expected, the result is as follows:

```
Aeroplane by Red Hot Chili Peppers
```

We've gone through a quick tour of how to set up text analysis for index and search, and how to index documents and retrieve them. You've also learned how to add synonym expansion capability. But it should be clear that this code can't be maintained in real life:

- You can't write code for each and every synonym you want to add.
- You need a synonym vocabulary that can be plugged in and managed separately, to avoid having to modify the search code every time you need to update it.
- You need to manage the evolution of languages—new words (and synonyms) are added constantly.

A first step toward resolving these issues is to write the synonyms into a file and let the synonym filter read them from there. You'll do that by putting synonyms on the same line, separated by commas. You'll build the `Analyzer` in a more compact way, by using a builder pattern (see https://en.wikipedia.org/wiki/Builder_pattern).

Listing 2.7 Feeding synonyms from a file

```
Map<String, String> sffargs = new HashMap<>();         Defines the file that
sffargs.put("synonyms", "synonyms.txt");               contains the synonyms
sffargs.put("ignoreCase", "true");
                                                                        Lets the
                                                                        analyzer use
CustomAnalyzer.Builder builder = CustomAnalyzer.builder()              a whitespace
    .withTokenizer(WhitespaceTokenizerFactory.class)                  tokenizer
    .addTokenFilter(SynonymGraphFilterFactory.class, sffargs)
return builder.build();
                                          Lets the analyzer use
                                          a synonym filter
```

Defines an analyzer →

Set up synonyms in the synonyms file:

```
plane,aeroplane,aircraft,airplane
boat,vessel,ship
...
```

This way, the code remains unchanged regardless of any change in the synonyms file; you can update the file as much as you need to. Although this is much better than having to write code for synonyms, you don't want to write the synonyms file by hand, unless you know that you'll have just a few fixed synonyms. Fortunately, these days there's lots of data that you can use for free or for a very low cost. A good, large resource for natural language processing in general is the WordNet project (http://wordnet.princeton.edu), a lexical database for the English language from Princeton University. You can take advantage of WordNet's large synonym vocabulary, which is constantly updated, and include it in your indexing analysis pipeline by downloading it as a file (called, for example, synonyms-wn.txt) and specifying that you want to use the WordNet format.

Listing 2.8 Using synonyms from WordNet

```
Map<String, String> sffargs = new HashMap<>();
sffargs.put("synonyms", "synonyms-wn.txt");        Sets up a synonym file using
sffargs.put("format", "wordnet");                   the WordNet vocabulary
CustomAnalyzer.Builder builder = CustomAnalyzer.builder()
    .withTokenizer(WhitespaceTokenizerFactory.class)    Specifies the
    .addTokenFilter(SynonymGraphFilterFactory.class, sffargs)   WordNet format
return builder.build();                              for the synonym file
```

With the WordNet dictionary plugged in, you have a very large, high-quality source of synonym expansion that should work well for English. But there are still a few problems. First, there's not a WordNet-type resource for every language. Second, even if you stick to English, the synonym expansion for a word is based on its *denotation* as defined by the rules of English grammar and dictionaries; this doesn't take into account its *connotation* as defined by the context in which those words appear.

I'm describing the difference between what linguists define as a synonym, based on strict dictionary definitions (denotation), versus how people commonly use language and words in real life (connotation). In informal contexts like social networks, chat rooms, and meeting friends in real life, people may use two words as if they were synonyms even if, by grammar rules, they aren't synonyms. To handle this issue, word2vec will kick in and provide a more advanced level of search than just expanding synonyms based on the strict syntax of a language. You'll see that using word2vec enables you to build synonym expansions that are language agnostic; it learns from the data which words are similar, without caring too much about the language used and whether it's formal or informal. This is a helpful feature of word2vec: words with similar contexts are considered similar exactly because of their context. There's no grammar or syntax involved. For each word, word2vec looks at the surrounding words, assuming that semantically similar words will appear in similar contexts.

2.2 The importance of context

The main problem with the approach outlined so far is that synonym mappings are static and not bound to the indexed data. For example, in the case of WordNet, synonyms strictly obey English grammar semantics but don't take into account slang or informal contexts where words are often used as synonyms even if they aren't synonyms according to strict rules of grammar. Another example is acronyms used in chat sessions and emails. For instance, it's not uncommon to see acronyms like ICYMI ("in case you missed it") and AKA ("also known as") in email. *ICYMI* and "in case you missed it" can't be called synonyms, and you probably won't find them in a dictionary, but they mean the same thing.

One approach to overcoming these limitations is to have a way to generate synonyms from the data to be ingested. The basic concept is that it should be possible to extract the *nearest neighbors* of a word by looking at the context of the word, which means analyzing the patterns of surrounding words that occur together with the word itself. A nearest neighbor of a word in this case should be its synonym, even if it's not strictly a synonym from the grammar perspective.

This idea that words that are used, and occur, in the same contexts tend to have similar meanings is called the *distributional hypothesis* (see https://aclweb.org/aclwiki/ Distributional_Hypothesis) and is the basis of many deep learning algorithms for text representations. The interesting thing about this idea is that it disregards language, slang, style, and grammar: every bit of information about a word is inferred from the word contexts that appear in the text. Think, for example, of how words representing cities (Rome, Cape Town, Oakland, and so on) are often used. Let's look at a few sentences:

- I like to live in Rome because …
- People who love surfing should go to Cape Town because …
- I would like to visit Oakland to see …
- Traffic is crazy in Rome …

Often the city names are used near the word "in" or a short distance from verbs like "live," "visit," and so on. This is the basic intuition behind the fact that the context provides a lot of information about each word.

With this in mind, you want to learn word representations for the words in the data to be indexed, so that you can generate synonyms from the data rather than manually building or downloading a synonym vocabulary. In the library example in chapter 1, I mentioned that it's best to have insight about what's in the library; with this additional insight, the librarian could help you more effectively. A student coming to the library could ask the librarian for, say, "books about artificial intelligence." Let's also suppose the library has only one book on the topic, and it's called *AI Principles*. If the librarian (or the student) were searching through book titles, they would miss this book, unless they knew that AI is an acronym (and, given previous assumptions, a synonym) for artificial intelligence. An assistant knowledgeable about these synonyms would be useful in this situation.

Let's imagine two hypothetical types of such an assistant: John, an English language expert who has studied English grammar and syntax for years; and Robbie, another student who collaborates weekly with the librarian and has the chance to read most of the books. John couldn't tell you that *AI* stands for *artificial intelligence*, because his background doesn't give him this information. Robbie, on the other hand, has far less formal knowledge of English, but he's an expert on the books in the library; he could easily tell you that *AI* stands for *artificial intelligence*, because he's read the book *AI Principles* and knows it's about the principles of artificial intelligence. In this scenario, John is acting like the WordNet vocabulary, and Robbie is the word2vec algorithm. Although John has proven knowledge of the language, Robbie may be more helpful in this particular situation.

In chapter 1, I mentioned that neural networks are good at learning representations (in this case, representations of words) that are sensitive to the context. That's the kind of capability you'll use with word2vec. In short, you'll use the word2vec neural network to learn a representation of the words that can tell you the most similar (or nearest neighbor) word for "plane": "aeroplane." Before we get deeper into that, let's take a closer look at one of the simplest forms of neural networks: feed-forward. Feed-forward neural networks are the basis for most more-complex neural network architectures.

2.3   *Feed-forward neural networks*

Neural networks are the key tool for neural search, and many neural network architectures extend from feed-forward networks. A *feed-forward neural network* is a neural network in which information flows from the input layer to hidden layers, if any, and finally to the output layer; there are no loops, because the connections among neurons don't form a cycle. Think of it as a magic black box with inputs and outputs. The magic mostly happens inside the net, thanks to the way neurons are connected to each other and how they react to their inputs. If you were looking for a house to buy in a specific country, for instance, you could use the "magic box" to predict a fair price you could expect to pay for a specific house. As you can see in figure 2.4, the magic box would learn to make predictions using input features such as house size, location, and a rating given by the seller.

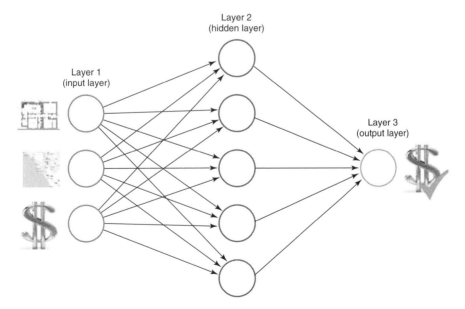

Figure 2.4   Predicting price with a feed-forward neural network with three inputs, five hidden units, and one output unit

A feed-forward neural network is composed of the following:

- *An input layer*—Responsible for gathering the inputs provided by the user. These inputs are usually in the form of real numbers. In the example of predicting a house price, you have three inputs: house size, house location, and amount of money required by the seller. You'll encode these inputs as three real numbers, so the input you'll pass to the network will be a three-dimensional vector: [size, location, price].
- *Optionally, one or more hidden layers*—Represents a more mysterious part of the network. Think of it as the part of the network that allows it to be so good at learning and predicting. In the example, there are five units in the hidden layer, all of which are connected to the units in the input layer and also to the units in the output layer. The connectivity in the network plays a fundamental role in the network activity dynamics. Most of the time, all units in a layer (x) are fully connected (forward) to the units in the next layer ($x+1$).
- *An output layer*—Responsible for providing the final output of the network. In the house price example, it will provide a real number representing what the network estimates the right price should be.

NOTE   Usually, it's a good idea to scale inputs so they're more or less in the same range of values—for example, between -1 and 1. In the example, a house's size in square meters is between 10 and 200, and its price range is in the order of tens of thousands. Preprocessing the input data so it's all in similar ranges of values allows the network to learn more quickly.

HOW IT WORKS: WEIGHTS AND ACTIVATION FUNCTIONS

As you've seen, a feed-forward neural network receives inputs and produces outputs. The fundamental building blocks of these networks are called *neurons* (even though a brain neuron is much more complex). Every neuron in a feed-forward neural network

- Belongs to a layer
- Smooths each input by its incoming weight
- Propagates its output according to an activation function

In the feed-forward neural network in figure 2.5, the second layer is composed of only one neuron. This neuron receives input from three neurons in layer 1 and propagates output to only one neuron in layer 3. It has an associated activation function, and its incoming links with the previous layer have associated weights (often, real numbers between -1 and 1).

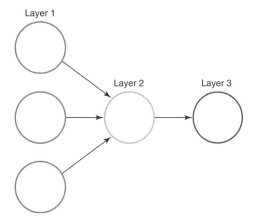

Figure 2.5   Propagating signals through the network

Let's assume that all the incoming weights of the neuron in layer 2 are set to 0.3 and that it receives from the first layer the inputs 0.4, 0.5, and 0.6. Each weight is multiplied by its input, and the results are summed together: $0.3 \times 0.4 + 0.3 \times 0.5 + 0.3 \times 0.6 = 0.45$. The activation function is applied to this intermediate result and then propagated to the outgoing links of the neuron. Common activation functions are hyperbolic tangent (`tanh`), `sigmoid`, and rectified linear unit (`ReLU`).

In the current example, let's use the `tanh` function. You'll have `tanh(0.45)` = `0.4218990053`, so the neuron in the third layer will receive this number as an input on its only incoming link. The output neuron will perform exactly the same steps the neuron from layer 2 does, using its own weights. For this reason, these networks are called *feed-forward*: each neuron transforms and propagates its inputs in order to feed the neurons in the next layer.

BACKPROPAGATION IN A NUTSHELL

In chapter 1, I mentioned that neural networks and deep learning belong to the field of machine learning. I also touched on the main algorithm used for training neural networks: backpropagation. In this section, we'll give it a closer look.

A fundamental point when discussing the rise of deep learning is related to how well and how quickly neural networks can learn. Although artificial neural networks are an old computing paradigm (circa 1950), they became popular again recently (around 2011) as modern computers' performance improved to a level that allowed neural nets to perform effective learning in a reasonable time.

In the previous section, you saw how a network propagates information from the input layer to the output layer in a feed-forward fashion. On the other hand, after a feed-forward pass, backpropagation lets the signal flow backward from the output layer to the input layer.

The values of the activations of the neurons in the output layer, generated by a feed-forward pass on an input, are compared the values in the desired output. This comparison is performed by a *cost function* that calculates a loss or cost and represents a measure of how much the network is wrong in that particular case. Such an error is sent backward through the incoming connections of the output neurons to the corresponding units in the hidden layer. You can see in figure 2.6 that the neuron in the output layer sends back its portion of error to the connected units in the hidden layer.

Once a unit receives an error, it updates its weights according to an *update algorithm*; usually, the algorithm used is *stochastic gradient descent*. This backward update of weights happens until the weights on the input layer connections are adjusted (note that updates are done only for output and hidden layer units, as input units don't have weights), and then the update stops. So a run of backpropagation updates all the weights associated with the existing connections. The rationale behind this algorithm is that each weight is responsible for a portion of the error and, therefore, backpropagation tries to adjust such weights in order to reduce the error for that particular input/output pair.

The gradient descent algorithm (or any other update algorithm for adjusting the weights) decides *how* the weights are changed with respect to the portion of error

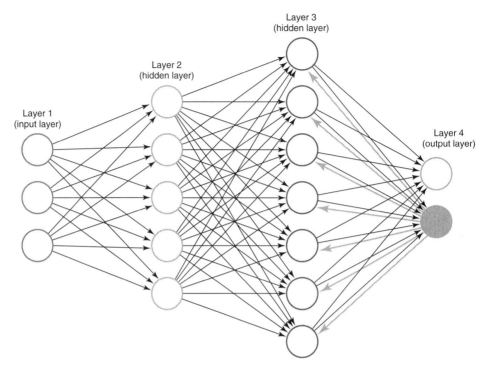

Figure 2.6   Backpropagating a signal from the output layer to the hidden layer

each weight contributes. A lot of math is involved in this concept, but you can think of it as if the cost function defines a shape like the one in figure 2.7, where the height of the hill defines the amount of error. A very low point corresponds to the combination of the neural network weights having a very low error:

- *Low*—The point with the lowest possible error, having optimal values for the neural network weights
- *High*—A point with high error; gradient descent tries to perform descent toward points with lower error

The coordinates of a point are given by the value of the weights in the neural network, so the gradient descent tries to find a value of the weights (a point) with very low error (a very low height) in the shape.

2.4   *Using word2vec*

Now that you understand what a generic feed-forward network is, we can focus on a more specific neural network algorithm based on feed-forward neural networks: word2vec. Although its basics are fairly easy to understand, it's fascinating to see the good results (in terms of capturing the semantics of words in a text) you can achieve. But what does it do, and how is it useful for the synonym expansion use case?

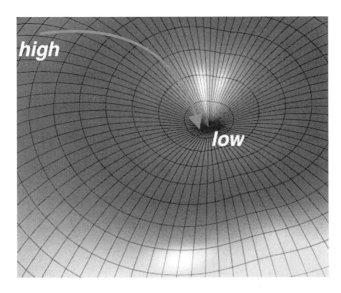

Figure 2.7   Geometric interpretation of backpropagation with gradient descent

Word2vec takes a piece of text and outputs a series of vectors, one for each word in the text. When the output vectors of word2vec are plotted on a two-dimensional graph, vectors whose words are very similar in terms of semantics are very close to one another. You can use a distance measures like the cosine distance to find the most similar words with respect to a given word. Thus, you can use this technique to find a word's synonyms. In short, in this section you'll set up a word2vec model, feed it the text of the song lyrics you want to index, get output vectors for each word, and use them to find synonyms.

Chapter 1 discussed using vectors in the context of search, when we talked about the vector space model and term frequency-inverse document frequency (TF-IDF). In a sense, word2vec also generates a vector space model whose vectors (one for each word) are weighted by the neural network during the learning process. Word vectors generated by algorithms like word2vec are often referred to as *word embeddings* because they map static, discrete, high-dimensional word representations (such as TF-IDF or one-hot encoding) into a different (continuous) vector space with fewer dimensions involved.

Let's get back to the example of the song "Aeroplane." If you feed its text to word2vec, you'll get a vector for each word:

```
0.7976110753441061, -1.300175666666296, i
-1.1589942649711316, 0.2550385962680938, like
-1.9136814615251492, 0.0, pleasure
-0.178102361461314, -5.778459658617458, spiked
0.11344064895365787, 0.0, with
0.3778008406249243, -0.11222894354254397, pain
-2.0494382050792344, 0.5871714329463343, and
-1.3652666102221962, -0.4866885862322685, music
-12.878251690899361, 0.7094618209959707, is
```

```
0.8220355668636578, -1.2088098678855501, my
-0.37314503461270637, 0.4801501371764839, aeroplane
...
```

You can see these in the coordinate plan shown in figure 2.8.

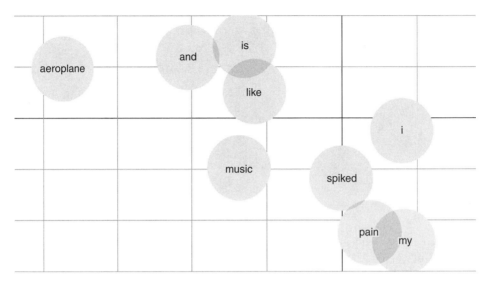

Figure 2.8   Plotted word vectors for "Aeroplane"

In the example output, two dimensions were used so those vectors are more easily plottable on a graph. But in practice, it's common to use 100 or more dimensions, and to use a dimensionality reduction algorithm like Principal Component Analysis or t-SNE to obtain two- or three-dimensional vectors that can be more easily plotted. (Using many dimensions lets you capture more information as the amount of data grows.) At this point, we won't discuss this tuning in detail, but we'll return to it later in the book as you learn more about neural networks.

Using cosine similarity to measure the distance among each of the generated vectors produces some interesting results:

```
music -> song, view
looking -> view, better
in -> the, like
sitting -> turning, could
```

As you can see, extracting the two nearest vectors for a few random vectors gives results, some good, and some, not so much:

- "Music" and "song" are very close semantically; you could even say they're synonyms. But the same isn't true for "view."
- "Looking" and "view" are related, but "better" has nothing to do with "looking."
- "In," "the," and "like" aren't close to each other.

- "Sitting" and "turning" are both verbs of the "ing" form, but their semantics are loosely coupled. "Could" is also a verb, but it doesn't have much else to do with "sitting."

What's the problem? Isn't word2vec up to the task?

There are two factors at play:

- The number of dimensions (two) of the generated word vectors is probably too low.
- Feeding the word2vec model the text of a single song probably doesn't provide enough contexts for each of the words to come with an accurate representation. The model needs more examples of the contexts in which the words "better" and "view" occur.

Let's assume you again build the word2vec model, this time using 100 dimensions and a larger set of song lyrics taken from the Billboard Hot 100 dataset (https://www.kaylinpavlik.com/50-years-of-pop-music):

```
music -> song, sing
view -> visions, gaze
sitting -> hanging, lying
in -> with, into
looking -> lookin, lustin
```

The results are much better and more appropriate: you could use almost all of them as synonyms in the context of search. You can imagine using such a technique at either query or indexing time. There would be no more dictionaries or vocabularies to keep up to date; the search engine could learn to generate synonyms from the data it handles.

You may have a couple of questions right about now: How does word2vec work? And how can you integrate it, in practice, into a search engine? The paper "Efficient Estimation of Word Representations in Vector Space"[1] describes two different neural network models for learning such word representations: *continuous-bag-of-words* (CBOW) and *continuous skip-gram*. We'll discuss both of them, and how to implement them, in a moment. Word2vec performs unsupervised learning of word representations; the mentioned CBOW and skip-gram models just need to be fed a sufficiently large text, properly encoded. The main concept behind word2vec is that the neural network is given a piece of text, which is split into fragments of a certain size (also called *windows*). Every fragment is fed to the network as a pair consisting of a *target word* and a *context*. In the case of figure 2.9, the target word is "aeroplane," and the context consists of the words "music," "is," and "my."

The hidden layer of the network contains a set of weights (in this case, 11 of them—the number of neurons in the hidden layer) for each word. These vectors will be used as the word representations when learning ends.

---

[1] Tomas Mikolov et al. (2013), https://arxiv.org/pdf/1301.3781.pdf.

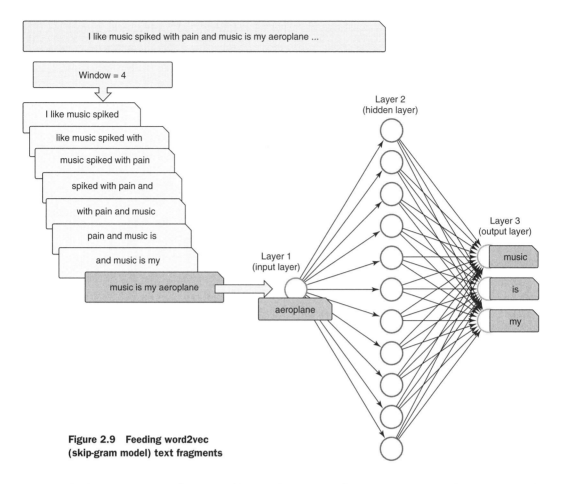

Figure 2.9   Feeding word2vec (skip-gram model) text fragments

An important note about word2vec is that you don't care much about the outputs of the neural network. Instead, you extract the internal state of the hidden layer at the end of the training phase, which yields exactly one vector representations for each word.

During training, a portion of each fragment is used as target word, and the rest is used as context. With the CBOW model, the target word is used as the output of the network, and the remaining words of the text fragment (the context) are used as inputs. The opposite is true with the continuous skip-gram model: the target word is used as input and the context words as outputs (as in the example). In practice, both work well, but skip-gram is usually preferred because it works slightly better with infrequently used words.

For example, given the text "she keeps moet et chandon in her pretty cabinet let them eat cake she says" from the song "Killer Queen" (by the band Queen), and a window of 5, a word2vec model based on CBOW will receive a sample for each five-word fragment. For example, for the fragment | she | keeps | moet | et | chandon |, the input will consist of the words | she | keeps | et | chandon | and the output will consist of the word moet.

As you can see from figure 2.10, the neural network is composed of an input layer, a hidden layer, and an output layer. This kind of neural network, with one hidden layer, is referred to as *shallow*. Neural networks with more than one hidden layer are referred to as *deep*.

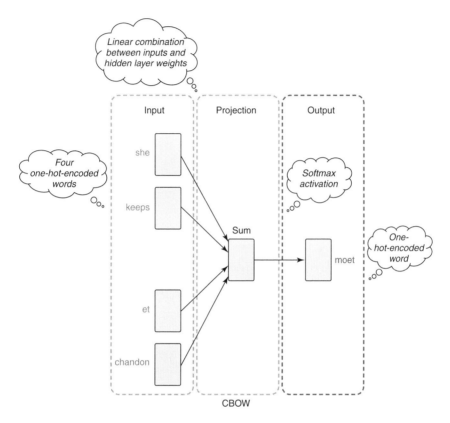

Figure 2.10   Continuous-bag-of-words model

The neurons in the hidden layer have no activation function, so they linearly combine weights and inputs (multiply each input by its weight and sum all of the results together). The input layer has a number of neurons equal to the number of words in the text for each word; word2vec requires each word to be represented as a *one-hot-encoded* vector.

Let's see what a one-hot-encoded vector looks like. Imagine that you have a dataset with three words: [cat, dog, mouse]. You have three vectors, each with all the values set to 0 except one, which is set to 1 (that one identifies that specific word):

```
dog   : [0,0,1]
cat   : [0,1,0]
mouse : [1,0,0]
```

If you add the word "lion" to the dataset, one-hot-encoded vectors for this dataset will have dimension 4:

```
lion  : [0,0,0,1]
dog   : [0,0,1,0]
cat   : [0,1,0,0]
mouse : [1,0,0,0]
```

If you have 100 words in your input text, each word will be represented as a 100-dimensional vector. Consequently, in the CBOW model, you'll have 100 input neurons multiplied by the value of the `window` parameter minus 1. So, if `window` is 4, you'll have 300 input neurons.

The hidden layer has a number of neurons equal to the desired dimensionality of the resulting word vectors. This parameter must be set by whoever sets up the network.

The size of the output layer is equal to the number of words in the input text: in this example, 100. A word2vec CBOW model for an input text with 100 words, embeddings dimensionality equal to 50, and `window` set to 4 will have 300 input neurons, 50 hidden neurons, and 100 output neurons. Note that, while input and output dimensionalities depend on the size of the vocabulary (in this case, 100) and the `window` parameter, the dimensionality of the word embeddings generated by the CBOW model is a parameter, to be chosen by the user. For example, in figure 2.11 you can see the following:

- The input layer has a dimensionality of C × V, where C is the length of the context (corresponding to the `window` parameter minus 1) and V is the size of the vocabulary.
- The hidden layer has a dimensionality of N, defined by the user.
- The output layer has a dimensionality equal to V.

For word2vec, CBOW model inputs are propagated through the network by first multiplying the one-hot-encoded vectors of the input words by their input-to-hidden weights; you can imagine that as a matrix containing a weight for each connection between an input and a hidden neuron. Those are combined (multiplied) with the hidden-to-output weights, producing the outputs; and these outputs are then passed through a softmax function. Softmax "squashes" a K-dimensional

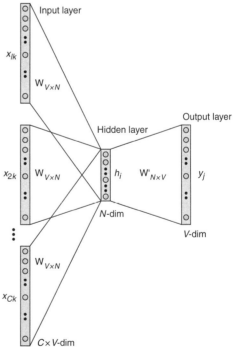

Figure 2.11 Continuous-bag-of-words model weights

vector (the output vector) of arbitrary real values to a K-dimensional vector of real values in the range (0, 1) that add up to 1, so that they can represent a probability distribution. Your network tells you the probability that each output word will be selected, given the context (the network input).

You now have a neural network that can predict the most likely word to appear in the text, given a context of a few words (the `window` parameter). This neural network can tell you that given a context like "I like eating," you should expect the next word to be something like "pizza." Note that because word order isn't taken into account, you could also say that given the context "I eating pizza," the next word most likely to appear in the text is "like."

But the most important part of this neural network for the goal of generating synonyms isn't learning to predict words given a context. The surprising beauty of this method is that, internally, the weights of the hidden layer adjust in a way that makes it possible to determine when two words are semantically similar (because they appear in the same or similar contexts).

After forward propagation, the backpropagation learning algorithm adjusts the weights of each neuron in the different layers, so the neural network will produce a more accurate result for each new fragment. When the learning process has finished, the hidden-to-output weights represent the vector representation (embedding) for each word in the text.

Skip-gram looks reversed with respect to the CBOW model. The same concepts apply: the input vectors are one-hot encoded (one for each word), so the input layer has a number of neurons equals to the number of words in the input text. The hidden layer has the dimensionality of the desired resulting word vectors, and the output layer has a number of neurons equal to the number of words multiplied by `window` minus 1. Using the same example as before, given the text "she keeps moet et chandon in her pretty cabinet let them eat cake she says" and a `window` value of 5, a word2vec model based on the skip-gram model will receive a first sample for | she | keeps | moet | et | chandon | with the input moet and the output | she | keeps | et | chandon | (see figure 2.12).

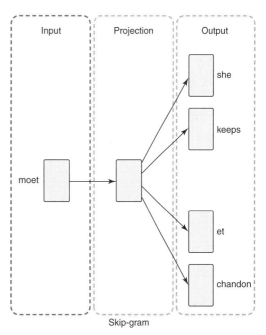

Figure 2.12 Skip-gram model

Figure 2.13 is an example excerpt of word vectors calculated by word2vec for the text of the Hot 100 Billboard dataset. It shows a small subset of words plotted, for the sake of appreciating word semantics being expressed geometrically.

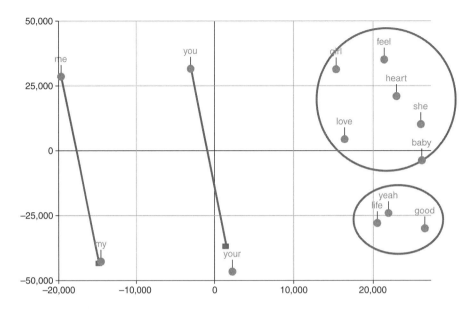

Figure 2.13   Highlights of word2vec vectors for the Hot 100 Billboard dataset

Notice the expected regularities between "me" and "my" with respect to "you" and "your." Also note the groups of similar words, or words used in similar contexts, which are good candidates for synonyms.

Now that you've learned a bit about how the word2vec algorithm works, let's write some code and see it in action. Then you'll be able to combine it with the search engine for synonym expansion.

Deeplearning4j

Deeplearning4j (DL4J) is a deep learning library for the Java Virtual Machine (JVM). It has good adoption among Java users and a not-too-steep learning curve for early adopters. It also comes with an Apache 2 license, which is handy if you want to use it within a company and include it in a possibly non-open source product. Additionally, DL4J has tools to import models created with other frameworks such as Keras, Caffe, TensorFlow, Theano, and so on.

2.4.1 Setting up word2vec in Deeplearning4j

In this book, we'll use DL4J to implement neural network–based algorithms. Let's see how to use it to set up a word2vec model.

DL4J has an out-of-the-box implementation of word2vec, based on the skip-gram model. You need to set up its configuration parameters and pass the input text you want to feed the search engine.

Keeping the song lyrics use case in mind, let's feed word2vec the Billboard Hot 100 text file. You want output word vectors of a suitable dimension, so set that configuration parameter to 100 and the window size to 5.

Listing 2.9 DL4J word2vec example

Reads the corpus of text containing the lyrics

Sets up an iterator over the corpus

```
String filePath = new ClassPathResource(
    "billboard_lyrics_1964-2015.txt").getFile()
    .getAbsolutePath();
SentenceIterator iter = new BasicLineIterator(filePath);

Word2Vec vec = new Word2Vec.Builder()
    .layerSize(100)
    .windowSize(5)
    .iterate(iter)
    .elementsLearningAlgorithm(new CBOW<>())
    .build();
vec.fit();

String[] words = new String[]{"guitar", "love", "rock"};
for (String w : words) {
    Collection<String> lst = vec.wordsNearest(w, 2);
    System.out.println("2 Words closest to '"
        + w + "': " + lst);
}
```

Creates a configuration for word2vec

Sets the number of dimensions the vector representations should have

Sets the window parameter

Sets word2vec to iterate over the selected corpus

Uses the CBOW model

Performs training

Obtains the closest words to an input word

Prints the nearest words

You obtain the following output, which seems good enough:

```
2 Words closest to 'guitar': [giggle, piano]
2 Words closest to 'love': [girl, baby]
2 Words closest to 'rock': [party, hips]
```

Note that you can alternatively use the skip-gram model by changing the elements-LearningAlgorithm.

Listing 2.10 Using the skip-gram model

```
Word2Vec vec = new Word2Vec.Builder()
    .layerSize(...)
    .windowSize(...)
    .iterate(...)
    .elementsLearningAlgorithm(new SkipGram<>())
    .build();
vec.fit();
```

Uses the skip-gram model

As you can see, it's straightforward to set up such a model and obtain results in a reasonable time (training the word2vec model took around 30 seconds on a "normal" laptop). Keep in mind that you'll now aim to use this in conjunction with the search engine, which should yield a better synonym-expansion algorithm.

2.4.2 *Word2vec-based synonym expansion*

Now that you have this powerful tool in your hands, you need to be careful! When using WordNet, you have a constrained set of synonyms, so you can't blow up the index. With word vectors generated by word2vec, you can ask the model to return the closest words for each word to be indexed. This might not be acceptable from a performance perspective (for both runtime and storage), so you have to come up with a strategy for using word2vec responsibly. One thing you can do is constrain the types of words for which you ask word2vec to get the nearest words. In natural language processing, it's common to tag each word as a *part of speech* (PoS) that labels its syntactic role in a sentence. Common parts of speech are NOUN, VERB, and ADJ; there are also finer-grained ones like NP and NC (proper and common noun, respectively). For example, you might decide to use word2vec only for words whose PoS is either NC or VERB, to avoid bloating the index with synonyms for adjectives. Another technique would be to look at how informative the document is. A short text has a relatively poor probability of being hit with a query, because it's composed of only a few terms. So you might decide to focus on such documents and expand their synonyms, rather than focusing on longer documents.

On the other hand, the "informativeness" of a document doesn't only depend on its size. Thus you might use other techniques, such as looking at term *weights* (the number of times a term appears in a piece of text) and skipping those that have a low weight.

You could also choose to use word2vec results only if they have a good similarity score. If you use cosine distance to measure the nearest neighbors of a word vector, such neighbors may be too far away (a low similarity score) but still be the nearest. In that case, you could decide not to use those neighbors.

Now that you've trained a word2vec model on the Hot 100 Billboard dataset using Deeplearning4j, let's use it in conjunction with the search engine to generate synonyms. As explained in chapter 1, a token filter performs operations on the terms provided by a tokenizer, such as filtering them or, as in this case, adding other terms to be indexed. A Lucene `TokenFilter` is based on the `incrementToken` API, which returns a `boolean` value that is false at the end of the token stream. Implementors of this API consume one token at a time (for example, by filtering or expanding a token). Figure 2.14 shows a diagram of how word2vec-based synonym expansion is expected to work.

You're finished with word2vec training, so you can create a synonym filter that will use the learned model to predict term synonyms during filtering. You'll build a Lucene `TokenFilter` that can use DL4J word2vec on input tokens. This means implementing the left side of figure 2.14.

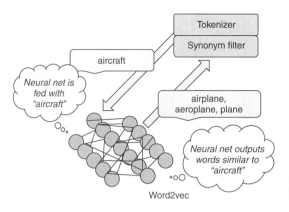

Figure 2.14 Synonym expansion at search time, with word2vec

The Lucene APIs for token filtering require you to implement the `incrementToken` method. This method will return `true` if there are still tokens to consume from the token stream or `false` if there are no more tokens left to consider for filtering. The basic idea is that the token filter will return `true` for all original tokens and `false` for all the related synonyms you get from word2vec.

Listing 2.11 Word2vec-based synonym expansion filter

```
protected W2VSynonymFilter(TokenStream input,
    Word2Vec word2Vec) {
  super(input);
  this.word2Vec = word2Vec;
}

@Override
public boolean incrementToken()
    throws IOException {
  if (!outputs.isEmpty()) {
    ...
  }

  if (!SynonymFilter.TYPE_SYNONYM.equals(
     typeAtt.type())) {
    String word = new String(termAtt.buffer())
        .trim();
    List<String> list = word2Vec.
        similarWordsInVocabTo(word, minAcc);
    int i = 0;
    for (String syn : list) {
      if (i == 2) {
        break;
      }
      if (!syn.equals(word)) {
        CharsRefBuilder charsRefBuilder = new CharsRefBuilder();
        CharsRef cr = charsRefBuilder.append(syn).get();

        State state = captureState();
        outputs.add(new PendingOutput(state, cr));
```

Creates a token filter that takes an already-trained word2vec model

Implements the Lucene API for token filtering

Adds cached synonyms to the token stream (see the next code listing)

Expands a token only if it's not a synonym (to avoid loops in the expansion)

For each term, uses word2vec to find the closest words that have an accuracy higher than a minAcc (for example, 0.35)

Records no more than two synonyms for each token

Records the current state of the original term (not the synonym) in the token stream (for example, starting and ending position)

Records the synonym value

Creates an object to contain the synonyms to be added to the token stream after all the original terms have been consumed

```
        i++;
      }
    }
  }
  return !outputs.isEmpty() || input.incrementToken();
}
```

This code traverses all the terms and, when it finds a synonym, puts the synonym in a list of pending outputs to expand (the `outputs` list). You apply those pending terms to be added (the actual synonyms) after each original term has been processed, as shown next.

Listing 2.12   Expanding pending synonyms

```
...
  if (!outputs.isEmpty()) {                                    Gets the first pending
    PendingOutput output = outputs.remove(0);                  output to expand
    restoreState(output.state);
    termAtt.copyBuffer(output.charsRef.chars, output          Retrieves the state of
      .charsRef.offset, output.charsRef.length);              the original term,
    typeAtt.setType(SynonymFilter.TYPE_SYNONYM);              including its text, its
    return true;                                              position in the text
  }                                                           stream, and so on
```

**Sets the synonym text to that given
by word2vec and previously saved
in the pending output**

**Sets the type of the
term as synonym**

You use the word2vec output results as synonyms only if they have an accuracy greater than a certain threshold, as discussed in the previous section. The filter picks only the two words closest to the given term (according to word2vec) having an accuracy of at least 0.35 (which isn't that high), for each term passed by the tokenizer. If you pass the sentence "I like pleasure spiked with pain and music is my airplane" to the filter, it will expand the word "airplane" with two additional words: "airplanes" and "aeroplane" (see the final part of the expanded token stream shown in figure 2.15).

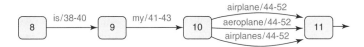

Figure 2.15   Token stream after word2vec synonym expansion

2.5   *Evaluations and comparisons*

As mentioned in chapter 1, you can usually capture metrics, including precision, recall, query with zero results, and so on, both before and after the introduction of query expansion. It's also usually good to determine the best configuration set for all the parameters of a neural network. A generic neural network has many parameters you can adjust:

- The general network architecture, such as using one or more hidden layers
- The transformations performed in each layer

- The number of neurons in each layer
- The connections between neurons belonging to different layers
- The number of times (also called *epochs*) the network should read through all the training sets in order to reach its final state (possibly with a low error and high accuracy)

These parameters also apply to other machine learning techniques. In the case of word2vec, you can decide

- The size of the generated word embeddings
- The window used to create fragments for unsupervised training of models
- Which architecture to use: CBOW or skip-gram

As you can see, there are many possible parameter settings to try.

Cross validation is a method of optimizing the parameters while making sure a machine learning model performs well enough on data that's different from the one used for training. With cross validation, the original dataset is split into three subsets: a training set, a validation set, and a test set. The training set is used as the data source to train the model. In practice, it's often used to train a bunch of separate models with different settings for the available parameters. The cross-validation set is used to select the model that has the best-performing parameters. This can be done, for example, by taking each pair of input and desired output in the cross-validation set and seeing whether a model gives results equal or close to the desired output, when given that particular input. The test set is used the same way as the cross-validation set, except it's only used by the model selected by testing on the cross-validation set. The accuracy of results on the test set can be considered a good measure of the model's overall effectiveness.

2.6   *Considerations for production systems*

In this chapter, you've seen how to use word2vec to generate synonyms from data to be indexed and searched. Most existing production systems already contain lots of indexed documents, and in such cases it's often impossible to access the original data as it existed before it was indexed. In the case of indexing the top 100 songs of the year to build a search engine of song lyrics, you have to take into account that the rankings of the most popular songs change every day, week, month, and year. This implies that the dataset will change over time; therefore, if you don't keep old copies in separate storage, you won't be able to build a word2vec model for all indexed documents (song lyrics) later.

The solution to this problem is to work with the search engine as the primary data source. When you set up word2vec using DL4J, you fetched sentences from a single file:

```
String filePath = new ClassPathResource("billboard_lyrics.txt").getFile()
    .getAbsolutePath();
SentenceIterator iter = new BasicLineIterator(filePath);
```

Given an evolving system that's fed song lyrics from different files daily, weekly, or monthly, you'll need to take the sentences directly from the search engine. For this reason, you'll build a SentenceIterator that reads stored values from the Lucene index.

Listing 2.13   Fetching sentences for word2vec from the Lucene index

```
public class FieldValuesSentenceIterator implements
    SentenceIterator {

  private final IndexReader reader;              View of the index used to
                                                 fetch the document values
  private final String field;
  private int currentId;                         Specific field to fetch
                                                 the values from
  public FieldValuesSentenceIterator(
      IndexReader reader, String field) {
    this.reader = reader;                        The identifier of the current
    this.field = field;                          document being fetched,
    this.currentId = 0;                          because this is an iterator
  }

  ...

  @Override
  public void reset() {              First document
    currentId = 0;                   ID is always 0
  }

}
```

In the example of the song lyrics search engine, the text of the lyrics were indexed into the text field. You therefore fetch the sentences and words to be used for training the word2vec model from that field.

Listing 2.14   Reading sentences from the Lucene index

```
Path path = Paths.get("/path/to/index");
Directory directory = FSDirectory.open(path);
IndexReader reader = DirectoryReader.open(directory);
SentenceIterator iter = new FieldValuesSentenceIterator(reader, "text");
```

Once you've set things up, you pass this new SentenceIterator to the word2vec implementation:

```
SentenceIterator iter = new FieldValuesSentenceIterator(reader, "text");
Word2Vec vec = new Word2Vec.Builder()
  .layerSize(100)
  .windowSize(5)
  .iterate(iter)
  .build();
vec.fit();
```

During the training phase, the SentenceIterator is asked to iterate over Strings.

Listing 2.15 For each document, passing field values to word2vec for training

```
@Override
public String nextSentence() {
  if (!hasNext()) {
    return null;
  }
  try {
    Document document = reader.document(currentId,
        Collections.singleton(field));
    String sentence = document.getField(field)
        .stringValue();
    return preProcessor != null ? preProcessor
        .preProcess(sentence) :
    sentence;
  } catch (IOException e) {
    throw new RuntimeException(e);
  } finally {
    currentId++;
  }
}

@Override
public boolean hasNext() {
  return currentId < reader.numDocs();
}
```

The iterator has more sentences if the current document identifier isn't bigger than the number of documents contained in the index.

Gets the document with the current identifier (only the field you need is fetched)

Gets the value of the text field from the current Lucene Document as a String

Returns the sentence, which is preprocessed if you set a preprocessor (for example, to remove unwanted characters or tokens)

Increments the document ID for the next iteration

This way, word2vec can be retrained frequently on existing search engines without having to maintain the original data. The synonym expansion filter can be kept up to date as the data in the search engine is updated.

2.6.1 Synonyms vs. antonyms

Imagine that you have the following sentences: "I like pizza," "I hate pizza," "I like pasta," "I hate pasta," "I love pasta," and "I eat pasta." This would be a small set of sentences for word2vec to use to learn accurate embeddings in real life. But you can clearly see that the terms "I" on the left and "pizza" and "pasta" on the right all share verbs in between. Because word2vec learns word embeddings using similar text fragments, you may end up with similar word vectors for the verbs "like," "hate," "love," and "eat." So word2vec may report that "love" is close to "like" and "eat" (which is fine, given that the sentences are all related to food) but also to "hate," which is definitely not a synonym for "love."

In some cases, this issue may not be important. Suppose you want to go out to dinner, and you're searching for a nice restaurant on the internet. You write the query "reviews of restaurants people love" in a search engine. If you get reviews about "restaurants people hate," then you'll know where *not* to go. But this is an edge case; generally, you don't want antonyms (the opposite of a synonym) to be expanded like synonyms.

Don't worry—usually, the text has enough information to tell you that although "hate" and "love" appear in similar contexts, they aren't proper synonyms. The fact that this corpus of text is only made of sentences like "I hate pizza" or "I like pasta" makes it more difficult: usually, "hate" and "like" also appear in other contexts, which helps word2vec figure out that they aren't similar. To see that, let's evaluate the nearest words of the word "nice" together with their similarity:

```
String tw = "nice";
Collection<String> wordsNearest = vec.wordsNearest(tw, 3);
System.out.println(tw + " -> " + wordsNearest);
for (String wn : wordsNearest) {
  double similarity = vec.similarity(tw, wn);
  System.out.println("sim(" + tw + "," + wn + ") : " + similarity);
  ...
}
```

The similarity between word vectors can help you exclude nearest neighbors that aren't similar enough. A sample word2vec run over the Hot 100 Billboard dataset indicates that the nearest words of the word "nice" are "cute," "unfair," and "real":

```
nice -> [cute, unfair, real]
sim(nice,cute) : 0.6139052510261536
sim(nice,unfair) : 0.5972062945365906
sim(nice,real) : 0.5814308524131775
```

"Cute" is a synonym. "Unfair" isn't an antonym but an adjective that expresses negative feelings; it's not a good result, because it's in contrast with the positive nature of "nice" and "cute." "Real" also doesn't express the same general semantics as "nice." To fix this, you can, for example, filter out the nearest neighbors whose similarity is less than the absolute value 0.5, or less than the highest similarity minus 0.1. You assume that the first nearest neighbor is usually good enough, as long as its similarity is greater than 0.5; once this applies, you exclude words that are too far from the nearest neighbor. In this case, filtering out words whose similarity is less than the highest nearest neighbor similarity (0.61) minus 0.1, you filter out both "unfair" and "real" (each has a similarity less than 0.60).

Summary

- Synonym expansion can be a handy technique to improve recall and make the users of your search engine happier.
- Common synonym-expansion techniques are based on static dictionaries and vocabularies that might require manual maintenance or are often far from the data they're used for.
- Feed-forward neural networks are the basis of many neural network architectures. In a feed-forward neural network, information flows from an input layer to an output layer; in between these two layers, there may be one or more hidden layers.
- Word2vec is a feed-forward neural network–based algorithm for learning vector representations for words that can be used to find words with similar mean-

ings—or that appear in similar contexts—so it's reasonable to use it for synonym expansion, too.

- You can either use the continuous-bag-of-words or skip-gram architecture for word2vec. In CBOW, the target word is used as the output of the network, and the remaining words of the text fragments are used as inputs. In the skip-gram model, the target word is used as input, and the context words are outputs. Both work well, but skip-gram is usually preferred, because it works better with infrequent words.
- Word2vec models can provide good results, but you need to manage word senses or parts of speech when using it for synonyms.
- In word2vec, be careful to avoid letting antonyms be used as synonyms.

Part 2

Throwing neural nets at a search engine

Now that you know something about the fundamentals of search and deep learning, you can start throwing neural networks at a search engine wherever you see fit, right? In theory, yes; in practice, no. Deep neural networks aren't magic: you need to use extreme care when deciding where and how using such powerful techniques makes sense. Chapters 3–6 look at tasks that every modern search engine commonly performs and highlight their limitations. As we identify them, we'll explore how to use deep learning to mitigate such issues. You'll see how to better solve the search engine task, either by looking at example output or by using more rigorous information-retrieval metrics.

From plain retrieval to text generation

This chapter covers

- Expanding queries
- Using search logs to build training data
- Understanding recurrent neural networks
- Generating alternative queries with RNNs

In the early days of the internet and search engines (late 1990s), people only searched for keywords. Users might have typed "movie zemeckis future" to find information about the movie *Back to the Future*, directed by Robert Zemeckis. Although search engines have evolved, and today we can type queries using natural language, many users still rely on keywords when searching. For these users, it would be advantageous if the search engine could generate a proper query based on the keywords they type: for example, taking "movie Zemeckis future" and generating "Back to the Future by Robert Zemeckis." Let's call the generated query an *alternative query*, in the sense that it's an alternative (text) representation of the information need expressed by the user.

This chapter will teach you how to add text-generation capabilities to your search engine so that, given a user query, it will generate a few alternative queries to run under the hood together with the original one. The goal is to express the query in additional ways so as to widen the net of the search—without asking the user to think of or type in alternatives. To add text generation to a search engine, you'll use a powerful architecture for neural networks called a *recurrent neural network* (RNN).

Recurrent neural networks have the same flexibility as the unembellished feed-forward networks you learned about in chapter 2. But RNNs also have the advantage of being able to deal with long sequences of inputs and outputs.

Before you learn how to use RNNs, let's remember what you did with feed-forward networks. You used them with a specific model, word2vec, to improve synonym expansion so a query could be expanded using one (or more) of its synonyms. Better synonym expansion increases the effectiveness of the search engine by returning more-relevant documents. Word2vec uses a specifically designed neural network to generate dense vector representations for words. Such vectors can be used to calculate the similarity of two words by their vectors' distances, as in the synonym expansion case. But they can also be used as inputs for more complex neural network architectures, like RNNs. This is exactly how you'll use them in this chapter.

> **NOTE** In practice, it's common to train neural networks to accomplish specific tasks by arranging neuron activation functions, layers, and their connections, depending on the problem at hand. The rest of this book will introduce you to various neural network architectures, each addressing a different kind of problem. For example, in the computer vision field, where network inputs are usually images or videos, it's common to use *convolutional neural networks* (CNNs). In CNNs, each layer has a distinct, specific function: there are convolutional layers, pooling layers, and so on. At the same time, the aggregation of these layers allows you to build a deep neural network where pixels are incrementally transformed into something more abstract: for instance, pixels → edges → objects →. We looked briefly at these in chapter 1 and will take a closer look in chapter 8.

In chapter 1, you saw how a user can express an information need as a variety of slightly different versions, and how even small changes in the way a query is written can influence which documents are returned first. So when training a neural network to generate output queries from input queries, it's useful to go beyond just the words in a query, apart from their context. The aim is to generate text queries that are semantically similar to the input query; doing so enables the search engine to return search results based on different ways of expressing the same fundamental need (via the query). You can use an RNN to generate text in natural language and then integrate that generated text into a search engine. The rest of this chapter will teach you how RNNs work, how to tune them to generate alternative queries, and how an RNN-backed search engine offers improved effectiveness in returning relevant results for end users.

3.1 Information need vs. query: Bridging the gap

Chapter 1 talked about the fundamental problem of how users can best express an information need. But as a user, do you really want to spend a lot of time thinking about how to word a query? Imagine yourself on your way to work on public transport early in the morning, searching for information on your phone. You don't have the time or the brainpower (it's early!) to come up with the best way to interact with a search engine.

If you ask users to explain the information they need in three or four sentences, you're likely to get a detailed explanation of the specific need and its detailed context. But if you ask the same person to express what they're looking for in a short query of no more than five or six words, the chances are high that they won't be able to do it, because it's not always easy to compress a detailed requirement into a short sequence of words. As search engineers, we need to do something to bridge this gap between user intent and the resulting queries.

3.1.1 Generating alternative queries

A well-known technique to help users write queries is providing a hint with suggested text while the user is typing the query. This lets the search engine UI guide the user while they write. The search engine makes an explicit effort to help the user type a "good" query (we'll take a detailed look at how it does this in chapter 4). Another approach to fill the gap between information need and the user-entered query is to postprocess the query right after it enters the search engine system but before it's executed. Such a postprocessing task's responsibility is to use the entered query to create a new one that's "better" to some extent. Of course, "better" can mean different things in this context; this chapter focuses on producing a query that expresses the same information need in various ways, to increase the likelihood that

- A relevant document is included in the result set
- More-relevant documents are ranked first in the search results

This is usually done manually and incrementally these days—you might fire a first query about, for instance, "latest research in artificial intelligence"; then a second one such as "what is deep learning"; and then a third one, like "recurrent neural networks for search." The term *manually* refers to the fact that in this example, you run a query, look at the results, reason about them, write and run another query, look at the results, reason about them, and so on, until you either get the knowledge you're looking for, or you give up.

The goal is to produce a set of alternative queries without any interaction with the user. Such queries should have the same or similar meaning with respect to the original query, but using different words (while still being correctly spelled). To see how this should work, let's go back to the example of the query "movie Zemeckis future." If you enter that phrase, the search engine should do the following:

1 Accept the user-entered query "movie Zemeckis future."

2 Pass the query through the query time-analysis chain and produce the transformed version of the user query—in this case, assuming you've configured a filter to lowercase capital letters.

3 Pass the filtered query "movie zemeckis future" to the RNN and obtain one or more alternative queries as output, such as "Back to the Future by Robert Zemeckis."

4 Transform the original filtered query and the generated alternative query into a form that's implementation-specific to the search engine (a *parsed* query).

5 Run the queries against the inverted indexes.

As you can see in figure 3.1, you'll be setting up the search engine to use a neural network at search time to generate appropriate alternative queries to add to the query entered by the user. You'll keep the original query as it was written by the user and add the generated queries as additional *optional* queries. Toward the end of the chapter, we'll discuss how to best use the generated queries.

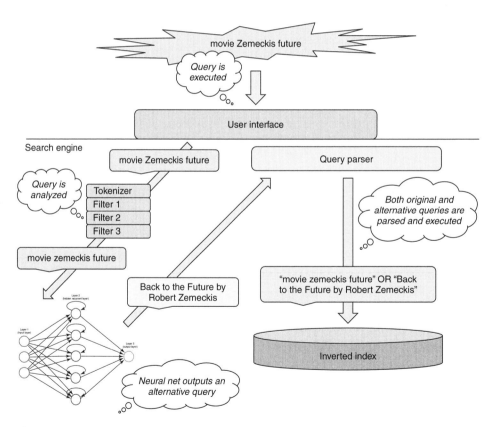

Figure 3.1 Alternative query generation

Automatic query expansion is the name of the technique of generating (portions of) queries under the hood to maximize the number of relevant results for the end user. In some sense, synonym expansion (which you saw in chapter 2) is a special case of automatic query expansion if you use it at query time only (not to index synonyms, but only to expand synonyms for terms in the query).

Your goal is to use this query-expansion feature to improve the query engine as follows:

- Minimizing queries with zero results. Providing an alternative text representation for a query is more likely to produce hits on search results.
- Improving recall (the fraction of relevant documents that are retrieved, with respect to a certain query) by including results you'd have missed otherwise.
- Improving precision by giving a boost to results that match both the original query and an alternative query (which implies that the alternative queries are close to the original).

NOTE Query expansion isn't just for neural networks; this approach can be implemented using various algorithms. You could, theoretically, replace the neural network in the query-expansion model with a black box. Before the advent of (deep) RNNs, other approaches existed for generating natural language (this is a subfield of natural language processing called *natural language generation*). At the end of the chapter, I'll offer a brief comparison to other methods, to illustrate "the unreasonable effectiveness of recurrent neural networks."[1]

Before seeing RNNs in action, as is the case with many machine learning scenarios, it's crucial to take a close look at how you train the model, along with what kind of data you should use and why. As you may recall, in supervised learning, you tell the algorithm how you want the model to produce an output with respect to a certain input. Thus the way you structure inputs and outputs depends a lot on what you want to achieve. The next section takes a quick tour of three possible ways to prepare the data to be fed into the RNN.

3.1.2 Data preparation

I've chosen RNNs to implement query expansion because they're surprisingly good at and flexible for learning to generate sequences of text, including sequences that don't appear in the training data but that still "make sense." Additionally, RNNs usually require less tuning compared to other natural language generation algorithms that use grammars, Markov chains, and so on. All this sounds great, but what do you expect to happen when generating alternative queries in practice? What should the generated queries look like? As is all too often true in computer science, the answer is *... it depends!*

---

[1] See Andrej Karpathy, "The Unreasonable Effectiveness of Recurrent Neural Networks," May 21, 2015, http://mng.bz/Mxl2.

It's important to define what you want to achieve. If you think about the case where a user enters the query "books about artificial intelligence," you could provide other queries (or sentences) that carry the same semantic information, like "publications from the field of artificial intelligence" or "books dealing with the topic of intelligent machines." At the same time, you need to consider how useful such alternative representations would be in your search engine—the possible alternative queries may give zero results if you have no documents dealing with the topic of artificial intelligence! You don't want to generate an alternative query representation that's perfect but not useful. Instead, you can look closely at user queries and provide alternative representations that are built on the information they contain; or you can make the query-generation algorithm obtain information from the indexed data rather than the user data, so that the generated alternative queries better reflect what's already in the search engine (and mitigate the problem of an alternative query returning no results).

In real life, you often have access to *query logs*, which are flat records of what users have queried via the search engine with minimal information about the results. You can gain many insights from looking at query logs. For instance, you can clearly see when people fail to find what they're looking for, because they will submit queries that are similar in meaning. You can also observe how users switch from searching for one topic to another. For the sake of an example, let's say you're building a search engine for a media company that provides political, cultural, and fashion news to users. Here's a sample query log:

```
time: 2017/01/06 09:06:41, query:{"artificial intelligence"}, results:
    {size=10, ids:["doc1","doc5", ...]}
time: 2017/01/06 09:08:12, query:{"books about AI"}, results:
    {size=1, ids:["doc5"]}
time: 2017/01/06 19:21:45, query:{"artificial intelligence hype"}, results:
    {size=3, ids:["doc1","doc8", ...]}
time: 2017/05/04 14:12:31, query:{"covfefe"}, results:
    {size=100, ids:["doc113","doc588", ...]}       ◁
time: 2017/10/08 13:26:01, query:{"latest trends"}, results:
    {size=15, ids:["doc113","doc23", ...]}
...
```

The query "covfefe" returned 100 results, and the first two resulting document identifiers are doc113 and doc588.

Assume that this is part of a huge query log of user activity on the search engine. Now, imagine you have to build a *training set* from this query log—a collection of examples of inputs associated with desired outputs—correlating similar queries so that you can build training examples where the input is a query and the target output is one or more correlated queries. In this case, each example will consist of one input query and one or more output queries. In practice, it's common to use query logs for such learning tasks because

- Query logs reflect the behavior of users on that specific system, so the resulting model will behave relatively close to the actual users and data.

- Using or generating other datasets may incur additional costs while possibly training a model that's based on different data, users, domains, and so on.

In the current example, imagine that you have two related queries: "men clothing latest trends" and "Paris fashion week." You can use them interchangeably as input and output for training a neural network. A nontrivial decision you need to make is how to measure the correlation (similarity) of two queries. Your general knowledge tells you that the two queries are similar in the sense that the Paris fashion week event has a significant influence on clothing (fashion) trends (for both men and women), so you may decide to set "Paris fashion week" as an alternative representation of the "men clothing latest trends" query; see figure 3.2. But in this context, neither the search engine nor the neural network knows anything about the topic of fashion—they just see input and output texts and vectors.

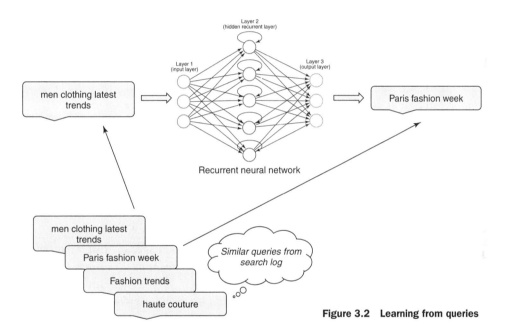

Figure 3.2 Learning from queries

Each line from the query log contains a user-entered query associated with its search results: more precisely, the document IDs of the matching results. But this isn't what you need. Your training examples have to be composed of an input query and one or more output queries that are similar or by some means correlated to the input. So before you can train the network, you need to process the lines of the search log and create a training set. This type of work, which involves manipulating and tweaking the data, is often called *data preparation* or *preprocessing*. Although it may sound a bit tedious, it's crucial for the effectiveness of any associated machine learning task.

The following sections look at three different ways of selecting input and output sequences for a neural network to use to learn to generate alternative queries:

correlating queries that generate similar search result sets, that come from the same users in specific time windows, or that contain similar search terms. Each of these options will yield specific side effects related to the way the neural network will learn to generate new queries.

CORRELATING QUERIES THAT GENERATE SIMILAR SEARCH RESULT SETS

The first approach groups queries that share a portion of their associated search result. For example, you could extract the following from the example query log.

Listing 3.1   Correlating queries using shared results

```
query:{"artificial intelligence"} -> {"books about AI"
    , "artificial intelligence hype"}   <--- Shares doc1 and doc5
query:{"books about AI"} -> {
    "artificial intelligence"}   <--- Shares doc5
query:{"artificial intelligence hype"} -> {
    "artificial intelligence"}            <--- Shares doc1
query:{"covfefe"} -> {"latest trends"}
query:{"latest trends"} -> {"covfefe"}      Shares doc113
```

By correlating queries having shared documents in the search log, you can see that "latest trends" can generate "covfefe" and vice versa, and the artificial intelligence–related queries seem to suggest good alternatives.

Note that "latest trends" refers to a relative concept: the latest trends one day may (or will) be significantly different than those tomorrow or next week. If you assume the *covfefe* trend lasted one week, it would be bad for the neural network to generate "covfefe" as an alternative query for "latest trends" one month after *covfefe* showed up in the news. As the real world outside of a search engine changes, you need to be careful about using data that is up to date, or at least avoid potential problems by removing training examples that may cause bad results, as in this case.

CORRELATING QUERIES THAT COME FROM THE SAME USERS IN SPECIFIC TIME WINDOWS

The second potential approach relies on the assumption that users search for similar things in small time windows. For example, if you're searching for "that specific restaurant I went to, but I can't recall its name," you'll perform multiple searches that relate to the same information need. The key point of this approach is to identify accurate time windows in the query logs so that queries related to the same information need can be grouped together (regardless of their results). In practice, identifying search sessions that relate to the same need isn't necessarily simple and depends on how informative the search logs are. For instance, if the search log is a flat list of concurrent anonymous searches for all users, it will be difficult to say which queries were performed by a single user. If you instead have information about every user, such as their IP address, you can try to identify a search session per topic.

Let's assume that the sample search log comes from a single user. The time information on each line indicates that the first two queries were run in a two-minute window, whereas the others were run a long time apart. So you could correlate the first two queries—"artificial intelligence" and "books about AI"—and skip the others. But in real life, people may be doing multiple things concurrently, like wanting to get information about a technical topic while going to work but also needing information about public transport time tables or traffic on the highway. In such cases, it's difficult to distinguish which queries are semantically correlated without looking at the query terms, which you do in the third approach.

CORRELATING QUERIES THAT CONTAIN SIMILAR SEARCH TERMS

Using similar terms to correlate queries is tricky to implement. On one hand, it sounds simple. You can find common terms among the queries in the search log, as shown next.

Listing 3.2 Correlating queries using search terms

```
query:{"artificial intelligence"} ->
    {"artificial intelligence hype"}    <--- Shares "artificial" and "intelligence" terms
query:{"books about AI"} -> {}          <--- Shares nothing
query:{"artificial intelligence hype"} ->
    {"artificial intelligence"}    <--- Shares "artificial" and "intelligence" terms
query:{"covfefe"} -> {}          <--- Shares nothing
query:{"latest trends"} -> {}          <--- Shares nothing
```

Here, you've lost some information that was carried by the query results, as you can see in comparison with the previous listing; in addition, the training set is much smaller and poorer. Let's look at "books about AI." This is surely related to "artificial intelligence" and, perhaps, to "artificial intelligence hype." But simple term matching fails to capture the fact that *AI* is short for *artificial intelligence*. You can mitigate that issue by applying synonym expansion techniques, as you learned in chapter 2; doing so requires an additional preprocessing step to generate new search log lines in which synonyms are expanded. In this example, if your synonym expansion algorithm can map the term "AI" to the composite term "artificial intelligence," you'll get the following input/output pairs.

Listing 3.3 Correlating queries using search terms and synonym expansion

```
query:{"artificial intelligence"} -> {"artificial intelligence hype"}
query:{"books about AI"} -> {}
query:{"books about artificial intelligence"} ->
    {"artificial intelligence",                  Additional mapping;
    "artificial intelligence hype"}    <------    shares "artificial" and
query:{"artificial intelligence hype"} -> {"artificial intelligence"}    "intelligence terms"
query:{"covfefe"} -> {}
query:{"latest trends"} -> {}
```

With respect to the former results, you now have an additional mapping: using synonyms generated by the new input query "books about artificial intelligence," which didn't exist in the original search log. Although this seems fine, be careful, because there may be more than one synonym for each term in each query. That's often the case with large dictionaries like WordNet and also when using word embeddings based on similarity (such as word2vec) to expand synonyms. Having more data for training neural networks is usually desirable, but it has to be of good quality to give good results. Let's not forget that this is a preprocessing stage to train a neural network that will be used to generate sequences. If you feed the neural network with text sequences that don't make much sense (not all synonyms of a certain word fit well in every possible context), it will generate sequences with little or no meaning.

If you plan to use synonym expansion, you probably should *not* expand on every possible synonym; you could instead do so only for input queries that don't have a corresponding alternative query, such as "books about AI" in the previous example.

SELECTING OUTPUT SEQUENCES FROM THE INDEXED DATA

If the techniques described so far don't work well enough on your data—for example, user-entered queries often give too few or zero results—you can get some help from the indexed data. In many real-life scenarios, indexed documents have a title, which is usually relatively short. Such a title can be used as a query if it's correlated to the original input query. Let's again choose the query "movie Zemeckis future." Running it on a movie search engine (such as IMDB) would probably return something like this:

```
title: Back to the Future
director: Robert Zemeckis
year: 1985
writers: Robert Zemeckis, Bob Gale
stars: Michael J. Fox, Christopher Lloyd, Lea Thompson, ...
```

Let's imagine how this document was retrieved:

- The term "movie" is on a stopword list on a search engine about movies, so it didn't match.
- The term "Zemeckis" matched in both the `writers` and `director` fields.
- The term "future" matched in the `title` field.

Put yourself in the shoes of someone looking at both the queries and the results: as the user types a query, if you saw the user entering "movie Zemeckis future," you could immediately tell they should have typed a query like "back to the future" instead. That's exactly the type of training example you can pass to a neural network, composed of an input ("movie Zemeckis future") and a target output ("back to the future"). You can preprocess the search log so that the target alternative query to be generated by the neural network is the query that would return the best result. Doing so will likely help reduce the number of queries with zero results, because the hints in the alternative queries don't come from the user-generated queries but rather from the text of relevant documents. To build training examples, you associate a query with the titles of the top two or three relevant documents from the search log, as in figure 3.3.

You may wonder, why not use the search engine instead of a neural network to generate alternative queries? That approach would constrain the set of alternative queries for a certain input text to what the search engine can already do in terms of matching. For example, "movie Zemeckis future" will always give the same set of alternative queries if you use the search engine to generate them. In the case of the example query,

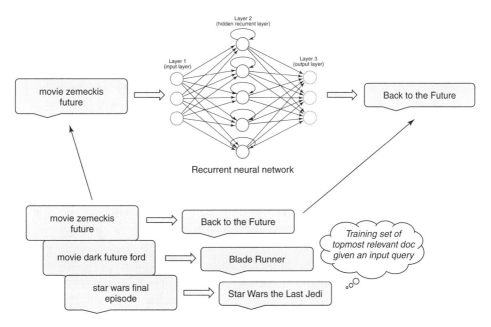

Figure 3.3 Learning from the titles of relevant documents

that would work—but what if the user typed "movie spielberg future" (confusing the movie's producer with its director)? There's no match in the search engine with the term "spielberg." So the search engine might return a lot of movies Steven Spielberg has directed that involve the term "future," but it wouldn't return *Back to the Future*. The key takeaway is that you aren't limited to using queries to train the neural network, as long as the target output is correlated with the input in a way that's useful for representing an alternative query.

UNSUPERVISED STREAMS OF TEXT SEQUENCES

A completely different approach for feeding an RNN for text generation is to perform unsupervised learning over streams of text. As mentioned in chapter 1, this is a form of machine learning where the learning algorithm isn't told anything about good (or bad) output; the algorithm just builds a model of the data as accurately as possible. You'll see that this is probably the most surprising way RNNs can learn to generate text: no one is telling them what good output is, so they learn to reproduce good-quality text sequences on the basis of the inputs.

In the search log example, you take the queries one after the other, removing everything else:

```
artificial intelligence
books about AI
artificial intelligence hype
covfefe
latest trends
```

As you can see, this is plain text. All you need to do is decide how to identify the end of a query. In this case, you might use the carriage return character (\n) as a delimiter for two consecutive queries, and the text-generation algorithm will stop whenever it generates a carriage return. This approach is tempting, because it requires almost no preprocessing: the data to be used can come from anywhere because it's just plain text. You'll see the pros and cons later in this chapter.

3.1.3 Wrap-up of generating data

Here's a quick summary of what we've discussed in this section:

- Performing supervised learning over similar queries gives you the advantage of being able to specify what you think are good, similar queries. The downside is that the neural network's effectiveness will be based on how good you are at defining when two queries are similar during the data-preparation phase.
- You may not want to explicitly specify when two queries are similar, but rather let the relevant documents for a query provide the alternative query text. This will make the neural network generate alternative queries whose text comes from the indexed documents (for example, the document titles) and will likely reduce the number of queries with few or zero results.
- An unsupervised approach considers the stream of queries from the search log as a sequence of plausible consecutive words, so little data preparation is needed. The advantages of this approach are that it's simple to implement and can closely capture which consecutive queries (and hence topics) users tend to be interested in.

There are many alternatives and considerable room for creativity to build new ways to generate data that suits the need of your users. The key point is to be careful how you prepare data for your system. We'll assume that you've chosen one of the approaches discussed here; next, we'll examine how RNNs learn to generate sequences of text.

3.2 Learning over sequences

In chapter 1, you saw what the general architecture of a neural network looks like, with input and output layers at the edges of the network and hidden layers in between. Then, in chapter 2, we started looking at two less-general neural network models (continuous-bag-of-words and skip-gram) used to implement the word2vec algorithm. The architectures discussed so far can be used to model how an input can be mapped into its corresponding output. In the case of the skip-gram model, you map an input vector representing a certain word to an output vector representing a fixed number of words.

Let's think of a simple feed-forward neural network you could use to detect the language used in text sentences: for example, for the four languages English, German, Portuguese, and Italian. This is called a *multiclass classification task*, where the input is a piece of text and the output is one of three or more possible classes assigned to that input (the document-categorization example from chapter 1 is also a multi-class classification task). In this example, a neural network that can perform such a task will have four output neurons, one for each class (language). Only one output neuron will be set to 1 in the output layer, to signal that the input belongs to a certain class. For example, if the value of output neuron 1 is 1, then the input text is classified as English; if the value of output neuron 2 is 1, then the input text is classified as German; and so on.

The dimension of the input layer is much trickier to define. If you assume you're working with fixed-size text sequences, you can design the input layer accordingly. For language detection, you need several words, so let's assume you'll set up the input layer with nine neurons: one per input word; see figure 3.4.

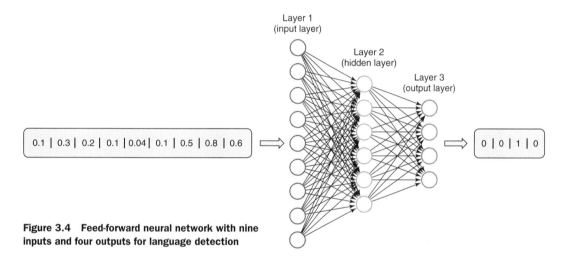

Figure 3.4 Feed-forward neural network with nine inputs and four outputs for language detection

> **NOTE** In practice, it would be difficult to use such one-to-one mapping between words and neurons: as you saw with the one-hot-encoding technique described for word2vec, each word is represented as a vector of all zeros except one, whose size is equal to the size of the entire vocabulary. In this case, if you were to use one-hot encoding, the input layer would contain $9 * size(vocabulary)$ neurons. But because we're focusing on fixed-size inputs, this isn't important here.

Clearly, you have a problem if a text sequence has fewer than nine words: you need to fill (or *pad*) it with some fake filler words. For longer sequences, you'll do language detection nine words at a time. Consider the text of a movie review. The contents might be in one language—for example, Italian—but deal with a movie whose title is in its original language—for example, English. If you split the review text into nine-word sequences, the output may be in either "Italian" or "English," depending on the portion of text fed into the neural network.

With this limitation in mind, how can you make a neural network learn from sequences of inputs whose size isn't known in advance? If you knew the size of each sequence you wanted the network to learn, you could make the input layer long enough to include the entire sequence. But doing so would hurt performance in the case of long sequences, because learning from a larger input requires more neurons in the hidden layer in order for the network to give accurate results. Thus this solution wouldn't scale well. RNNs can handle unbounded sequences of text by keeping their input and output layer sizes fixed, so they're perfect for learning to generate sequences of text in the use case of automatically expanding queries.

3.3   *Recurrent neural networks*

You can think of an RNN as a neural network that can remember information about its inputs as it processes them, so that the outputs produced by subsequent inputs also depend on previously seen inputs. At the same time, the size of the input layer (and the output layer, if the RNN generates sequences) is fixed.

For now, this is a bit abstract, but you'll come to understand how it works in practice and why it's important. Let's try to generate text sequences *without* an RNN, using a feed-forward neural network with five inputs and four outputs. The language-detection example used one input for each word, but in practice it's often more convenient to use characters instead of strings. The reason is that the number of possible words is much larger than the number of available characters, and it can be easier for the network to learn how to handle all possible combinations of 255 characters than all possible combinations of more than 300,000 words.[2] Using the one-hot-encoding technique, a character would be represented with a vector of size 255, and a word taken from the *Oxford English Dictionary* would be represented as a vector of size 301,000! The neural network input layer would need 301,000 neurons for one word, as opposed to 255 neurons for one character. On the other hand, a word represents a combination of characters that has meaning. At the character level, such information isn't available, and therefore a neural network with character inputs must first learn to generate meaningful words from characters; that isn't the case if you use words as inputs. In the end, it's a trade-off.

For example, when using characters, the sentence "the big brown fox jumped over the lazy dog" can be split into chunks of five characters. Then, each input is fed into the neural network with five input neurons; see figure 3.5. You can pass an entire sequence to the network regardless of the size of the input layer. It appears that you can use a "simple" neural network—you don't need an RNN.

But imagine if humans listening to someone talking had to understand what that person was saying by only hearing words composed of five characters and forgetting each sequence as soon as they heard the next. For example, if someone said "my

---

[2] This number is constantly increasing; see the *Oxford English Dictionary*, www.oed.com.

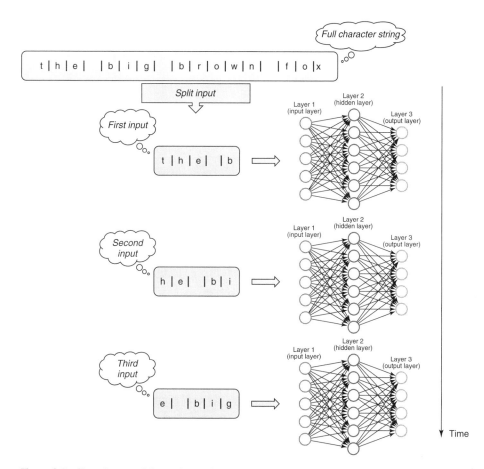

Figure 3.5 Neural network ingesting an input sequence with a fixed input layer of five neurons

name is Yoda," you'd get each of the following sequences, without remembering all the others:

```
my na
y nam
 name
name
ame i
me is
e is
 is Y
is Yo
s Yod
 Yoda
```

Now you're asked to repeat what you heard. Weird! With such a short fixed input, you may rarely get entire words, and each input is always detached from the rest of the sentence.

What makes it possible to understand a sentence is that each time you hear a five-character sequence, you keep track of what you received immediately before that. Let's say you have a memory of size 10:

```
my na ()
y nam (m)
 name (my)
name  (my )
ame i (my n)
me is (my na)
e is  (my nam)
 is Y (my name)
is Yo (my name )
s Yod (my name i)
 Yoda (my name is)
```

This is a huge simplification of how both humans and neural networks work with input and memory, but it should be enough for you to see the rationale behind the effectiveness of RNNs (a simple one is shown in figure 3.6) in working with sequences versus plain feed-forward neural networks.

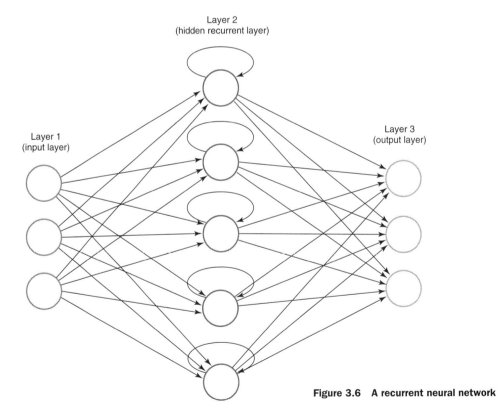

Figure 3.6   A recurrent neural network

3.3.1 RNN internals and dynamics

These special neural networks are called *recurrent* because, via simple looping connections in the hidden-layer neurons, the network becomes capable of operations that depend on the current input and the previous state of the network with respect to the previous input. In the case of learning to generate the text "my name is Yoda," the internal state of the RNN can be thought of as the memory that makes it possible to understand the sentence. Let's pick a single neuron in the hidden layer in an RNN, as shown in figure 3.7.

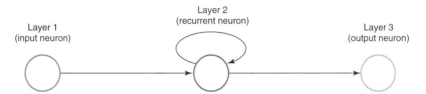

Figure 3.7   A recurrent neuron in the hidden layer of an RNN

The recurrent neuron combines the signal from the input neuron (the arrow from the neuron on the left) *and* a signal stored internally (the looping arrow), which plays the role of the memory in the Yoda example. As you can see, this single neuron processes an input, transforming it into an output, given its internal state (the hidden-layer weights and activation function). It also updates its state as a function of the new input and its current state. This is exactly what the neuron needs to do to learn to relate subsequent inputs. By *relate*, I mean that during training, the network will learn, for example, that characters that form meaningful words are more likely to appear nearby.

Going back to the Yoda example, the RNN would learn that, having seen the characters *Y* and *o*, the most probable character to generate is *d*, because the sequence "Yod" has already been seen. This is a significant simplification of the learning dynamics of an RNN, but it gives you a basic overview.

COST FUNCTIONS

As in many machine learning algorithms, a neural network learns to minimize the errors it commits when trying to create "good" outputs from inputs. The good outputs you provide during training, together with the inputs, tell the network how much it's wrong when it then performs a prediction. The amount of such error is usually measured by a *cost function* (also called a loss function). The aim of a learning algorithm is to optimize the algorithm parameters (in the case of a neural network, optimize the weights) so that the loss (or cost) is as low as possible.

I mentioned earlier that an RNN for text generation implicitly learns how likely certain sequences of text are in terms of probability. In the previous example, the sequence "Yoda" could have probability 0.7, whereas the sequence "ode " may have a probability of 0.01. An appropriate cost function compares the probabilities calculated by the neural network (with its current weights) against the actual probabilities in the input text; for example, the sequence "Yoda" would have an actual probability of about 1 in the example text. This gives the amount of loss (the error). Several different cost functions exist, but one that intuitively performs this type of comparison is called a *cross-entropy cost function*; we'll use it in the RNN examples. You can think of such a cost function as measuring how much the probabilities calculated by the neural network differ from what they should be with respect to a certain output. For example, if a network learning over the Yoda sentence says the probability of the word "Yoda" is 0.00000001, it's probably going to have a high loss: the correct probability should be high, because "Yoda" is one of the few known good sequences in the input text.

Cost functions play a key role in machine learning, because they define the goal of the learning algorithm. Different cost functions are used for different types of problems. For example, the cross-entropy cost function is useful for classification tasks, whereas a *mean squared error* cost function is useful when a neural network needs to predict real values.

The mathematical foundations of cost functions would probably require an entire chapter; because the focus of this book is the applications of deep learning for search, we won't go into more detail. But I'll suggest the right cost function to use, depending on the specific problem being solved, as we proceed through the book.

UNROLLING RNNS

You may have noticed that the only aesthetic difference between a feed-forward network and an RNN is in some looping arrows in the hidden layers. The word *recurrent* refers to such loops.

A better way to visualize how an RNN works in practice is to *unroll* it. Imagine unrolling an RNN into a set of finite connected copies of the same network. This is useful in practice when implementing an RNN, but it also makes it easier to see how RNNs naturally fit into sequence learning.

In the Yoda example, I said that a memory of 10 characters helps you keep in mind the previously entered characters as you see new inputs. An RNN has this capability of keeping track of previous inputs (with respect to context) by means of recurrent neurons or layers. If you let the recurrent layer of an RNN "explode" into a set of 10 copies of the layer, you *unroll* the RNN by 10 (see figure 3.8).

You're feeding the sentence "my name is Yoda" to an RNN unrolled for 10 steps. Let's focus on the highlighted node in figure 3.8: you can see that it receives inputs from its input (the character *s*) and the previous node in the hidden (unrolled) layer, which in turn receives input from the character *i* and the previous node in the hidden layer; this goes back until the first input. The idea is that each node receives information about plain input (a character of the sequence) and, backward, from previous inputs and internal states of the network for such previous inputs.

On the other hand, going forward, you can see that the output to the first character (*m*) only depends on the input and the internal state (weights) of the network;

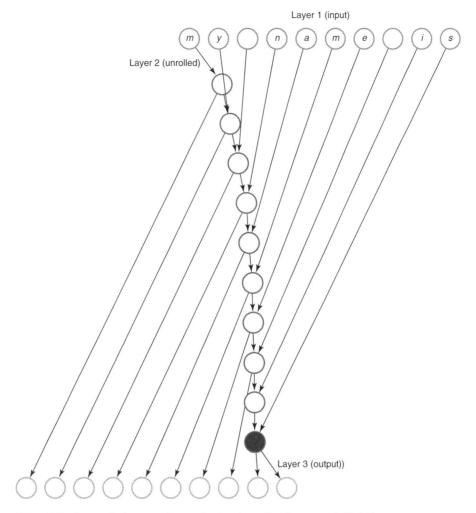

Figure 3.8 An unrolled recurrent neural network reading "my name is Yoda"

whereas the output to character *y* depends on the input, the current state, *and* the previous state as it was for the first character, *m*.

Thus the `unrolls` parameter is the number of steps the network can look back in time when generating the output for the current input. In practice, when setting up RNNs, you can decide how many steps you want to use to unroll the network. The more steps you have, the better the RNNs will be able to handle longer sequences, although they will also require more data and more time to train. Now you should have a basic idea of how an RNN handles sequences of inputs like text and keeps track of past sequences, when generating values in the output layers.

BACKPROPAGATION THROUGH TIME: HOW RNNS LEARN

Chapter 2 briefly introduced backpropagation, the most widely used algorithm for feed-forward neural network training. RNNs can be thought as feed-forward networks with an additional dimension: time. The effectiveness of RNNs lies in their ability to learn to correctly take into account information from previous input, using a learning algorithm called *backpropagation through time*. It's essentially an extension of simple backpropagation where the number of weights to learn is much higher than in plain feed-forward neural networks, due to the loops in the recurrent layer, because RNNs have weights that control how past information flows through. We just looked at the concept of unrolling an RNN. Backpropagation through time (BPTT) adjusts the weights of the recurrent layers; so, the more unrolls you have, the more parameters must be adjusted to get good results. Essentially, BPTT makes the (recurrent) neural network automatically learn not just the weights on the connections between neurons belonging to different layers, but also how past information needs to be combined with the current inputs, via additional weights.

The reasons for unrolling an RNN should now be clearer. It's a way to limit the number of recursions the loop performs into a recurrent neuron or layer so learning and predicting are bounded and don't recur indefinitely (which would make it difficult to compute the value in a recurrent neuron).

3.3.2 *Long-term dependencies*

Let's consider what an RNN for generating queries would look like. Imagine that you have two similar queries, such as "books about artificial intelligence" and "books about machine learning." (This is a simple example: the two sequences are exactly the same length.) One of the first things to do is decide the size of the hidden layers and the number of unrolls. In the previous section, you learned that the number of unrolls controls how far the network can look back in time. For that to work properly, the network needs to be powerful enough, which means it needs more neurons in the hidden layer to correctly handle the information coming from the past as the number of unrolls grows. The number of neurons in a layer defines the maximum *power* of the network. It's also important to note that if you want a network with many neurons (and layers), you'll need to provide lots of data in order for the network to perform well in terms of the accuracy of the outputs.

The number of unrolls is related to *long-term dependency*: a scenario where words may have semantic correlations even though they appear further from each other in a sequence of text. For instance, look at the following sentence, where words that are distant from each other are highly correlated:

> *In 2017, despite what happened during the 2016 Finals, Golden State Warriors won the championship again.*

Reading this phrase, you can easily understand that the word "championship" refers to the year "2017." But a not-so-smart algorithm may link "championship" to "2016," because that's also a likely pair to generate. This algorithm would fail to take into account that the word "2016" refers to "Finals" in the incidental sentence. This is an example of a long-term dependency. Depending on the data you're dealing with, you may need to take this into account to make an RNN work effectively.

Using more unrolls helps mitigate long-term dependency problems, but in general you may never know how far apart two correlated words can be (or characters, or even phrases). To fix this problem, researchers came up with an improved RNN architecture called a *long short-term memory* (LSTM) network.

3.3.3 Long short-term memory networks

So far, you've seen that a layer in a normal RNN is composed of a number of neurons with looping connections. On the other hand, an LSTM network layer is slightly more complex.

LSTM layers can decide the following:

- Which information should go through the next unroll
- Which information should be used to update the values of the LSTM internal state
- Which information should be used as the next possible internal state
- Which information to output

With respect to vanilla RNNs (the most basic form, as shown in the previous section), there are many more parameters to learn in an LSTM. It's the equivalent of a sound engineer in a recording studio tweaking an equalizer (the LSTM), versus turning the volume knob (the RNN): an equalizer is much more complex to operate, but if you tune it correctly, you can get much better sound quality. The neurons of an LSTM layer have more weights, which are adjusted to make them learn when to remember information and when to forget it. This makes training LSTM networks more computationally expensive than training RNNs.

A lighter-weight version of LSTM neurons, but still slightly more complex than vanilla RNN neurons, is the *gated recurrent unit* (GRU).[3] There's a lot more to know about LSTMs, but the key point here is that they perform extremely well with long-term dependencies and therefore are a good fit for the use case of generating queries.

3.4 LSTM networks for unsupervised text generation

In Deeplearning4j, you can use an out-of-the-box implementation of LSTM networks. Let's set up a simple neural network configuration for an RNN with one hidden LSTM layer. You'll build an RNN that can sample text outputs of 50 characters. Although this isn't a long sequence, it should be enough to handle short text queries (for example, "books about artificial intelligence" is 35 characters).

The unroll parameter should ideally be larger than the target text sample (output) size, so you can handle longer sequences of input. The following code will configure

---

[3] See Kyunghyun Cho et al., "Learning Phrase Representations Using RNN Encoder-Decoder for Statistical Machine Translation" (September 3, 2014), https://arxiv.org/abs/1406.1078v3.

an RNN with 50 neurons in the input and output layers and 200 neurons in the hidden (recurrent) layer, unrolling it 10 time steps.

Listing 3.4   Sample LSTM configuration

Number of neurons in the hidden (LSTM) layer

Number of neurons in the input and output layers

```
int lstmLayerSize = 200;
int sequenceSize = 50;
int unrollSize = 10;
MultiLayerConfiguration conf = new NeuralNetConfiguration.Builder()
    .list()
    .layer(0, new LSTM.Builder()
        .nIn(sequenceSize)
        .nOut(lstmLayerSize)
        .activation(Activation.TANH).build())
    .layer(2, new RnnOutputLayer.Builder(LossFunctions
        .LossFunction.MCXENT)
        .activation(Activation.SOFTMAX)
        .nIn(lstmLayerSize)
        .nOut(sequenceSize).build())
    .backpropType(BackpropType.TruncatedBPTT)
        .tBPTTForwardLength(unrollSize)
        .tBPTTBackwardLength(unrollSize)
    .build();
```

Number of unrolls for the RNN

Declares the LSTM layer with 50 inputs (nIn) and 200 outputs (nOut), using the tanh activation function

Declares the output layer with 200 inputs (nIn) and 50 outputs (nOut), using the softmax activation function. The cost function is also declared here.

Declares the time dimension of the RNN (LSTM) with unrollSize as a parameter of the backpropagation-through-time algorithm

It's important to note a few details about this architecture:

- You specify the loss-function parameter for the cross-entropy cost function.
- You use the tanh activation function on input and hidden layers.
- You use a softmax activation function in the output layer.

Using the cross-entropy cost function is closely tied to the use of a softmax function in the output layer. A softmax function in the output layer transforms each of its incoming signals into an estimated probability with respect to the other signals, generating a *probability distribution*, where each such value is between 0 and 1 and the sum of all the resulting values is equal to 1.

In the context of character-level text generation, you'll have one neuron for each character in the data used to train the network. Once the softmax function is applied to the values generated by the hidden LSTM layer, each character will have an assigned probability (a number between 0 and 1). In the Yoda example, the data consists of 10 characters, so the output layer will contain 10 neurons. The softmax function makes the output layer contain a probability for each character:

```
m -> 0.031
y -> 0.001
n -> 0.022
a -> 0.088
```

```
e -> 0.077
i -> 0.063
s -> 0.181
Y -> 0.009
o -> 0.120
d -> 0.408
```

As you can see, the most probable character comes from the neuron associated with the character *d* (probability = 0.408).

Let's pass some sample text to this LSTM network and see what it learns to generate. Before generating text for your queries, though, let's first try something simpler to understand. This will help you make sure the network is doing its job correctly. We'll use some text written in natural language: specifically, pieces of literature taken from the Gutenberg project (www.gutenberg.org), such as "Queen. This is mere madness; And thus a while the fit will work on him." You're going to teach the RNN to (re)write Shakespearean poems and comedies (see figure 3.9)!

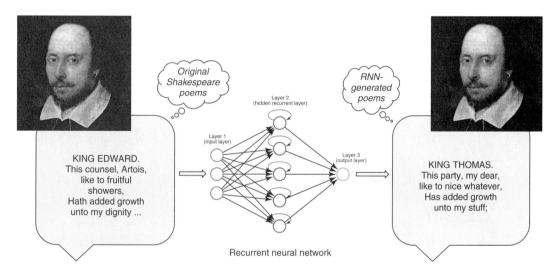

Figure 3.9   Generating Shakespearean text

This will be your first experience with an RNN, so it's good to start with the simplest possible approach to train it. You'll perform unsupervised training of the network by feeding it text from Shakespeare's works, one line at a time, as illustrated in figure 3.10. (The input and output layer sizes are set to 10 for the sake of readability). As you go through the text of Shakespeare's works, you take excerpts of *unroll size* + 1 and feed them, one character at a time, into the input layer. The expected result in the output layer is the next character in the input excerpt: for example, given the sentence "work on him," you'll see the inputs receiving characters for "work on hi," and the corresponding outputs "ork on him." This way, you train the network to generate the next character, by also looking back at the previous 10 characters.

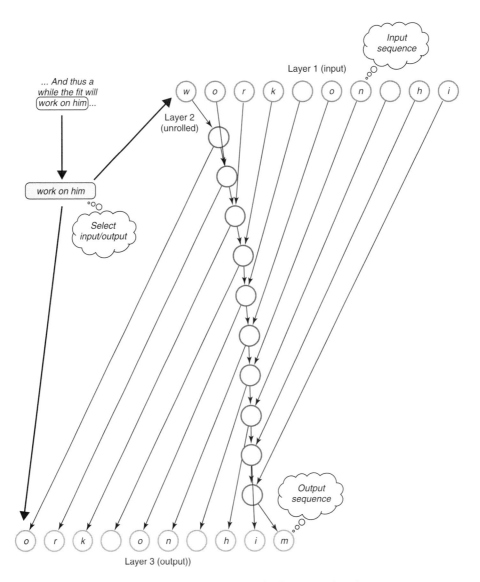

Figure 3.10   Feeding the unrolled RNN with unsupervised sequence learning

You configured the LSTM earlier; now you'll train it by iterating over the character sequences from the Shakespearean texts. First, you initialize the network with the configuration defined earlier:

```
MultiLayerNetwork net = new MultiLayerNetwork(conf);
net.init();
```

As mentioned, you're building an RNN that generates text sequences one character at a time. Therefore, you'll use a `DataSetIterator` (the DL4J API for iterating over datasets) that creates character sequences: a `CharacterIterator` (http://mng.bz/y1ZJ). You can skip some of the details regarding the `CharacterIterator`. You initialize it with

- The source file that contains the text to perform unsupervised training
- The number of examples that should be fed together into the network before it updates its weights (called the *mini-batch* parameter)
- The length of each example sequence

Here's the code to iterate over Shakespearean text characters:

```
CharacterIterator iter = new CharacterIterator("/path/to/shakespeare.txt",
    miniBatchSize, exampleLength);
```

Now you have all the pieces of the puzzle to train the network. Training a `MultiLayer-Network` is done with the `fit(Dataset)` method:

```
MultiLayerNetwork net = new MultiLayerNetwork(conf);
net.init();
net.setListeners(new ScoreIterationListener(1));    ⊲ You can set listeners to look
while (iter.hasNext()) {    ⊲                          into the training process (for
    net.fit(iter);    ⊲                               example, to check that the loss
}                                                     is going down over time).
```

Iterates over the dataset content

Trains the network on each portion of the dataset

You want to check that the value of the loss generated by the network during training steadily declines over time. This is useful as a sanity check: a neural network with appropriate settings will see this number steadily decline. The following log shows that over 10 iterations, the loss went from 4176 to 3490 (with some ups and downs in between):

```
Score at iteration 46 is 4176.819462796047
Score at iteration 47 is 3445.1558312409256
Score at iteration 48 is 3930.8510119434372
Score at iteration 49 is 3368.7542747804177
Score at iteration 50 is 3839.2150762596357
Score at iteration 51 is 3212.1088334832025
Score at iteration 52 is 3785.1824493103672
Score at iteration 53 is 3104.690257065846
Score at iteration 54 is 3648.584794826596
Score at iteration 55 is 3064.9664614373564
Score at iteration 56 is 3490.8566755252486
```

If you plot the score and loss of more such values (for example, 100), you may see something like figure 3.11.

Let's see some sequences (of 50 characters each) generated by this RNN after a few minutes of learning:

- …o me a fool of s itter thou go A known that fig..
- ..ou hepive beirel true; They truth fllowsus; and..
- ..ot; suck you a lingerity again! That is abys. T…
- ..old told thy denuless fress When now Majester s…

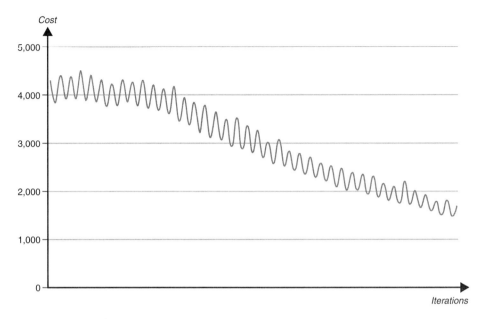

Figure 3.11 Plotting a loss trend

Although you can recognize that the grammar isn't too bad, and some portions may even make sense, you can clearly see that this isn't something of good quality. You probably wouldn't want to use this network to write a query in natural language for an end user, given its poor outcomes. A complete example of Shakespeare text generation with a similar LSTM (with one hidden recurrent layer) can be found in the DL4J examples project (http://mng.bz/7ew9).

One good thing about RNNs is that it's been demonstrated that adding more hidden layers often improves the accuracy of the generated results.[4] This means that, given enough data, increasing the number of hidden layers can make deeper RNNs work better. To see if this applies in this use case, let's build an LSTM network with two hidden layers.

Listing 3.5 Configuring an LSTM with two hidden layers

```
MultiLayerConfiguration conf = new NeuralNetConfiguration.Builder()
        .list()
        .layer(0, new LSTM.Builder()
        .nIn(sequenceSize)
        .nOut(lstmLayerSize)
        .activation(Activation.TANH).build())
    .layer(1, new LSTM.Builder()          ⟵   In this new configuration, you
        .nIn(lstmLayerSize)                    add a second hidden LSTM
                                               layer identical to the first.
```

[4] See Razvan Pascanu et al., "How to Construct Deep Recurrent Neural Networks" (April 24, 2014), https://arxiv.org/abs/1312.6026.

```
      .nOut(lstmLayerSize)
      .activation(Activation.TANH).build())
.layer(2, new RnnOutputLayer.Builder(LossFunctions.LossFunction.MCXENT)
      .activation(Activation.SOFTMAX)
      .nIn(lstmLayerSize)
      .nOut(sequenceSize).build())
.backpropType(BackpropType.TruncatedBPTT)
      .tBPTTForwardLength(unrollSize).tBPTTBackwardLength(unrollSize)
.build();
```

With this configuration, you again train the neural network using the same dataset, so the code for training remains the same. Note how you generate the output text from the trained network. Because this is an RNN, you use the DL4J API `network.rnnTime-Step(INDArray)`, which takes an input vector, produces an output vector using the previous RNN state, and then updates it. A further call to `rnnTimeStep` will use this previously stored internal state to produce the output.

As discussed earlier, the input to this RNN is a sequence of characters, each of which is represented in a one-hot-encoded manner. The Shakespearean text contains 255 distinct characters, so a character input will be represented by a size-255 vector whose values are all set to 0 except one that has a value of 1. Each position corresponds to a character, so setting the vector value at a certain position to 1 means that input vector represents that specific character. The output generated by the RNN with respect to the input will be a probability distribution, because you're using the softmax activation function in the output layer. Such a distribution will tell you which characters are more likely to be generated in response to the corresponding input character (and previous inputs, as per information stored in the RNN layer). A probability distribution is like a mathematical function that can output all possible characters, but with a greater probability of outputting some than others. For example, in a vector generated by an RNN trained over the sentence "my name is Yoda," the character *y* is more likely to be generated by such a distribution than the character *n* when the previous input character is *m* (and hence the sequence *my* is more likely than *mn*). Such a probability distribution is used to generate the output character.

You first convert an initialization character sequence (for example, a user query) to a sequence of character vectors.

Listing 3.6 One-hot-encoding a character sequence

```
INDArray input = Nd4j.zeros(sequenceSize,        ┐ Creates an input vector
    initialization.length());          ◁━━━━━━━━━┘ of the required size
char[] init = initialization.toCharArray();
for (int i = 0; i < init.length; i++) {      ◁━━━━┐ Iterates over each
                                                  │ character in the input
  int idx = characterIterator.convertCharacterToIndex(  │ sequence
   ▷ init[i]);

  input.putScalar(new int[] {idx, i}, 1.0f);   ◁━━┐ Creates a one-hot-encoded vector
}                                                 │ for each character, with the value
                                                  │ at position "index" set to 1
 Gets the index of each character
```

For each character vector, you generate an output vector of character probabilities and convert it into an actual character by sampling (extracting a probable result) from the generated distribution:

```
INDArray output = network.rnnTimeStep(input);          ◁──┐  Predicts the probability
                                                            distribution over the given
                                                            input character (vector)
int sampledCharacterIdx = sampleFromDistribution(
    output);                         ◁────────────────  Samples a probable
                                                        character from the
char c = characterIterator.convertIndexToCharacter(     generated distribution
    sampledCharacterIdx);  ◁────┐
                                 Converts the index of the
                                 sampled character to an
                                 actual character
```

In the Shakespearean text, you initialize the input sequence with a random character, and then the RNN generates subsequent characters. With the text-generation part covered, you can see that having two hidden LSTM layers gives better results:

- … ou for Sir Cathar Will I have in Lewfork what lies …
- … , like end. OTHELLO. I speak on, come go'ds, and …
- … , we have berowire to my years sword; And more …
- … Oh! nor he did he see our strengh …
- … WARDEER. This graver lord. CAMILL. Would I am be …
- … WALD. Husky so shall we have said? MACBETH. She h …

As expected, the generated text looks more accurate than the text generated with the first LSTM, which had one hidden layer. At this point, you may be wondering what would happen if you added another hidden LSTM layer. Would the results be even better? How many hidden layers should a perfect network for this text-generation case have? You can easily answer the first question by trying the example with a network that has three LSTM hidden layers. It's more difficult, and perhaps impossible, to come up with an accurate response for the second question. Finding the best architecture and network settings is a complex process; you'll find more details about RNNs toward the end of this chapter when we talk about using them in production.

Using the same configuration as earlier, but with an additional (third) hidden LSTM layer, the samples look like these:

- … J3K. Why, the saunt thou his died There is hast …
- … RICHERS. Ha, she will travel, Kate. Make you about …
- … or beyond There the own smag; know it is that l …
- … or him stepping I saw, above a world's best fly …

Given the parameters you set in the neural network (layer size, sequence size, unroll size, and so on), adding a fourth hidden LSTM layer wouldn't improve the results. In fact, they'd be slightly worse (for example, "… CHOPY. Wencome. My lord 'tM times our mabultion …"): adding more layers means adding power but also complexity to the network. Training requires more and more time and data; sometimes it isn't possible to generate better results just by adding another hidden layer. In chapter 9, we'll discuss a few techniques for addressing this balance between the needs of computational resources (CPU, data, time) and result accuracy in practice.

3.4.1 Unsupervised query expansion

Now that you've seen how an RNN based on LSTMs works in the case of literary text, let's assemble a network to generate alternative queries. In the literature example, you passed the text to the RNN (unsupervised learning) because that was the simplest way to understand and visualize how such a network works. Now, let's look at using this same approach for query expansion. You can try it on publicly available resources like the web09-bst dataset (http://boston.lti.cs.cmu.edu/Data/web08-bst/planning.html), which contains queries from actual information retrieval systems. You expect that the RNN will learn to generate queries similar to those found in a search log, one per line. Consequently, the data-preparation task consists of grabbing all the queries from the search log and writing them in a single file, one after the other.

Here's an excerpt from the query log :

```
query:{"artificial intelligence"}, results:{          The query part consists of
    size=10, ids:["doc1","doc5", ...]}        ◁──┘   "artificial intelligence."
query:{"books about AI"}, results:{
    size=1, ids:["doc5"]}            ◁─────────────────  The query part consists
query:{"artificial intelligence hype"}, results:{       of "books about AI."
    size=3, ids:["doc1","doc8", ...]}
query:{"covfefe"}, results:{size=100, ids:["doc113","doc588", ...]}
query:{"latest trends"}, results:{size=15, ids:["doc113","doc23", ...]}
...
```

Using only the query part of each line, you get a text file like this:

```
artificial intelligence
books about AI
artificial intelligence hype
covfefe
latest trends
...
```

Once you have that, you can pass it to an LSTM network like that described in the previous section. The number of hidden layers depends on various constraints; two is usually a good starting value. As shown in the graph back in figure 3.1, you'll build your query-expansion algorithm in a query parser, so the user isn't exposed to the alternative query generation. For the sake of this example, you'll extend a Lucene `Query-Parser`, whose responsibility is to build a Lucene `Query` from a `String` (a user-entered query, in this case).

Listing 3.7 Lucene query parser for alternative query expansion

```
public class AltQueriesQueryParser
    extends QueryParser {

  private final MultiLayerNetwork rnn;
  private CharacterIterator characterIterator;

  public AltQueriesQueryParser(String field, Analyzer a,
        MultiLayerNetwork rnn, CharacterIterator characterIterator) {
    super(field, a);
    this.rnn = rnn;
    this.characterIterator = characterIterator;
  }

  @Override
  public Query parse(String query) throws ParseException {
    BooleanQuery.Builder builder =
        new BooleanQuery.Builder();
    builder.add(new BooleanClause(super.parse(
        query), BooleanClause.Occur.MUST));

    String[] samples = sampleFromNetwork(query);

    for (String sample : samples) {
      builder.add(new BooleanClause(super.parse(
        sample), BooleanClause.Occur.SHOULD));
    }

    return builder.build();
  }

  private String[] sampleFromNetwork(String query) {
    // where the "magic" happens ...
  }

}
```

The query parser translates a String into a parsed query to be run against the Lucene index.

RNN used by the custom query parser to generate alternative queries

Initializes a Lucene Boolean query to contain the original user-entered query and the optional queries created by the RNN

Adds a mandatory clause for the user-entered query (the results for that query need to be shown)

Lets the RNN generate some samples to be used as additional queries

Parses text generated by the RNN and includes it as an optional clause

Builds and returns the final query as a combination of the user-entered query and the RNN-generated queries

This method does query encoding, RNN prediction, and output decoding into a new query, as in the Shakespearean example.

You initialize the query parser with the RNN and use it to build a number of alternative queries that are added as optional clauses appended to the original query. All the magic is contained in the portion of the code that generates new query strings from the original one.

The RNN receives the user-entered query as an input and produces a new query as output. Remember, neural networks "talk" by means of vectors, so you need to transform the text query into a vector. You perform one-hot encoding of the characters of the user-entered query. Once the input text is converted into a vector, you can sample the output query one character at a time. Looking back at the Shakespearean example, you did the following:

1   Encoded the user-entered query into a series of one-hot-encoded character vectors
2   Fed this sequence to the network
3   Got the first output character vector, transformed it into a character, and fed this generated character back into the network
4   Iterated the previous step until an ending character was found (such as the carriage return character, in this case)

Practically, this means if you feed the RNN a user-entered query that's something like a common term, the RNN will probably "complete" the query by adding relevant terms. If you instead feed the RNN a query that looks like a finished query, the RNN will probably generate a query that you could find near the user-entered query in a search log. With all this in place, you can now generate alternative queries by using the following settings.

Listing 3.8 Trying `AltQueriesQueryParser` using an LSTM with two hidden layers

Number of examples to put into a mini-batch

The size of LSTM layers

Length of each input sequence to make the RNN learn to generate new ones

Unroll size (as a parameter of backpropagation through time)

```
int lstmLayerSize = 150;
int miniBatchSize = 10;
int exampleLength = 50;
int tbpttLength = 40;
int epochs = 1;
int noOfHiddenLayers = 2;
double learningRate = 0.1

String file = getClass().getResource("/queries.txt")
    .getFile();
CharacterIterator iter = new CharacterIterator(file,
    miniBatchSize, exampleLength);

MultiLayerNetwork net = NeuralNetworksUtils
    .trainLSTM(
    lstmLayerSize, tbpttLength, epochs, noOfHiddenLayers, iter, learningRate,
    WeightInit.XAVIER,
    Updater.RMSPROP,
    Activation.TANH,
    new ScoreIterationListener(10));

Analyzer analyzer = new EnglishAnalyzer(null);
AltQueriesQueryParser altQueriesQueryParser =
    new AltQueriesQueryParser("text",
        analyzer, net, iter);
```

Number of times the RNN should iterate over the same data

Number of hidden LSTM layers in the RNN network

Gradient descent learning rate

Source file containing the queries

Builds an iterator over text characters of the file containing queries

Algorithm used to initialize the network weights

Update algorithm used to update parameters while performing gradient descent

Analyzer used to identify terms in the query text

Sets up a score-iteration listener that outputs the value of loss every 10 iterations (of backpropagation through time)

Instantiates the AltQueriesQueryParser

Activation function to be used in the hidden layers

```
String[] queries = new String[] {"latest trends",
    "covfefe", "concerts", "music events"};   ⟵——— Creates a few sample queries
for (String query : queries) {
  System.out.println(altQueriesQueryParser
    .parse(query));   ⟵——  Prints the alternative queries
}                              generated by the custom parser
```

The standard output will contain the following:

> The query "latest trends" is expanded in a more specific query about trends about AI; this boosts AI-related results.

```
latest trends -> (latest trends) about AI,
    (latest trends) about artificial intelligence  ⟵——
```

```
covfefe -> books about coffee   ⟵————
```

> The second query looks weird, but it isn't from the RNN perspective: the characters composing "covfefe" and "coffee" are almost identical and in similar positions.

```
concerts -> gigs in santa monica
music events -> concerts in california  ⟵——
```

> The alternative query for "music events" is similar but more specific.

Note that no terms are shared between the input and output queries.

The first alternative queries generated sound like more specific versions of the original, which may not be what the user wants. You can see that "latest trends" is in parentheses: the RNN is generating "about AI" and "about artificial intelligence" to sort of complete the sentence. If you ask a generic question about "latest trends," the query parser will be cautious in generating more-specific versions of an original query, if no more context is given (in this example case, "latest trends" is too generic). If you don't want alternative queries like those for the first query here, you can use a trick to hint to the RNN that it should try to generate a completely new query. The data you feed the RNN is split into sequences, one per line, delimited by a carriage return, so here's the trick: add a carriage return character at the end of the user-entered query. The RNN is used to observing sequences of the form wordA wordB wordC CR (or, more precisely, character streams that often have a space character in between), where CR is a carriage return. Implicitly, the CR character tells the RNN that the sequence of text before CR is finished and that a new sequence of text is starting. If you take the user-entered query "latest trends" and let the query parser add CR at the end of it, the RNN will try to generate a new sequence starting from a carriage return character. This makes it much more likely that the RNN will generate text that sounds like a new query rather than a more specific version of the original query.

3.5   *From unsupervised to supervised text generation*

The approach that you've just seen for generating alternative queries is nice, but you want something better than nice; you're focused on providing a tool that changes the lives of your end users. You want to make sure the search engine operates better than before, or all this effort will have been useless.

In the query expansion use case, a key role is defined by the way the RNN learns. You've seen how the RNN performs unsupervised learning from a text file containing many user queries that aren't directly related. Section 3.1.2 also mentioned more-complex alternatives, creating examples that had the desired alternative query with respect to a certain input query.

In this section, I'll briefly introduce supervised text generation for search (for example, using search logs) with two different algorithms.

3.5.1 Sequence-to-sequence modeling

You've learned about LSTMs and how they're good at handling sequences. Doing supervised learning for the task of building alternative queries requires providing a desired target sequence to be generated with respect to an input sequence. In section 3.1.2, where we discussed data preparation, you saw that you can obtain training examples by deriving them from the search logs.

So if you have pairs like "latest research in AI" → "recent publications in artificial intelligence," you can use them in an RNN architecture, as shown in figure 3.12.

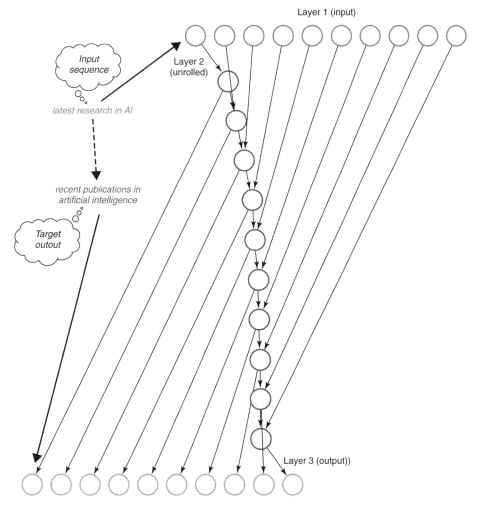

Figure 3.12 Supervised sequence learning with a single LSTM

With such input/output pairs, it's much more difficult for the RNN (or LSTM) to learn. In the previous unsupervised approach, the network was learning to generate the next character in the sequence in order to teach the RNN to reproduce the input sequence.

In a supervised learning scenario, you're instead trying to teach the neural network to generate a sequence of output characters that might be completely different from the input characters. Let's look at an example. If you have the input sequence "latest resea," it's easy to guess that the next character will be *r*. The RNN output to be learned looks one character ahead in time:

```
l -> a
la -> at
lat -> ate
late -> ates
lates -> atest
latest -> atest
latest  -> atest r
latest r -> atest re
latest re -> atest res
latest res -> atest rese
latest rese -> atest resea
latest resea -> atest resear
```

On the other hand, if you use the portion of the sentence "recent pub" as the target output, the RNN should do something like this:

```
l -> r
la -> re
lat -> rec
late -> rece
lates -> recen
latest -> recent
latest  -> recent
latest r -> recent p
latest re -> recent pu
latest res -> recent pub
latest rese -> recent publ
latest resea ->  recent publi
```

This task is clearly much more difficult, so I'll now introduce a fascinating architecture called *sequence-to-sequence* models. This architecture uses two LSTM networks:

- The *encoder* takes the input sequence as a sequence of word vectors (not characters). It generates an output vector called a *thought vector* that corresponds to the last hidden state of the LSTM, rather than generating a probability distribution like the previous model.
- The *decoder* takes the thought vector as an input and generates an output sequence that represents a probability distribution to be used to sample the output sequence.

This architecture is also called *seq2seq* (see figure 3.13). We'll inspect it in more detail in chapter 7, because it's also used to perform machine translation (transforming one sequence written in a certain language into a corresponding sequence in another target language). Seq2seq is also often used to build conversational models for chatbots. In the context of search, what's interesting is the concept of the thought vector: a vectorized representation of the user's intent. There's a lot of research in this area.[5] Although it's called a thought vector, what the RNN learns is based on the given inputs and outputs. In this case, if the input is a query and the output is another query, the thought vector can be seen as the vector that can map the input query to the output query. If the output query is relevant with respect to the input query, then the thought vector encodes the information about how a relevant alternative query can be generated from that input query, a distributed representation of user intent.

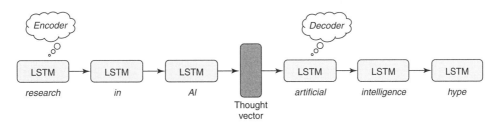

Figure 3.13   **Sequence-to-sequence modeling for queries**

Because we'll take a closer look at sequence-to-sequence models in chapter 7, for now we'll use a previously trained seq2seq model where related input and desired output queries have been extracted from a search log on the basis of two measures:

- How close in time they were fired, as seen in the search log
- Whether they share at least one search result

In DL4J, you load this previously created model from the filesystem and pass it to the previously defined `AltQueriesQueryParser`:

```
MultiLayerNetwork net = ModelSerializer
    .restoreMultiLayerNetwork(
    "/path/to/seq2seq.zip");
AltQueriesQueryParser altQueriesQueryParser = new
    AltQueriesQueryParser("text", new
    EnglishAnalyzer(null), net, null);
```

Restores a previously persisted neural network model from a file

Builds the AltQueriesQueryParser using the neural network implementing the seq2seq model. Note that you no longer need the CharacterIterator.

---

[5] See, for example, Ryan Kiros et al., "Skip-Thought Vectors" (June 22, 2015), https://arxiv.org/pdf/1506.06726v1.pdf; Shuai Tang et al., "Trimming and Improving Skip-thought Vectors" (June 9, 2017), https://arxiv.org/abs/1706.03148; and Yoshua Bengio, "The Consciousness Prior" (September 25, 2017), https://arxiv.org/abs/1709.08568.

In order to use the sequence-to-sequence model, you need to change the way you generate the sequence. In the unsupervised approach, you sampled characters from the output probability distributions. In this case, you'll instead generate the sequence from the `decoder` LSTM at the word level. Here are some results given by the `AltQueryParser` using the seq2seq model:

This result may look weird at first, but there's actually a foundation for the **Museum of Contemporary Art in Chicago.**

```
museum of contemporary art chicago -> foundation

joshua music festival -> houston monmouth

mattel toys -> mexican yellow shoes
```

The input query about a music event generates a query that contains a city and the name of another event (although the Monmouth Festival takes place in Oregon).

A query about toys for kids generates a query for Mexican yellow shoes. If it's Christmas, this is a good result (gift for kids and for ... someone who may like yellow shoes)!

3.6   *Considerations for production systems*

Training RNNs was tedious, and it was even worse with LSTMs. Nowadays, we have frameworks like DL4J that can run on CPUs or on graphical processing units (GPUs), or can even run in a distributed manner (for example, via Apache Spark). Other frameworks like TensorFlow have dedicated hardware (tensor-processing units [TPUs]!), and so on. But it's not trivial to set up an RNN to work well. You may have to train several different models to come up with the one that works best on your data. By the way, not only are there theoretical constraints around setting up LSTMs, but the data you use to train also defines what they can do at test time: for example, when using them on unseen queries.

In practice, it took several hours of trial and error to come up with good settings for the different parameters in the unsupervised approach. This process will take less time as you become more experienced with the dynamics of LSTMs (and, in general, of neural networks). For instance, the Shakespeare example contains sequences that are much longer than queries. Queries are short—on average, between 10 and 50 characters—whereas lines from *Macbeth* can contain 300 characters. So the example-length parameter for the Shakespeare example (200) is longer than that used for learning to generate queries (50).

Also consider the hidden structures in text. Text from Shakespearean comedies usually has the following pattern: CHARACTERNAME : SOMETEXT PUNCTUATION CR, whereas queries are just sequences of words followed by a carriage return. Queries can contain both formal and informal sentences, with words like "myspaceeee" that can confuse the RNN. So whereas the Shakespearean text needed only one hidden layer to give okay results, the LSTM needed at least two hidden layers to perform in a useful way.

The decision about whether to perform unsupervised LSTM training over characters versus using a sequence-to-sequence model depends first on the data you have. If you aren't able to generate good training examples (where the output query is a relevant alternative to the input query), you should probably go with the unsupervised approach. The architecture is also lighter, and training will likely take less time.

A key point to take into account is that during training, the loss values should be tracked to make sure they're steadily declining. You saw a graph of the loss generated by plotting the values outputted by the `ScoreIterationListener` while training the unsupervised LSTM. It's useful to do this to make sure training is going well. If the loss begins to increase or stops decreasing at a value far from zero, you probably need to tune the network parameters.

The most important parameter is the learning rate. This value (usually between 0 and 1) determines the speed at which the gradient descent algorithm goes downhill toward points where the error is low. If the learning rate is too high (closer to 1: for example, 0.9), it will result in the loss starting to diverge (increasing to infinity). If the learning rate is instead too low (closer to 0: for example, 0.0000001), the gradient descent may take too long to reach a point with low error.

Summary

- Neural networks can learn to generate text, even in the form of natural language. This is useful for silently generating queries that are executed together with user-entered queries to provide better search results.
- Recurrent neural networks are helpful for the task of text generation, because they're adept at handling even long sequences of text.
- Long short-term memory networks are an extension of RNNs that can deal with long-term dependencies. They work better than plain RNNs when dealing with natural language text where related concepts or words may be a significant distance apart in a sentence.
- Providing deeper layers in neural networks can help in cases where the network requires more computational power for handling larger datasets and/or more-complex patterns.
- Sometimes it's useful to look closely at how a neural network is generating its outputs. Small adjustments (like the CR trick) can make a difference in the quality of the results.
- Sequence-to-sequence models and thought vectors are powerful tools for learning to generate sequences of text in a supervised manner.

More-sensitive
query suggestions

We've covered the fundamentals of neural networks and looked at the construction of both shallow and deep architectures for these networks. In practical terms, you now know how to integrate neural networks into a search engine to boost the search engine with two key features: synonym expansion and alternative query generation. Both of these features work on the search engine to make it smarter and return better results to the user. But can you do anything to improve the wording of the query itself? In particular, can you do anything to help the user write better queries—queries that deliver the results that come closest to what the user is looking for?

The answer, of course, is yes. You're no doubt accustomed to a search engine providing you with suggestions as you type in your query. This autocomplete function is designed to speed up the querying process by suggesting words or sentences that could make up a meaningful query. For instance, if a user starts typing "boo," the autocomplete feature may provide the rest of the word the user is likely to be writing: "book," for example, or a complete sentence that starts with "boo," such as "books about deep learning." Helping users compose their queries is likely to speed things up and help users avoid typos and similar errors. But this functionality also gives the search engine the opportunity to provide hints to help the user compose a better query. These hints are words or sentences that make sense in the context of the specific query the user is writing. The words "book" and "boomerang" share the same "boo" prefix, so if a user starts typing "boo," the search engine might suggest that they choose either "book" or "boomerang" to complete the query. But if the user types "big parks where I can play boo," it's clear that suggesting "boomerang" would make more sense than suggesting "book."

By generating these hints, autocomplete also has an impact on the effectiveness of the search engine. Imagine if, instead of "big parks where I can play boomerang," the search engine suggested "big parks where I can play book." That would certainly return fewer relevant search results.

Suggestions also give the search engine a chance to favor certain queries (and therefore documents to be matched) over others. This can be useful, for example, for marketing purposes. If the owner of the search engine of an e-commerce website wants to sell books more than boomerangs, they may want to suggest "big parks where I can play book" rather than "big parks where I can play boomerang." If you know the topics that users look for most often, you may want to suggest terms related to those recurring topics more frequently.

Autocomplete is a common feature in search engines, so there are already plenty of algorithms to create it. What can neural networks help you with here? In a word: sensitivity. A *sensitive* suggestion is one that accurately interprets what the user is looking for and rewords it in a manner that will more likely deliver relevant results. This chapter will build on what you've learned about neural nets to get them to generate more-sensitive suggestions.

4.1 Generating query suggestions

You know from chapter 3 that deep neural networks can learn to generate text that looks like it was written by a human. You saw this at work when you generated alternative queries. Now you'll see how to use and extend such neural nets so they can outperform the current most widely used algorithms for autocompletion by generating better, more-sensitive query suggestions.

4.1.1 Suggesting while composing queries

In chapter 2, we discussed how to help users of a search engine look for song lyrics, in the common scenario in which the user doesn't recall a song title exactly. In that context, we introduced the synonym-expansion technique, to allow users to fire a possibly incomplete or incorrect query (for example, "music is my aircraft") that was fixed by expanding synonyms under the hood ("music is my aeroplane") using the word2vec algorithm. Synonym expansion is a useful technique, but perhaps you could do something simpler to help a user recall that the song chorus is "music is my *aeroplane*" and not "music is my aircraft" by suggesting the right words while the user types the query. You can avoid letting the user run a suboptimal query, in the sense that they already know "aircraft" isn't the right word.

Having good autocompletion algorithms offers two benefits:

- Fewer queries with few or zero results (affects recall)
- Fewer queries with low relevance (affects precision)

If the *suggester* algorithm is good, it won't output nonexistent words, or terms that never occurred in the indexed data. This means it's unlikely that a query using terms suggested by such algorithm will return no results. Let's think about the "music is my aircraft" example. Provided you don't have synonym expansion enabled, there's probably no song that contains all such terms; therefore, the best results will contain "music" and "my," or "my" and "aircraft," with low relevance to the user's information need (and hence a low *score*). Ideally, once the user enters "music is my," the suggester algorithm will offer the hint "aeroplane," because that's a sentence the search engine has already seen (indexed).

We just touched an important point that plays a key role in generating effective suggestions: where do suggestions come from? Most commonly, they originate from the following places:

- Static (handcrafted) dictionaries of words or sentences to be used for suggestions
- Chronology of previously entered queries (for example, taken from a query log)
- Indexed documents taken from various portions of the documents (title, main text content, authors, and so on)

In the rest of this chapter, we'll explore obtaining suggestions from these sources by using common techniques from the fields of information retrieval and natural language processing (NLP). You'll also see how they compare with suggesters based on neural network language models, a longstanding NLP technique implemented through neural networks, in terms of features and accuracy of results.

4.1.2   Dictionary-based suggesters

Back in the old days, when search engines required many handcrafted algorithms, a common approach was to build a dictionary of words that could be used to help users type queries. Such dictionaries usually contained important words only, such as main concepts that were closely related to that specific domain. For example, a search engine for a shop selling musical instruments might have used a dictionary containing terms like "guitar," "bass," "drums," and "piano." It would have been very difficult to fill the dictionary with all the relevant English words by hand-compiling it. Instead, it's possible to make such dictionaries build themselves (for example, using a script) by looking at the query logs, getting the user-entered queries, and extracting a list of the

1,000 (for example) most frequently used terms. That way, you can avoid misspelled words in the dictionary, by means of the frequency threshold (hopefully, people type queries without typos most of the times). Given this scenario, dictionaries can still be a good resource for query history–based suggestions: you can use that data to suggest the same queries or portions of them.

Let's build a dictionary-based suggester using Lucene APIs, with terms from previous queries. Over the course of the chapter, you'll implement this API using different sources and suggestion algorithms; this will help you compare them and evaluate which one to choose, depending on the use case.

4.2 Lucene Lookup APIs

Suggestion and autocompletion features are provided by means of the `Lookup` API in Apache Lucene (http://mng.bz/zM0a). The life cycle of a lookup usually includes the following phases:

- *Build*—The lookup is built from a data source (for example, a dictionary).
- *Lookup*—The lookup is used to provide suggestions based on a sequence of characters (and some other, optional, parameters).
- *Rebuild*—The lookup is rebuilt if the data to be used for suggestion is updated or a new source needs to be used.
- *Store and load*—The lookup is persisted (for example, for future reuse) and loaded (for example, from a previously saved lookup on disk).

Let's build a lookup using a dictionary. You'll use a file containing the 1,000 previously entered queries as recorded in the search engine log. The queries.txt file looks like this, with one query per line:

```
...
popular quizzes
music downloads
music lyrics
outerspace bedroom
high school musical sound track
listen to high school musical soundtrack
...
```

You can build a `Dictionary` from this plain text file and pass it to `Lookup` to build the dictionary-based suggester:

```
Lookup lookup = new JaspellLookup();       ◁—— Instantiates a Lookup

Path path = Paths.get("queries.txt");      ◁—┐ Locates the input file containing
                                              the queries (one per line)
Dictionary dictionary = new
    PlainTextDictionary(path);             ◁—┐ Creates a plain text dictionary
                                              that reads from the queries file
lookup.build(dictionary);                  ◁—┐ Builds the Lookup using the
                                              data from the Dictionary
```

As you can see, the `Lookup` implementation called `JaspellLookup`, which is based on a *ternary search tree*, is fed data from a dictionary containing past queries. A ternary search tree (TST; https://en.wikipedia.org/wiki/Ternary_search_tree) like that shown in figure 4.1 is a data structure in which strings are stored in a way that recalls the shape of a tree. A TST is a particular type of tree called a *prefix tree* (or *trie*), where each node in the tree represents a character and has a maximum of three child nodes.

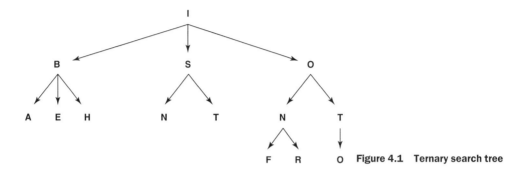

Figure 4.1   Ternary search tree

Such data structures are particularly useful for autocompletion, because they're efficient in terms of speed when searching for strings that have a certain prefix. That's why prefix trees are often used in the context of autocompletion: as a user searches for "mu," the trie can efficiently return all the strings in the tree that start with "mu."

Now that you've built your first suggester, let's see it in action. You'll split the query "music is my aircraft" into progressively bigger sequences and pass them to the lookup to get suggestions, simulating the way a user types a query in a search engine user interface. You'll start with "m," then "mu," "mus," "musi," and so on, and see what kind of results you get based on past queries. To generate such *incremental inputs*, use the following code:

```
List<String> inputs = new LinkedList<>();
for (int i = 1; i < input.length(); i++) {
  inputs.add(input.substring(0, i));
}
```

Each step creates a substring of the original input where the ending index i is bigger.

Lucene's `Lookup#lookup` API accepts a sequence of characters (the input of the user typing the query) and a few other parameters, such as if you only want more-popular suggestions (for example, strings found more frequently in the dictionary) and the maximum number of such suggestions to retrieve. Using the list of incremental inputs, you can generate the suggestions for each such substring:

```
List<Lookup.LookupResult> lookupResults = lookup.lookup(substring, false, 2);
```

Uses Lookup to obtain a maximum of two results for a given substring (such as "mu"), regardless of their frequency (morePopular is set to false)

You obtain a `List` of `LookupResults`, each composed of a `key` that's the suggested string and a `value` that's the `weight` of that suggestion; this weight can be thought of as a measure of how relevant or frequent the suggester implementation thinks the related string is, so its value may vary depending on the lookup implementation used. Let's show each suggestion result together with its weight:

```
for (Lookup.LookupResult result : lookupResults) {
    System.out.println("--> " + result.key + "(" + result.value + ")");
}
```

If you pass all the generated substrings of "music is my aircraft" to the suggester, the results are as follows:

```
'm'
--> m
--> m &
----
'mu'
--> mu
--> mu alumni events
----
'mus'
--> musak
--> musc
----
'musi'
--> musi
--> musi for wish you could see me now
----
'music'
--> music
--> music &dvd whereeaglesdare
----
'music '
--> music &dvd whereeaglesdare
--> music - mfs curtains up
----
'music i'
--> music i can download for free no credit cards and music parental advisory
--> music in atlanta
----
'music is'
----
```
... ⟵— **No more suggestions**

You get no suggestions for inputs beyond "music i." Not too good. The reason is that you've built a lookup based solely on entire query strings; you didn't provide a means for the suggester to split such lines into smaller text units. The lookup wasn't able to suggest "is" after "music" because no previously entered query started with "music is." That's a significant limitation. On the other hand, this kind of suggestion is handy for chronological autocompletion, where a user sees queries they entered in the past as soon as they begin typing a new query. For example, if a user ran a query that was the same as one they ran a week before, it would appear as a suggestion if the implementation used a dictionary of previously entered queries.

But you want to do more:

- Suggest not just entire strings that the user typed in the past, but also the words that composed past queries (for example, "music," "is," "my," and "aircraft").
- Suggest query strings even if the user types a word that's in the middle of a previously entered query. For example, the previous method gives results if the query string *starts* with what that user is typing, but you'd like to suggest "music is my aircraft" even if the user types "my a."
- Suggest word sequences that are grammatically and semantically correct, but may not have been previously typed by any user.

The suggestion functionality should be able to compose natural language to help users write better-sounding queries:

- Make suggestions that reflect the data from the search engine. It would be extremely frustrating for a user if a suggestion led to an empty list of results.
- Help users disambiguate when a query may have different scopes among the possible interpretations.

Imagine a query like "neuron connectivity," which could relate to the field of neuroscience as well as to artificial neural networks. It would be helpful to give the user a hint that such a query might hit very different domains, and let them filter the results before firing the query.

In the following sections, we'll examine each of these points and see how using neural networks allows you to achieve more accurate suggestions when compared to other techniques.

4.3   Analyzed suggesters

Think about typing a query in a web search engine. In many cases, you don't know the entire query you're going to write. This wasn't true years ago, when most web search was based on keywords and people had to think in advance: "What are the most important words I have to look for in order to get search results that are relevant?" That approach involved a lot more trial and error than searching does now. Today, good web search engines give useful hints while you're typing a query; so you type, look at the suggestions, select one, begin typing again, and look for additional suggestions, select another one, and so on.

Let's run a simple experiment and see what suggestions I got when I searched for "books about search and deep learning" on Google. When I typed "book," the results were generic, as shown in figure 4.2 (as you might expect, because "book" can have a lot of different meanings in various contexts). One of the suggestions was about bookings for going on vacation in Italy (Roma, Ischia, Sardegna, Firenze, Ponza). At this stage, the suggestions weren't much different than what you created using the dictionary-based suggester with Lucene in the previous section: all the suggestions started with "book."

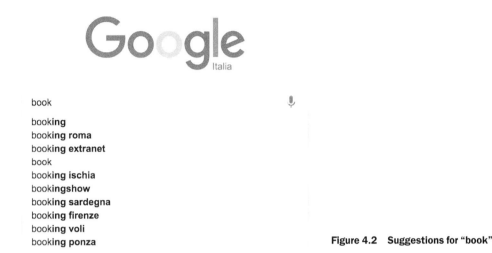

Figure 4.2 Suggestions for "book"

I didn't select any of the suggestions, because none of them were relevant to my search intent. So I continued typing: "books about sear" (see figure 4.3).

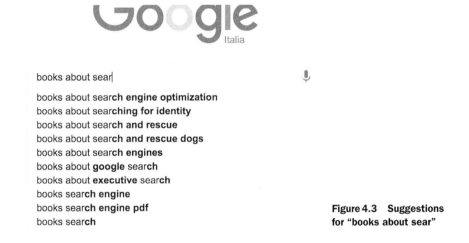

Figure 4.3 Suggestions for "books about sear"

The suggestions became more meaningful and closer to my search intent, although the first results weren't relevant (books about search engine optimization, books about searching for identity, books about search and rescue). The fifth suggestion was probably the closest. It's interesting to note that I also got the following:

- An *infix* suggestion (a suggestion string containing new tokens placed infix—between two existing tokens of the original string). In the "books about google search" suggestion, the word "google" is between "about" and "sear" in the query I typed. Keep this in mind, because this is something you'll want to achieve later; but we'll skip it for now.

- A suggestion that skipped the word "about" (the last three, "books search…"). Keep this in mind also; you can discard terms from the query while giving suggestions.

I selected the "books about search engines" suggestion, typed "and," and got the results shown in figure 4.4. Looking at the results, you probably realize that the topic of integration of search engines and deep learning doesn't have much book coverage: none of the suggestions hints "deep learning." A more important thing to note is that the suggester seems to have discarded some of the query text when giving me hints; in the suggestions box, the results all start with "engine and." But this might be a user interface issue, because the suggestions seem accurate; they're not about engines in general, but rather clearly reflect that *engine* refers to a search engine. Here's another idea to keep in mind for later: you may want to discard some of the query text as is becomes longer.

Figure 4.4   Suggestions for "books about search engines and"

I kept trying. The final suggestion, shown in figure 4.5, was the query I intended to type initially, with a small modification: I planned to type "books about search and deep learning," and the suggestion was "books about search engines and deep learning."

Figure 4.5   Suggestions for "books about search engines and dee"

This experiment wasn't intended to demonstrate how the Google search engine implements autocompletion. Rather, we wanted to observe some of the possibilities when working with autocompletion:

- Suggestions of single words ("books")
- Suggestions of multiple words ("search engines")
- Suggestions of whole phrases

This will help you reason and decide what's useful in practice for your own search engine applications.

Beyond the granularity of the suggestions (single word, multiword, sentence, and so on), we observed that some suggestions had these characteristics:

- Words removed from the query ("books search engines")
- Infix suggestions ("books about google search")
- Prefix removed ("books about" wasn't part of the final suggestions)

All this, and much more, is possible by applying text analysis to the incoming query and the data from the dictionary you use to build a suggester. You can, for example, remove certain terms by using a stopword filter. Or you can break long queries into multiple subsequences, and generate suggestions for each subsequence by using a filter that breaks a text stream at a certain length. This fits nicely with the fact that text analysis is heavily used within search engines. Lucene has such a lookup implementation, called `AnalyzingSuggester`. Instead of relying on a fixed data structure, it uses text analysis to let you define how text should be manipulated, first when building the lookup and again when passing a piece of text to the lookup to get suggestions:

```
Analyzer buildTimeAnalyzer =
    new StandardAnalyzer();

Analyzer suggestTimeAnalyzer =
    new StandardAnalyzer();

Directory dir = FSDirectory.open(
    Paths.get("suggestDirectory"));

AnalyzingSuggester lookup = new AnalyzingSuggester(
    dir, "prefix", buildTimeAnalyzer,
    suggestTimeAnalyzer));
```

When you build the lookup, you use a StandardAnalyzer that removes stopwords and splits tokens on whitespace.

When you look for suggestions, you use the same analyzer used at build time.

You need to provide a Directory on the filesystem because the AnalyzingSuggester uses it internally to create the required data structures for generating suggestions.

Creates an AnalyzingSuggester instance

The `AnalyzingSuggester` can be created using separate `Analyzers` for build and lookup times; this allows you to be creative when setting up the suggester.

Internally, this lookup implementation uses a *finite state transducer*: a data structure used in several places in Lucene. You can think of a finite state transducer (FST) as a graph in which each edge is associated with a character and, optionally, a weight (see figure 4.6). At build time, all possible suggestions that come from applying the build-time

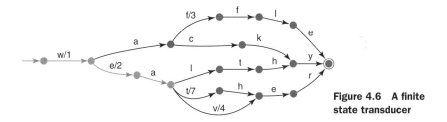

Figure 4.6   A finite state transducer

analyzer to the dictionary entries are compiled into a big FST. At query time, traversing the FST with the (analyzed) input query will produce all the possible paths and, consequently, suggestion strings to output:

```
'm'
--> m
--> .m
----
'mu'
--> mu
--> mu'
----
'mus'
--> musak
--> musc
----
'musi'
--> musi
--> musi for wish you could see me now
----
'music'
--> music
--> music'
----
'music '
--> music'
--> music by the the
----
'music i'
--> music i can download for free no credit cards and music parental advisory
--> music industry careers
----
'music is'
--> music'
--> music by the the
----
'music is '
--> music'
--> music by the the
----
'music is m'
--> music by mack taunton
--> music that matters
```

The dictionary-based suggester wasn't able to provide suggestions past this point.

```
----
'music is my'                        <——————————
--> music of my heart by nicole c mullen
--> music in my life by bette midler
----
'music is my '                       <——————————
--> music of my heart by nicole c mullen
--> music in my life by bette midler
----
'music is my a'                      <——————————
--> music of my heart by nicole c mullen
--> music in my life by bette midler
----
'music is my ai'
----
...    <——  No more suggestions
```

The dictionary-based suggester wasn't able to provide suggestions past this point.

The earlier ternary search tree–based suggester stopped providing suggestions beyond "music i," because no entry in the dictionary started with "music is." But this analyzed suggester, even though the dictionary is the same, is able to provide more suggestions.

In the case of "music is," the token "music" matches some suggestions, and therefore the related results are provided, even though "is" doesn't give any suggestions. Even more interestingly, when the query becomes "music is my," some suggestions contain both "music" and "my." But at a certain point, where there are too many tokens that don't match (starting with "music is my ai"), the lookup stops providing suggestions because they might be too poorly related to the given query. This is a definite improvement on the previous implementation and solves one of the issues: you can provide suggestions based on single tokens, not just on entire strings.

You can also enhance things by using a slightly modified version of `Analyzing-Suggester` that works better with infix suggestions:

```
AnalyzingInfixSuggester lookup = new AnalyzingInfixSuggester(dir,
    buildTimeAnalyzer, lookupTimeAnalyzer, ... );
```

By using this infix suggester, you get fancier results:

```
'm'
--> 2007 s550 mercedes
--> 2007 qualifying times for the boston marathon
----
'mu'
--> 2007 nissan murano
--> 2007 mustang rims com
----
'mus'
--> 2007 mustang rims com
--> 2007 mustang
```

You don't get results starting with "m," "mu," or "mus"; instead, such sequences are used to match the most important part of a string, like "2007 s550 mercedes," "2007 qualifying times for the boston marathon," "2007 nissan murano," and "2007 mustang rims com." Another noticeable difference is that token matching can happen in the middle of a suggestion (that's why it's called *infix*):

```
'music is my'
--> 1990's music for myspace
--> words to music my humps
----
'music is my '
--> words to music my humps
--> where can i upload my music
----
'music is my a'
--> words to music my humps
--> where can i upload my music
```

With the `AnalyzingInfixSuggester`, you get infix suggestions. It takes the input sequence, analyzes it so that tokens are created, and then suggests matches based on prefix matches of any such tokens. But you still have the problems of making suggestions closer to the data stored in the search engine, making suggestions look more like natural language, and being able to better disambiguate when two words have different meanings. Additionally, you aren't getting any suggestions when you begin typing "aircraft," as not enough tokens match.

Now that you have some experience with the problem of providing good suggestions, we'll discuss language models. First we'll explore models implemented through natural language processing (*ngrams*), and then we'll look at those implemented via neural networks (neural language models).

4.4   *Using language models*

In the suggestions shown in the previous sections, some text sequences made little sense: for example, "music by the the." You fed the suggester data from previously entered queries, so in some entry a user must have made a mistake by typing "the" twice. Beyond that, you've provided suggestions consisting of the entire query. Although this is fine if you want to use autocompletion to return the entire text of previous queries (this might be useful if you were searching for a book in an online bookstore), it doesn't work well for composing new queries.

In medium to large search engines, the search logs contain a huge number of diverse queries—coming up with a good suggester algorithm is difficult because of the number and diversity of such text sequences. For example, if you look at the web09-bst dataset (http://boston.lti.cs.cmu.edu/Data/web08-bst/planning.html), you'll find queries such as "hobbs police department," "ipod file sharing," and "liz taylor's biography." Such queries look good and can be used as sources for the suggester algorithm. On the other hand, you can also find queries like "hhhhh," "hqwebdev," and "hhht hootdithuinshithins." You probably don't want the suggester to provide similar suggestions! The problem isn't filtering out "hhhh," which can be cleared out of the dataset by removing all lines or words that contain three or more consecutive characters that are the same. Filtering out "hqwebdev" is much harder: it contains the word "webdev" (shortened version of "web developer"), prefixed by "hq." Such a query might make sense (for example, there's a website with this name), but you don't want to use over-specific suggestions for a general-purpose suggester service. The challenge is to work with diverse text sequences, some of which may not make sense to use because they're too specific and therefore rare. One way to address this is to use *language models.*

Language models

In the NLP field, a language model's main task is to predict the probability of a certain sequence of text. Probability is a measure of how likely a certain event is, and it ranges between 0 and 1. So if you take the weird query we saw earlier—"music by the the"—and pass it to a language model, you'll get a low probability (for example, 0.05). Language models represent a probability distribution and therefore can help predict the likelihood of a certain word or character sequence in a certain context. Language models can help with excluding sequences that are unlikely (low probability) and with generating previously unseen word sequences, because they capture which sequences are most likely (even though they may not appear in the text).

Language models are often implemented by calculating the probabilities of ngrams.

Ngrams

An *ngram* is a sequence of characters made up of *n* consecutive *units*, where a unit can be a character ("a," "b," "c," …) or a word ("music," "is," "my," …). Imagine an ngram language model (using words as units) where $n = 2$. An ngram with $n = 2$ is also known as a *bigram*; an ngram with $n = 3$ is also known as a *trigram*. A bigram language model can estimate the probability of pairs of words like "music concert" or "music sofa." A good language model would assign a probability to the bigram "music concert" that's higher with respect to the probability of the "music sofa" bigram.

As an implementation note, the probability of (a sequence of) ngrams for a language model can be calculated in a number of ways. Most of them rely on the *Markov assumption* that the probability of some future event (for example, the next character or word) depends only on a limited history of preceding events (characters or words). So if you use an ngram model with $n = 2$, also called a *bigram model*, the probability of the *next* word, given a *current* word, is given by counting the number of occurrences of the two words "music is" and dividing that result by the number of occurrences of the current word ("music") alone. For example, the probability that the next word is "is," given the current word "music," can be written as $P(is|music)$. To calculate the probability of a word given a sequence of words greater than two—for example, the probability of "aeroplane" given "music is my," you split that sentence into bigrams, calculate the probabilities of all such bigrams, and multiply them:

$$P(music\ is\ my\ aeroplane) = P(is|music) * P(my|is) * P(aeroplane|my)$$

For reference, many ngram language models use a slightly more advanced method called *stupid backoff*[1] that tries first to calculate the probability of ngrams with a higher n (for example, $n = 3$) and then recursively falls back to smaller ngrams (such as $n = 2$) if an ngram with the current n doesn't exist in the data. Such fallback probabilities are discounted so that probabilities from bigger ngrams have more positive influence on the overall probability measure. Lucene has an ngram-based language model lookup called `FreeTextSuggester` (using the stupid backoff algorithm) that uses an analyzer to decide how to split ngrams:

```
Lookup lookup = new FreeTextSuggester(new WhitespaceAnalyzer());
```

Let's see it in action, with n set to 2, on the query "music is my aircraft":

```
'm'
--> my
--> music
----
'mu'
--> music
--> museum
----
'mus'
--> music
--> museum
----
'musi'
--> music
--> musical
----
'music'
--> music
--> musical
----
'music '
--> music video
--> music for
----
'music i'
--> music in
--> music industry
----
'music is'
--> island
--> music is
----
'music is '
--> is the
--> is a
----
'music is m'
--> is my
```

One of the suggestions for "music is m" matched the desired query ("is my") one character in advance.

[1]   See section 4 of Thorsten Brants et al., "Large Language Models in Machine Translation," http://www.aclweb .org/anthology/D07-1090.pdf.

```
--> is missing
----
'music is my'
--> is my
--> is myspace.com
----
'music is my '
--> my space
--> my life
----
'music is my a'
--> my account
--> my aol
----
'music is my ai'
--> my aim
--> air
----
'music is my air'
--> air
--> airport
----
'music is my airc'
--> aircraft
--> airconditioning
----
'music is my aircr'
--> aircraft
--> aircraftbarnstormer.com
----
...
```

The suggestions for "music is my " ("my space," "my life") aren't what you're looking for, but they sound good.

The suggestions for "music is my ai" aren't much good ("my aim," "air") but are closer to what you wanted.

The suggestions for "music is my airc" caused a match four characters in advance ("aircraft") and a funny sentence ("airconditioning").

One positive thing is that the language model–based suggester always gives suggestions. There's no point when the end user can't count on suggestions, even if they aren't particularly accurate. That's an advantage over previous methods. Most important, you can see the stream of suggestions from "music" onward.

> **NOTE** You may wonder how bigram-based models can predict entire words from portions of words. Similarly to the `AnalyzingSuggester`, the `FreeText-Suggester` builds a finite state transducer from the ngrams.

With the ngram language model, you can generate queries like "music is my space," "music is my life," and even "music is my airconditioning" that don't appear in the search log. So you've reached the goal of generating new sequences of words. But due to the nature of ngrams (a fixed sequence of tokens), longer queries aren't provided with full suggestions: thus "music is my aircraft" wasn't included in the suggestions in the final stages, just "aircraft." This isn't necessarily bad, but it highlights the fact that such ngram language models aren't very effective for calculating good probabilities for long sentences; therefore they may give weird suggestions like "music is my airconditioning."

All that you've just learned relates to existing methods for generating suggestions. I wanted you to see all the issues that affect these approaches before diving into neural language models, which aggregate capabilities from each of these methods. Another disadvantage of these models that we've ignored so far is that they need manually curated dictionaries, as you saw in the word2vec example—something that isn't sustainable in practice. You need solutions that automatically adapt to changing data rather than requiring manual interventions. To do that, you'll use the search engine to feed the suggester. The suggestions generated with such data will be based on the indexed content. If documents are indexed, the suggester will be updated as well. In the next section, we'll look at these content-based suggesters.

4.5   Content-based suggesters

With *content-based* suggesters, the content comes directly from the search engine. Consider the search engine for a book shop. It's probable that users will look for book titles or authors much more often than they will search through the text of a book. Each book that's indexed has separate fields for title, author(s), and, eventually, the text of the book. Also, as new books are indexed and old ones go out of production, you need to add the new documents to the search engine and delete the ones related to books that can't be bought anymore. The same thing needs to happen for the suggestions: you don't want to miss suggesting new titles, and you want to avoid suggesting titles for books that are no longer being sold.

So the suggester must be kept up to date. If any document is removed from the index, the suggester may keep the suggestions that were built from that text, but they may be of little use. Suppose two books have been indexed: *Lucene in Action* and *Oauth2 in Action*. A suggester using only the text from the books' titles will be based on the following (lowercased) terms: "lucene," "in," "action," "oauth2." If you remove the *Lucene in Action* book, the list of terms will be trimmed down to this: "in," "action," "oauth2." You can keep the "lucene" token in the suggester; in that case, if the user types an "L," the suggester will suggest "lucene." The problem is that a query for "lucene" won't return any results. That's why you should remove terms from the suggester when they have no possible match at search time.

You can access the inverted index that contains data about the book titles and use those terms the same way you use the lines of a static dictionary. In Lucene, feeding lookups with data from the index can be done using a `DocumentDictionary`. A `DocumentDictionary` reads data from the search engine, specifically from an `Index-Reader` (a view on the search engine at a certain point in time), using one field for fetching the terms (to be used for suggestions) and another field to eventually calculate the suggestion weights (how important a suggestion is).

Let's build a dictionary from data indexed into the `title` field in the search engine. You'll give more weight to titles whose rating is higher. Suggestions coming from books with a higher rating will be shown first:

```
IndexReader reader = DirectoryReader.open(
    directory);
Dictionary dictionary = new DocumentDictionary(
    reader, "title", "rating");
lookup.build(dictionary);
```

Gets a view (an IndexReader) on the search engine

Creates a dictionary based on the contents of the title field, and lets rating decide how much weight a suggestion has

Builds the lookup with the data from the index, just as with a static dictionary

You can guide the user to select the search results you want them to find—for instance, as the owner of the book shop, you may be happier if higher-rated books are shown more often. Other metrics to boost the suggestion may be related to prices, so that a user is given more frequent suggestions of books that have higher or lower prices.

Now that you're all set as far as getting the data for suggestions from the search engine, we can look at neural language models. We expect them to be able to mix all the good things from the methods discussed so far with better accuracy, composing queries that sound like they were typed by a human.

4.6　*Neural language models*

A neural language model is supposed to have the same capabilities as other types of language models, such as the ngram models. The difference lies in how they learn to predict probabilities and how much better their predictions are. Chapter 3 introduced a recurrent neural network (RNN) that tried to reproduce text from Shakespeare's works. We were focused on how RNNs work, but in practice you were setting up a *character-level neural language model*! You saw that RNNs are very good at learning sequences of text in an unsupervised way, so that they can generate good new sequences based on previously seen ones. A language model learns to get accurate probabilities for text sequences, so this looks like a perfect fit for RNNs.

Let's start with a simple RNN that's *not* deep and that implements a character-level language model: the model will predict the probabilities of all the possible output characters, given a sequence of input characters. Let's visualize it:

```
LanguageModel lm = ...
for (char c : chars) {
    System.out.println("mus" + c + ":" + lm.getProbs("mus"+c));
}

....

musa:0.01
musb:0.003
musc:0.02
musd:0.005
muse:0.02
musf:0.001
musg:0.0005
```

```
mush:...
musi:...
...
```

You know that a neural network uses vectors for inputs and outputs; the output layer of the RNN you used for text generation in chapter 3 produced a vector holding a real number (between 0 and 1) for each possible output character. This number represents the probability of the character being outputted from the network. You also saw that generating probability distributions (the probability for all the possible characters, in this case) is accomplished by the softmax function. Now that you know what the output layer does, you can add a recurrent layer in the middle whose responsibility is to remember previously seen sequences, and an input layer for sending input characters to the network. The result is illustrated in the diagram in figure 4.7.

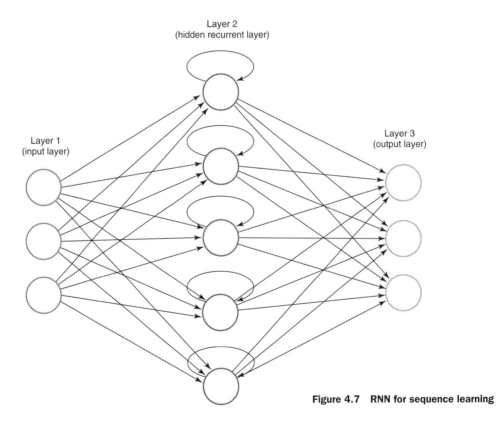

Figure 4.7   RNN for sequence learning

With DL4J, you configured such a network when generating alternative queries in chapter 3 as follows:

```
                            Size of the hidden layer
int layerSize = 50;   ◁
int sequenceSize = chars.length();   ◁─── Input and output size
int unrollSize = 100   ◁
                            Number of unrolls of the RNN
```

```
MultiLayerConfiguration conf = new NeuralNetConfiguration.Builder()
.layer(0, new LSTM.Builder().nIn(sequenceSize).nOut(layerSize)
    .activation(Activation.TANH).build())
.layer(1, new RnnOutputLayer.Builder(LossFunction.MCXENT).activation(
    Activation.SOFTMAX).nIn(layerSize).nOut(sequenceSize).build())
.backpropType(BackpropType.TruncatedBPTT).tBPTTForwardLength(unrollSize)
    .tBPTTBackwardLength(unrollSize)
.build();
```

Although the fundamental architecture is the same (LSTM network with one or more hidden layers), the goal here is different with respect to what you want to achieve in the alternative query generation use case. For alternative queries, you need the RNN to get a query and output a new query. In this case, you want the RNN to guess a good completion for the query the user is writing before they're finished typing it. This is exactly the same RNN architecture used for generating text from Shakespeare's works.

4.7 Character-based neural language model for suggestions

In chapter 3, you fed the RNN a `CharacterIterator` that iterated over the characters in a file. So far, you've built suggestions from text files. The plan is to use the neural network as a tool to help the search engine, so the data to feed it should come from the search engine itself. Let's index the Hot 100 Billboard dataset:

Creates an IndexWriter to put documents into the index

```
IndexWriter writer = new IndexWriter(directory, new IndexWriterConfig());

for (String line :
     IOUtils.readLines(getClass().getResourceAsStream("/billboard_lyrics_1964
     -2015.csv"))) {                    ⟵   Reads each line of the
                                             dataset, one at a time
  if (!line.startsWith("\"R")) {
```

Doesn't use the header line

```
    String[] fields = line.split(",");   ⟵
    Document doc = new Document();
    doc.add(new TextField("rank", fields[0],
        Field.Store.YES));      ⟵

    doc.add(new TextField("song", fields[1],
        Field.Store.YES));     ⟵

    doc.add(new TextField("artist", fields[2],
        Field.Store.YES));    ⟵

    doc.add(new TextField("lyrics", fields[3],
        Field.Store.YES));   ⟵

    writer.addDocument(doc);   ⟵   Adds the created
  }                                Lucene document
}                                  to the index
writer.commit();   ⟵
```

Persists the index into the filesystem

Each row in the file has the following attributes, separated by a comma: Rank, Song, Artist, Year, Lyrics, Source.

Indexes the rank of the song into a dedicated field (with its stored value)

Indexes the title of the song into a dedicated field (with its stored value)

Indexes the artist who played the song into a dedicated field (with its stored value)

Indexes the song lyrics into a dedicated field (with its stored value)

You can use the indexed data to build a character LSTM–based lookup implementation called `CharLSTMNeuralLookup`. Similarly to what you've been doing for the `FreeTextSuggester`, you can use a `DocumentDictionary` to feed the `CharLSTMNeuralLookup`:

**Creates a DocumentDictionary whose content
is fetched from the indexed song lyrics**

```
Dictionary dictionary = new DocumentDictionary(reader, "lyrics", null);
Lookup lookup = new CharLSTMNeuralLookup(...);
lookup.build(dictionary);
```

**Trains the charLSTM-
based lookup**

**Creates the lookup based on
the charLSTM**

The `DocumentDictionary` will fetch the text from the `lyrics` field. In order to instantiate the `CharLSTMNeuralLookup`, you need to pass the network configuration as a constructor parameter so that

- At build time, the LSTM will iterate over the characters of the Lucene document values and learn to generate similar sequences.
- At runtime, the LSTM will generate characters based on the portion of the query already written by the user.

Completing the previous code, the `CharLSTMNeuralLookup` constructor requires the parameters for building and training the LSTM:

```
int lstmLayerSize = 100;
int miniBatchSize = 40;
int exampleLength = 1000;
int tbpttLength = 50;
int numEpochs = 10;
int noOfHiddenLayers = 1;
double learningRate = 0.1;
WeightInit weightInit = WeightInit.XAVIER;
Updater updater = Updater.RMSPROP;
Activation activation = Activation.TANH;

Lookup lookup = new CharLSTMNeuralLookup(lstmLayerSize, miniBatchSize,
    exampleLength, tbpttLength, numEpochs, noOfHiddenLayers,
    learningRate, weightInit, updater, activation);
```

As mentioned earlier, neural networks require a lot of data to produce good results. Take care when choosing how the neural network is configured to work with these datasets. In particular, it's common for a configuration that made a neural network work well on one dataset not to result in the same quality on a different dataset. Consider the number of training samples with respect to the number of neural network weights to be learned by the network. The number of examples should always be greater than the number of learnable parameters: the neural network weights.

If you have a `MultiLayerNetwork` and a `DataSet`, you can compare them:

```
MultiLayerNetwork net = new MultiLayerNetwork(...);
DataSet dataset = ...;
System.out.println("params :" + net.numParams() + ," examples: "
    + dataset.numExamples());
```

Another aspect we haven't considered yet is the *initialization* of the network weights. When you start training a neural network, what are the initial values of the weights? Bad ideas for weight initialization are setting all the weights to the same value (zero is even worse), and setting the weights to random values. Weight initialization schemes are extremely important for the neural network's ability to learn quickly. In this case, good weight initialization schemes are NORMAL and XAVIER. Both refer to probability distributions with certain properties; you can read about them on the DL4J cheat sheet (http://mng.bz/K19K).

To predict outputs from the neural network, you use the same code used to generate alternative queries. Because this LSTM works at character level, you output one character at a time:

```
INDArray output = network.rnnTimeStep(input);     ⟵  Predicts a probability
                                                      distribution over the given
                                                      input character (vector)
int sampledCharacterIdx = sampleFromDistribution(
    output);     ⟵                                   Samples a probable
                                                      character from the
                                                      generated distribution
char c = characterIterator.convertIndexToCharacter(
    sampledCharacterIdx);     ⟵   Converts the index of the sampled
                                  character to an actual character
```

You can now implement the Lookup#lookup API with the neural language model. The neural language model has an underlying neural network and an object (Character-Iterator) that consults the dataset used for training. The primary reason to consult it is for one-hot-encoding mapping—for example, you need to be able to reconstruct which character corresponds to a certain one-hot-encoded vector (and vice versa):

```
public class CharLSTMNeuralLookup extends Lookup {

  private CharacterIterator characterIterator;
  private MultiLayerNetwork network;

  public CharLSTMNeuralLookup(MultiLayerNetwork net,
      CharacterIterator iter) {
    network = net;
    characterIterator = iter;                        Samples num text sequences
  }                                                  from the network, given the
                                                     input string entered by a user
  @Override
  public List<LookupResult> lookup(CharSequence key,
      boolean onlyMorePopular, int num) throws IOException {
    List<LookupResult> results = new
        LinkedList<>();
    Map<String, Double> output = NeuralNetworksUtils
        .sampleFromNetwork(network, characterIterator,
        key.toString(), num);     ⟵
    for (Map.Entry<String, Double> entry : output.entrySet()) {
      results.add(new LookupResult(entry.getKey(),
        entry.getValue().longValue()));     ⟵   Adds the sampled outputs to the list of
    }                                           results, using their probabilities (from the
    return results;                             softmax function) as suggestion weights
  }
  ...
```

Prepares the list of results

The `CharLSTMNeuralLookup` also needs to implement the build API. That's where the neural network will train (or retrain):

```
IndexReader reader = DirectoryReader.open(directory);
Dictionary dictionary = new DocumentDictionary(reader,
    "lyrics", "rank");
lookup.build(dictionary);
```

> **Extracts text to be used for suggestions from the lyrics field, weighted by the song's rank value**

Because the character LSTM uses a `CharacterIterator`, you convert data from the `Dictionary` (an `InputIterator` object) into a `CharacterIterator`, and pass it to the neural network for training (as a side effect, this means having a temporary file on disk to hold the data extracted from the index to train the network):

> **Fetches text coming from the lyrics field in the Lucene index (Lucene uses BytesRef instead of String for performance reasons)**

> **Creates a temporary file**

```
@Override
public void build(Dictionary dictionary) throws IOException {
    Path tempFile = Files.createTempFile("chars",
        ".txt");
    FileOutputStream outputStream = new FileOutputStream(tempFile.toFile());
    for (BytesRef surfaceForm; (surfaceForm = dictionary
            .getInputIterator().next()) != null;) {
        outputStream.write(surfaceForm.bytes);
    }
    outputStream.flush();
    outputStream.close();
    characterIterator = new CharacterIterator(tempFile
        .toAbsolutePath().toString(), miniBatchSize,
        exampleLength);
    this.network = NeuralNetworksUtils.trainLSTM(
        lstmLayerSize, tbpttLength, numEpochs, noOfHiddenLayers, ...);
    FileUtils.forceDeleteOnExit(tempFile.toFile());
}
```

> **Writes the text into the temporary file**

> **Releases resources for writing into the temporary file**

> **Creates a CharacterIterator (using the CharLSTMNeuralLookup configuration parameters)**

> **Removes the temporary file**

> **Builds and trains the LSTM (using the CharLSTMNeuralLookup configuration parameters)**

Before going forward and using this `Lookup` in a search application, you need to make sure the neural language model works well and gives good results. Like other algorithms in computer science, neural networks aren't magic: you need to set them up correctly if you want them to work well.

4.8   *Tuning the LSTM language model*

Instead of doing what you did in chapter 3 and adding more layers to the network, you'll start simple with a single layer and adjust other parameters, and see if one layer is sufficient. The most important reason to do this is that as the complexity of the network grows (for example, more layers), the data and time required for the training phase to generate a good model (which gives good results) grows as well. So although small, shallow networks can't beat deeper ones with lots of different data, this language-modeling example is a good place to learn to start simple and go deeper only when needed.

As you work more with neural networks, you'll get to know how to best set and tune them. For now, you know that when data is large and diverse, it may be a good idea to have a deep RNN for language modeling. But let's be pragmatic and see if that's true. To do so, you need a way to evaluate the neural network learning process. Neural network training is an *optimization problem*, where you want to optimize the weights in the connections between the neurons in order to let them generate the results you desire. In practice, this means you have an initial set of weights in each layer, according to a chosen weight-initialization scheme. These weights are adjusted during training so that the error the network commits when trying to predict outputs decreases as training goes on. If the error committed by the network doesn't decrease or, even worse, increases, you've done something wrong in your setup. In chapter 3, we talked about *cost functions* that measure such error, and the fact the neural network–training algorithm's objective is to minimize these cost functions. A good way to begin measuring whether the training is doing well is to plot the network cost (or loss) over time and make sure it keeps decreasing as backpropagation proceeds.

To make sure your neural language model will give good results, you need to track whether the cost decreases. In the case of DL4J, you can use `TrainingListeners` like the `ScoreIterationListener` from chapter 3 (which logs the loss value) or, even better, a `StatsListener`, which has a proper user interface and will collect and send statistics to a remote server so you can better monitor the learning process. Figure 4.8 shows how such a server displays the learning process.

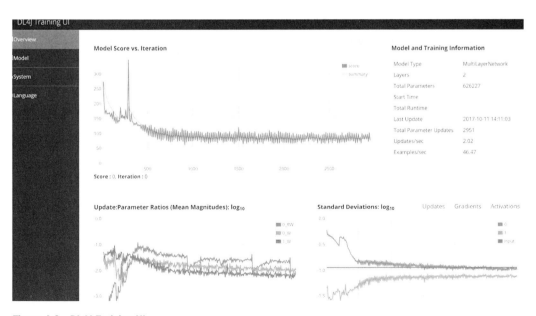

Figure 4.8   DL4J Training UI

The Overview page of the DL4J Training UI contains a lot of information about the training process; for now, we'll focus on the score versus iteration panel at upper left. That's where the score should decrease as the number of iterations grows over time, ideally to near zero. At upper right, you can see some general information about the network parameters and training speed. We'll skip the graphs at the bottom, because they show more detailed information about the size of the parameters (such as weights) and how they vary over time.

It's easy to set up this UI:

```
UIServer uiServer = UIServer.getInstance();      ◁──────┐  Initializes the user
                                                            interface backend

StatsStorage statsStorage = new InMemoryStatsStorage();   ◁────────────┐

uiServer.attach(statsStorage);   ◁──────┐
```

Attaches the StatsStorage instance to the UI so the contents of StatsStorage will be displayed

Configures where the network information is to be stored— in this case, in memory

Having configured and started the UI server, you now tell the neural network to send statistics to it by adding a `StatsListener`:

```
MultiLayerNetwork net = new MultiLayerNetwork(conf);   ◁──────┐  Neural network
                                                                  to monitor

net.init();   ◁──────────────

net.setListeners(new StatsListener(statsStorage));   ◁──────┐

net.fit()   ◁────── Lets training start
```

Initializes the network (for example, sets the initial weights in the layers)

Uses the StatsListener

As soon as training begins, you can access the DL4J UI at http://localhost:9000 from a web browser. When you do, you'll see the Overview page.

Let's start with a character LSTM network that has two hidden layers, and see how it performs on the queries dataset by looking at the DL4J training UI (see figure 4.9). As you can see, the score decreases very little with the number of iterations, which means you probably won't get good results. A common mistake is to overengineer the neural network: you started with two 300-dimensional hidden layers, and maybe that's too many. Earlier in the chapter, I mentioned that it's not a good idea to have more weights to be learned than training samples. Let's double-check the logs:

```
...
INFO o.d.n.m.MultiLayerNetwork - Starting MultiLayerNetwork ...
INFO c.m.d.u.NeuralNetworksUtils - params :1.197.977, examples: 77.141
INFO o.d.o.l.ScoreIterationListener - Score at iteration 0 is 174.1792
....
```

The number of training examples is 100 times smaller than the number of parameters to be learned. Because of that, it's unlikely that the training will achieve a good set of weights. You don't have enough data!

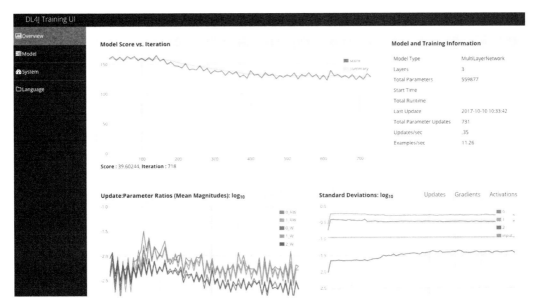

Figure 4.9 Character-level LSTM neural language model with 2 hidden layers (300 neurons each)

You need to either get more data or use a simpler neural network, with fewer parameters to be learned. Assuming you can't do the former, let's go for the latter: configure a simpler, smaller neural network that has one hidden layer with 80 neurons, and check the logs again:

```
...
INFO o.d.n.m.MultiLayerNetwork - Starting MultiLayerNetwork ...
INFO c.m.d.u.NeuralNetworksUtils - params :56.797, examples: 77.141
INFO o.d.o.l.ScoreIterationListener - Score at iteration 0 is 173.4444
...
```

Figure 4.10 shows a nicer loss curve; it degrades smoothly, although the final point isn't close to zero.

The goal is to have the final loss reach a value that steadily remains close to zero. Let's test it anyway, with the "music is my aircraft" query—you can expect suboptimal results because the neural network didn't find a combination of weights with a low cost:

```
'm'
--> musorida hosking floa
--> miesxams reald 20
----
...
----
```

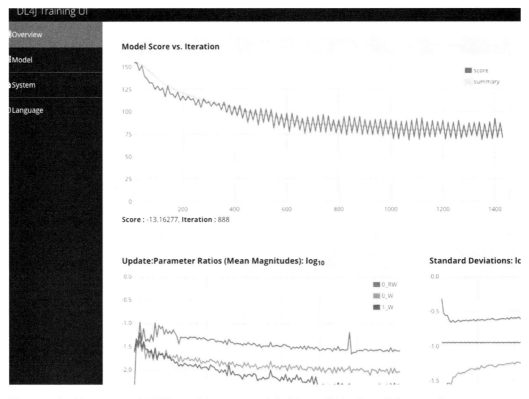

Figure 4.10   Character-level LSTM neural language model with one hidden layer (80 neurons)

```
'music '
--> music tents in sauraborls
--> music kart
----
'music i'
--> music instente rairs
--> music in toff chare sive he
----
'music is'
--> music island kn5 stendattion
--> music is losting clutple
----
'music is '
--> music is seill butter
--> music is the amehia faches of
----
...
----
'music is my ai'
--> music is my airborty cioderopaship
--> music is my air dea a
----
```

```
'music is my air'
--> music is my air met
--> music is my air college
----
'music is my airc'
--> music is my aircentival ad distures
--> music is my aircomute in fresight op
----
'music is my aircr'
--> music is my aircrichs of nwire
--> music is my aircric of
----
'music is my aircra'
--> music is my aircrations sime
--> music is my aircracts fast
----
'music is my aircraf'
--> music is my aircraffems 2
--> music is my aircrafthons and parin
----
'music is my aircraft'
--> music is my aircrafted
--> music is my aircrafts njrmen
```

These results are worse than those with previous solutions that weren't based on neural networks! Let's compare the results from this first neural language model to those from the ngram language model and from the `AnalyzingSuggester`. Table 4.1 shows that although the neural language model always gives results, many of them don't make much sense.

Table 4.1 Comparing results of different `Suggester` implementations

Input	Neural	Ngram	Analyzing
"m"	musorida hosking floa	my	m
"music"	music tents in sauraborls	music	music
"music is"	music island kn5 stendattion	island	music
"music is my ai"	music is my airborty cioderopaship	my aim	
"music is my aircr"	music is my aircrichs of nwire	aircraft	

What is "sauraborls" in the "music tents in sauraborls" suggestion? And what is "stendattion" from the "music island kn5 stendattion" suggestion? As the length of the text to be predicted grows, the neural language model starts returning sequences of characters that don't form meaningful words—it fails at estimating good probabilities for longer inputs. That's exactly what you expected after observing the learning curve.

You want the network to learn better, so let's look at one of the most important configuration parameters when setting up the training for a neural network: the *learning rate*. The learning rate defines how much the weights of the neural network are changed with respect to the (gradient) cost. A high learning rate may cause the neural network to never find a good set of weights, because the weights are changed too much and a good combination is never found. A low learning rate may slow learning so much that a good set of weights isn't found before all the data is used for learning.

Let's increase the number of neurons in the layer just a bit, to 90, and start the training again:

```
...
INFO o.d.n.m.MultiLayerNetwork - Starting MultiLayerNetwork ...
INFO c.m.d.u.NeuralNetworksUtils - params :67.487, examples: 77.141
INFO o.d.o.l.ScoreIterationListener - Score at iteration 0 is 173.9821
...
```

The number of neural network parameters is slightly smaller than the number of available training examples, so you shouldn't add more parameters going forward. Once you've finished training, let's get the lookup results:

```
'm'
--> month jeans of saids
--> mie free in manufact
----
'mu'
--> musications head socie
--> musican toels
----
'mus'
--> muse sc
--> muse germany nc
----
'musi'
--> musical federations
--> musicating outlet
----
'music'
--> musican 2006
--> musical swin daith program
----
'music '
--> music on the grade county
--> music of after
----
'music i'
--> music island fire grin school
--> music insurance
----
'music is'
--> music ish
--> music island recipe
----
'music is '
--> music is befied
--> music is an
```

```
----
'music is m'
--> music is michigan rup dogs
--> music is math sandthome
----
'music is my'
--> music is my labs
--> music is my less
----
'music is my '
--> music is my free
--> music is my hamby bar finance
----
'music is my a'
--> music is my acket
--> music is my appedia
----
'music is my ai'
--> music is my air brown
--> music is my air jerseys
----
'music is my air'
--> music is my air bar nude
--> music is my air ambrank
----
'music is my airc'
--> music is my airclass
--> music is my aircicle
----
'music is my aircr'
--> music is my aircraft
--> music is my aircross of mortgage choo
----
'music is my aircra'
--> music is my aircraft
--> music is my aircraft popper
----
'music is my aircraf'
--> music is my aircraft in star
--> music is my aircraft bouble
----
'music is my aircraft'
--> music is my aircraft
--> music is my aircraftless theatre
```

The quality of the suggested results has improved. Many of them are composed of correct English words; some of them are even funny, like "music is my aircraft popper" and "music is my aircraftless theatre"! Let's take another look at the Overview tab of the just-trained neural language model (see figure 4.11).

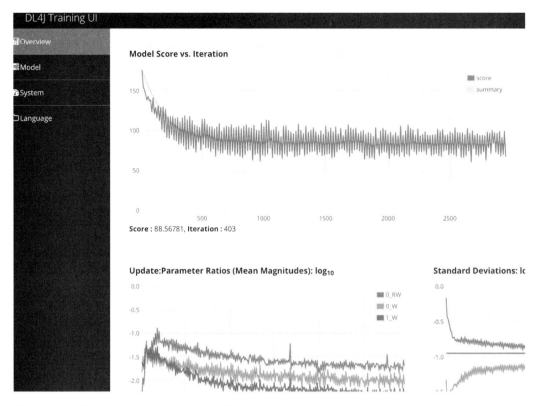

Figure 4.11   More parameters but still suboptimal convergence

The loss is decreasing better, but it still didn't reach a small enough value, so the learning rate probably isn't set correctly yet. Let's try to boost it by setting the learning rate to a higher value. It was set to 0.1, so let's try 0.4—a very high value! Figure 4.12 shows the network being trained again.

The result is a lower loss, and the neural network reached that with more parameters. This means it knows more about the training data. We'll stop here and consider ourselves satisfied with these outputs.

For optimal training, more iterations would be required; adjusting other parameters may give better-looking shapes and better-sounding suggestions. We'll discuss neural network tuning further in the final chapter of the book.

4.9   *Diversifying suggestions using word embeddings*

In chapter 2, you saw how useful it is to use word embeddings for synonym expansion. This section shows how to mix them with the results of LSTM-generated suggestions to provide more diverse suggestions for the end user. In production systems, it's common to combine the results of different models to provide a good user experience. The word2vec model lets you create a vectorized representation of a word. Such vec-

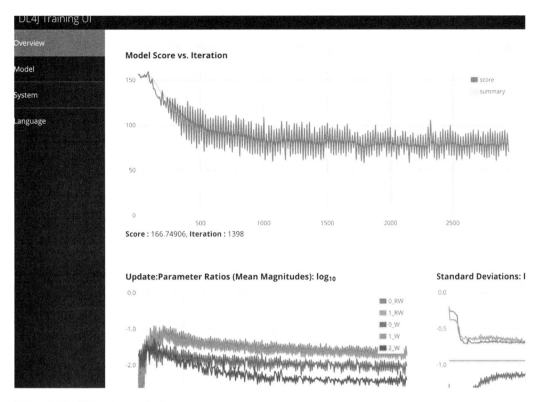

Figure 4.12   Higher learning rate

tors are learned by a shallow neural network by looking at the surrounding context (other nearby words) of each word. The nice thing about word2vec and similar algorithms for representing words as vectors is that they place similar words close together in the vector space: for example, the vectors representing "aircraft" and "aeroplane" will be very close to one another.

Let's build a word2vec model from the Lucene index containing the song lyrics, similar to what you did in chapter 2:

```
CharacterIterator iterator = ...
MultiLayerNetwork network = ...

FieldValuesSentenceIterator iterator = new
    FieldValuesSentenceIterator(reader, "lyrics");
Word2Vec vec = new Word2Vec.Builder()
    .layerSize(100)
    .iterate(iterator)
    .build();
vec.fit();

Lookup lookup = new CharLSTMWord2VecLookup(network,
    iterator, vec);
```

Creates a DataSetIterator over the contents of the Lucene lyrics field

Configures a word2vec model with word vectors of size 100

Builds the neural language model with the previously trained LSTM, the CharacterIterator, and the word2vec model

Performs word2vec model training

With the word2vec model trained on the same data, you can now combine it with the `CharLSTMNeuralLookup` and generate more suggestions. You'll define a `CharLSTM-Word2VecLookup` that extends the `CharLSTMNeuralLookup` class. This `Lookup` implementation requires a `Word2Vec` instance. At lookup time, it goes over the string suggested by the LSTM network, and then the word2vec model is used to find the nearest neighbor(s) for each word in the string. These nearest neighbors are used to create a new suggestion. For example, the sequence "music is my aircraft" generated by the LSTM will be split into its tokens "music," "is," "my," and "aircraft." The word2vec model will check, for example, the nearest neighbors of the word "aircraft" and find "aeroplane," and then create the additional suggestion "music is my aeroplane."

Listing 4.1   Extended neural language model with Word2Vec

```
public class CharLSTMWord2VecLookup extends CharLSTMNeuralLookup {

  private final Word2Vec word2Vec;

  public CharLSTMWord2VecLookup(MultiLayerNetwork net,
        CharacterIterator iter, Word2Vec word2Vec) {
    super(net, iter);
    this.word2Vec = word2Vec;
  }

  @Override
  public List<LookupResult> lookup(CharSequence key, Set<BytesRef> contexts,
        boolean onlyMorePopular, int num) throws IOException {
    Set<LookupResult> results = Sets.
        newCopyOnWriteArraySet(super.lookup(key,
        contexts, onlyMorePopular, num));              ⟵   Gets the suggestions generated
    for (LookupResult lr : results) {                      by the LSTM network
      String suggestionString = lr.key.toString();
      for (String word : word2Vec.
          getTokenizerFactory().create(
          suggestionString).getTokens()) {           ⟵   Divides the suggestion string
        Collection<String> nearestWords = word2Vec         into its tokens (words)
          .wordsNearest(word, 2);
        for (String nearestWord : nearestWords) {
          if (word2Vec.similarity(word, nearestWord)
              > 0.7) {                                 ⟵
            results.addAll(enhanceSuggestion(lr,           For each nearest neighbor,
              word, nearestWord));       ⟵                 checks whether it's similar
          }                                                enough to the input word
        }
      }
    }                                                  Creates an enhanced
    return new ArrayList<>(results);                   suggestion using the word
  }                                                    suggested by word2vec

  private Collection<LookupResult> enhanceSuggestion(LookupResult lr,
        String word, String nearestWord) {
    return Collections.singletonList(new LookupResult(
        lr.key.toString().replace(word, nearestWord),
        (long) (lr.value * 0.7)));       ⟵             Simple suggestion enhancement
  }                                                    implementation: substitutes the original
}                                                      word with its nearest neighbor word
```

Finds the top two nearest neighbors of each token

Back at the beginning of chapter 2, a user wanted to find the lyrics of a song whose title they couldn't exactly recall. With a word2vec model for synonym expansion, you can return the correct song even when the query doesn't match the title, by means of generated synonyms. With this combination of a neural language model and a word2vec model to generate suggestions, you manage to let the user avoid searching completely: the user types "music is my airc…" and gets the suggestion "music is my aeroplane," so no actual search is performed, but the user's information need is satisfied!

Summary

- Search suggestions are important to help users write good queries.
- The data for generating such suggestions can be static (for example, dictionaries of previously entered queries) or dynamic (such as documents stored in the search engine).
- You can use text analysis and/or ngram language models to build good suggester algorithms.
- Neural language models are language models based on neural networks, such as RNNs (or LSTMs).
- By using neural language models, you can get better-sounding suggestions.
- It's important to monitor the neural network training process to make sure you get good results.
- You can combine the results of the original suggester with word vectors to augment the diversity of the suggestions.

Ranking search results with word embeddings

Since chapter 2, we've been building components based on neural networks that can improve a search engine. These components aim to help the search engine better capture user intent by expanding synonyms, generating alternative representations of a query, and giving smarter suggestions while the user is typing a query. As these approaches show, a query can be expanded, adapted, and transformed before matching with the terms stored in the inverted indexes is performed. Then, as mentioned in chapter 1, the terms of the query are used to find matching documents.

These matching documents, also known as *search results*, are sorted according to how closely they're predicted to match the input query. This task of sorting the results is known as *ranking* or *scoring*. The ranking function has a fundamental impact on the *relevance* of search results, so getting it right means the search engine will have higher *precision,* and users will receive the most relevant and important information first. Getting ranking right isn't a one-shot process; rather, it's an incremental one. In real life, you'll use an existing ranking algorithm, create a new one, or use a combination of existing and new ranking functions. Many times you'll have to fine-tune them to accurately capture what your users are looking for, how they're writing queries, and so on.

In this chapter, you'll learn about common ranking functions, information retrieval models, and how a search engine "decides" which results to show first. Then I'll show you how to improve your search engine's ranking functions by using dense vector representations of text (words, sentences, documents, and so on). Also known as *embeddings,* these vector representations of text can help your ranking functions to do a better job matching and scoring documents according to the user's intent.

5.1 *The importance of ranking*

A somewhat funny meme that floated around on the internet for a while said, "The best place to hide a dead body is page two of Google." This is of course a hyperbolic sentence that applies mostly to web search (searching for content, such as pages, from websites). But it says a lot about the degree to which users expect search engines to be good at returning relevant results. It's often mentally easier for a user to write a better query than to scroll down and click the Page 2 button on the results page. The meme could be rephrased as, "If it didn't show up on the first page, it can't be relevant." This tells you why relevance is important. You can assume the following:

- *Users are lazy.* They don't want to scroll down or look at more than two or three results before deciding whether the search results are good. Returning thousands of results is often useless.
- *Users are uninformed.* They don't know how a search engine works internally; they just write a query and hope to get good results.

If a search engine ranking function works well, you can return the top 10 to 20 results, and the user will be satisfied. Note that this approach can also have a positive impact on the performance of the search engine, because the user won't browse through all the matching documents.

You may wonder if the relevance problem applies in all cases, though. For example, if you have a short query that consists of one or two words and that clearly identifies a small set of search results, the relevance problem is less evident. Think about all the search queries you've performed on Google just to retrieve a Wikipedia page. For example, imagine that you want to find the page that describes Bernhard Riemann. It's annoying to enter the en.wikipedia.org URL, type `Bernhard Riemann` in the Wikipedia Search text box, and click the magnifying glass button to get the results. It's much faster to type `Bernhard Riemann` in the Google search box—and you'll most probably get the Wikipedia page as the first or second search result on the first page. This is an example where you (think you) know in advance what you want to retrieve (you're lazy, but you were informed about what you wanted and you knew from prior experience how the search engine usually works when searching for people). But in many cases, this doesn't apply. Put yourself in the shoes of an undergrad math student who isn't interested in generic information about Riemann, but instead wants to understand why his works are considered important in several different fields of science. The student doesn't know in advance the specific resources they want; they know the *type* of resource needed and will type a query based on that. So such a student may type a query like `the importance of Bernhard Riemann works` or `Bernhard Riemann influence in academic research`. If you run these two queries on Google yourself,

- You'll see different search results for each query.
- Search results that appear in both cases are in a different order.

More notably, at the time of writing, the first query returns the Wikipedia page as the first result, whereas the second query's first result is "herbart's influence on bernhard riemann." That's odd because it turns the user's intent upside down: the student wanted to know how Riemann influenced others, not vice versa (the second result, "riemann's contribution to differential geometry," sounds much more relevant). This is the kind of problem that makes ranking search results difficult.

Let's now see how ranking comes into play in the life cycle of a query (see also figure 5.1):

1. A query written by the user is parsed, analyzed, and broken down into a set of term clauses (an encoded query).
2. The encoded query is executed against the search engine data structures (for each term, a lookup in the inverted index table is performed).
3. The matching documents are collected and passed to the ranking function.
4. Each document is scored by the ranking function.
5. Typically, the list of search results is composed of such documents, sorted according to their score in descending order (the first result has the highest score).

The ranking function takes a bunch of search results and assigns each one a score value that's an indicator of its importance with respect to the input query. The higher the score, the more important the document.

Additionally, when ranking results, a smart search engine should consider the following:

- *User history*—Record the past activity of a user and take it into consideration when ranking. For example, recurring terms in past queries may indicate a user's interest in a certain topic, so search results on that same topic should have a higher ranking.
- *User's geographical location*—Record the user's location, and increase the score of search results written in the appropriate language.

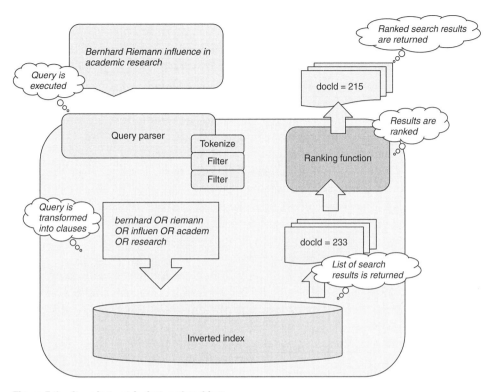

Figure 5.1 Querying, retrieving, and ranking

- *Temporal changes in information*—Recall the "latest trends" query from chapter 3. Such a query should match not only the words "latest" and/or "trends," but should also boost the score of newer documents (more recent information).
- *All possible context clues*—Look for signals to provide more context to the query. For example, look at the search logs to see whether a query was previously performed; if so, check the next query in the search log to see if there are any shared results, and give them a higher ranking.

We'll now dive into answering the key question: how does the search engine decide how to rank search results with respect to a given query?

5.2   *Retrieval models*

So far, we've talked about the task of ranking a document as a function that takes a document as input and generates a score value representing the document's relevance. In practice, ranking functions are often part of an *information retrieval model* (IR model). Such a model defines how the search engine tackles the entire problem of providing relevant results with respect to an information need: from query parsing to matching, retrieving, and ranking search results. The rationale for having a model is that it's hard to come up with a ranking function that gives an accurate score without knowing how the search engine handles a query. In a query like "+riemann -influenced influencing," if a document contains both the terms "riemann" and "influencing," the resulting final score should be a combination of the scores for the first and second terms (score = score(riemann) \+ score(influencing)); but the "riemann" term has a mandatory constraint (the \+ sign), so it should contribute a higher score than "influencing," which is optional.

Thus the way a search engine calculates the relevance of a document with respect to a query has an impact on the design and infrastructure behind the search engine. Since chapter 1, we've assumed that when text is fed into the search engine, it's analyzed and split into chunks that can be altered depending on tokenizers and token filters. This text analysis chain generates terms that end up in inverted indexes, also known as *posting lists*. The search-by-keyword use case motivated the choice of posting lists to efficiently retrieve documents by matching terms. Similarly, the choice of how to rank query-document pairs may impact system requirements: for example, the ranking function may need to access more information about the indexed data than just the presence or absence of a term in the posting list. A widely used set of retrieval models called *statistical models* makes decisions about ranking a certain document based on how frequently a matching term appears within a specific document and the entire document set.

In previous chapters, we've already gone beyond simple matching of terms between queries and documents. We've used synonym expansion to generate synonym terms: for example, at search time, to extend the number of possible ways a user can "say" the same thing (at a word level). We expanded this approach in chapter 3 by generating new alternative queries in addition to the original query entered by the user.

All this work aims to build a search engine that's eager to understand the semantics of text:

- *In the synonym expansion case*—Whether you type "hello" or "hi," you're *semantically* saying the same thing.
- *In the alternative query expansion case*—If you type "latest trends," you get alternative queries that are spelled differently but are semantically close to the original.

Overall, the (simplified) idea is that a document that's relevant with respect to a certain query should be returned even if there's no exact match between the query and the indexed terms. Synonyms and alternative query representations provide a wider range of relevant query terms that can match the document terms. Those methods make it more probable that you'll find a document using semantically similar words or queries. In an ideal world, a search engine would go beyond query-document term matching and understand the user's information need. Based on that, it would return results relevant to that need, again not constraining retrieval to term matching.

Creating a search engine with good semantic understanding capabilities is difficult. The good news is that, as you'll see, techniques based on deep learning can help a lot in reducing the gap between a plain query string and the actual user intent. Think about the *thought vector* you briefly met in chapter 3 when we looked at seq2seq models. You can think of it as the kind of representation of user intent you need in order to go beyond simple term matching.

A good retrieval model should consider semantics. As you can imagine, this semantic perspective applies to ranking documents, as well. For example:

- When ranking a result whose matching terms came from one of the alternative queries generated by a LSTM network, should such documents score differently than documents that matched based on terms from the original user query?
- If you plan to use representations generated via deep learning (for example, thought vectors) to capture user intent, how do you use them to retrieve and rank results?

We'll now begin an exploration that will touch on the following:

- More-traditional retrieval models
- Extending traditional models that use vector representations of text learned through neural networks (this will be our main focus)
- Neural IR models that rely purely on deep neural networks

5.2.1 *TF-IDF and the vector space model*

In chapter 1, I mentioned term frequency–inverse document frequency (TF-IDF) and the vector space model (VSM). Let's take a closer look at them to understand how they work. The fundamental purpose of a ranking function is to assign a score to a query-document pair. A common way to measure the importance of a document with respect to a query is based on calculating and fetching statistics for query and document terms. Such retrieval models are called *statistical models for information retrieval.*

Suppose you have the query "bernhard riemann influence" and two resulting documents: document1 = "riemann bernhard - life and works of bernhard riemann," and document2 = "thomas bernhard biography - bio and influence in literature." Both the query and the documents are made up of terms. When you look at which of them matched, you observe the following:

- Document1 matched the terms "riemann" and "bernhard." Both terms matched twice.
- Document2 matched the terms "bernhard" and "influence." Both terms matched once.
- The term frequency for document1 is 2 for each matching term, and document2's term frequency for its two matching terms is 1.
- The document frequency for "bernhard" is 2 (it appears in both documents; you don't count repeated occurrences in a singular document). The document frequency for "riemann" is 1, and the document frequency for "influence" is 1.

> ### Term frequency and document frequency
>
> Often, statistical models combine *term frequency* and *document frequency* to come up with a measure of the relevance of a document, given a query. The rationale behind the choice of these metrics is that calculating frequencies and statistics about terms give you a measure of how informative each of them is. More specifically, the number of times a query term appears in a document gives a measure of how pertinent that document could be to that query; this is the *term frequency*. On the other hand, terms that rarely appear in the indexed data are considered more important and informative than more common terms (terms like "the" and "in" usually aren't informative, because they're much too common). The frequency of a term within all the indexed documents is called the *document frequency*.

If you sum all the term frequencies of each matching term, the score is 4 for document1 and 2 for document2.

Let's add a document3 whose content is "riemann hypothesis - a deep dive into a mathematical mystery" and score it against the same query. Document3 has a score of 1 because only the "riemann" term matches. This isn't good, because document3 is more relevant than document2, although it isn't pertinent to Riemann's influence.

A better way to express ranking is to score each document using the sum of the logarithms of term frequencies divided by the logarithm of the document frequency. This famous weighting scheme is called TF-IDF:

$$\text{weight(term)} = (1 + \log(\text{tf(term)})) * \log(N/\text{df(term)})$$

N is the number of indexed documents. With the new document3 added, the document frequency for the term "riemann" is now 2. Using the previous equation for each matching term, you add each TF-IDF and obtain the following scores:

$$\text{score(document1)} = \text{tf-idf}(\textit{riemann}) \backslash\!+ \text{tf-idf}(\textit{bernhard}) = 1.28 \backslash\!+ 1.28 = 2.56$$
$$\text{score(document2)} = \text{tf-idf}(\textit{bernhard}) \backslash\!+ \text{tf-idf}(\textit{influence}) = 1 \backslash\!+ 1 = 2$$
$$\text{score(document3)} = \text{tf-idf}(\textit{riemann}) = 1$$

You've just seen that TF-IDF–based scoring only relies on pure frequencies of terms, so a document that isn't relevant (document2) is scored higher than a somewhat-relevant document (document3). This is a case where the retrieval model is missing semantic understanding of query intent, as discussed in the previous section.

In this book so far, you've encountered vectors many times. Using them in information retrieval isn't a novel idea; VSM relies on representing queries and documents as vectors and measures how similar they are based on a TF-IDF weighting scheme. Each document can be represented by a one-dimensional vector with size equal to the number of existing terms in the index. Each position in the vector represents a term having a value equal to the TF-IDF value for that document for that term.

The same can be done for queries, because they're also made up of terms; the only difference is the fact that term frequencies can be either local (frequency of query terms as they appear in the query) or from the index (frequency of query terms as they appear in the indexed data). This way, you represent documents and queries as vectors. This representation is called *bag-of-words*, because the information about positions of terms is lost—every document or query is represented as a collection of words, as in table 5.1.

Table 5.1   Bag-of-words representations

Terms	bernhard	bio	dive	hypothesis	in	influence	into	life	mathematical	riemann
doc1	1.28	0.0	0.0	0.0	0.0	0.0	0.0	1.0	0.0	1.28
doc2	1.0	1.0	0.0	0.0	1.0	1.0	0.0	0.0	0.0	0.0
doc3	0.0	0.0	1.0	1.0	0.0	0.0	1.0	0.0	1.0	1.0

The vectors of "bernhard riemann influence" and "riemann influence bernhard" look exactly the same: the facts that the two queries are different and that the first query is more meaningful than the second one aren't captured. Now that the documents and queries are represented in a vector space, you want to calculate which document best matches the input query. You do that by calculating the *cosine similarity* between each document and the input query; that will give you the final ranking for each document. The cosine similarity is a measure of the amplitude of the angle between a document and the query vectors. Figure 5.2 shows vectors for the input query, document1, and document2 in a (simplified, two-dimensional) vector space that only considers the terms "bernhard" and "riemann."

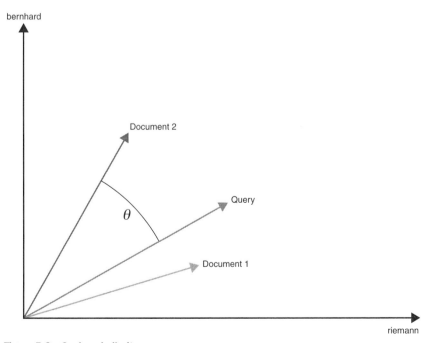

Figure 5.2   Cosine similarity

The similarity between the query vector and a document is evaluated by looking at the existing angle between the two vectors. The smaller the angle, the more similar the two vectors are. When you apply this to the vectors from table 5.1, you get the following similarity scores:

```
cosineSimilarity(query,doc1) = 0.51
cosineSimilarity(query,doc2) = 0.38
cosineSimilarity(query,doc3) = 0.17
```

With just three documents, the resulting vector's size is 10 (the number of columns equals the number of the terms used across the documents). In production systems, this value would be much higher. So one problem with this bag-of-words representation is that the size of vectors grows linearly with the number of existing terms (all the distinct words contained in the indexed documents). This is another reason word vectors like those generated by word2vec are better than bag-of-words vectors. Word2vec-generated vectors have a fixed size, so they don't grow with the number of terms in the search engine; therefore, resource consumption is much lower when using them. (Word2vec-generated vectors do better at capturing word semantics, as explained in chapter 2.)

Despite these limitations, VSM and TF-IDF are used often with good results in many production systems. Before discussing other information retrieval models, let's get pragmatic, ingest the documents with Lucene, and see how they're scored using TF-IDF and VSM.

5.2.2 *Ranking documents in Lucene*

In Lucene, the `Similarity` API serves as the base for ranking functions. Lucene comes with some information retrieval models implemented out of the box, such as VSM with TF-IDF (which was the default used up to version 5), Okapi BM25, Divergence from Randomness, language models, and others. `Similarity` needs to be set at both indexing and search time. In Lucene 7, the VSM + TF-IDF similarity is `ClassicSimilarity`.

At index time, `Similarity` is set in the `IndexWriterConfig`:

```
IndexWriterConfig config = new IndexWriterConfig();    ⟵⎯ Creates a configuration for indexing

config.setSimilarity(new ClassicSimilarity());    ⟵⎯ Sets the similarity to ClassicSimilarity
IndexWriter writer = new IndexWriter(directory, config);
```
Creates an IndexWriter using the configured Similarity

At search time, `Similarity` is set in the `IndexSearcher`:

```
IndexReader reader = DirectoryReader.open(directory);    ⟵⎯ Opens an IndexReader
IndexSearcher searcher = new IndexSearcher(reader);    ⟵⎯ Creates an IndexSearcher over the reader
searcher.setSimilarity(new ClassicSimilarity);
```
Sets Similarity in the IndexSearcher

If you index and search over the earlier three documents, you can see whether the ranking behaves as you expect:

You can define the features of a Lucene field yourself (storing values, storing term positions, and so on).

For each document, creates a new Document and adds the contents in a title field

```
FieldType fieldType = ...
Document doc1 = new Document();
doc1.add(new Field("title",
    "riemann bernhard - life and works of bernhard riemann", ft));
Document doc2 = new Document();
doc2.add(new Field("title",
    "thomas bernhard biography - bio and influence in literature", ft));
Document doc3 = new Document();
doc3.add(new Field("title",
    "riemann hypothesis - a deep dive into a mathematical mystery", ft));
writer.addDocument(doc1);
writer.addDocument(doc2);
writer.addDocument(doc3);
writer.commit();
```

Adds all three documents and commits the changes

To check how each search result is scored by the `Similarity` class with respect to a query, you can ask Lucene to "explain" it. The output of an `explain` consists of text describing how each matching term contributes to the final score of each search result:

Writes a query

Parses the user-entered query

Performs the search

```
String queryString = "bernhard riemann influence";
QueryParser parser = new QueryParser("title", new WhitespaceAnalyzer());
Query query = parser.parse(queryString);
TopDocs hits = searcher.search(query, 3);
for (int i = 0; i < hits.scoreDocs.length; i++) {
    ScoreDoc scoreDoc = hits.scoreDocs[i];
    Document doc = searcher.doc(scoreDoc.doc);
    String title = doc.get("title");
    System.out.println(title + " : " + scoreDoc.score);
    System.out.println("--");
    Explanation explanation = searcher.explain(query, scoreDoc.doc);
    System.out.println(explanation);
}
```

Prints the document title and score on the standard output

Gets an explanation of how the score was calculated

With `ClassicSimilarity`, you get the following `explain` output:

```
riemann bernhard - life and works of bernhard riemann : 1.2140384
--
1.2140384 = sum of:
  0.6070192 = weight(title:bernhard in 0) [ClassicSimilarity], result of:
    0.6070192 = fieldWeight in 0, product of:
      ...
  0.6070192 = weight(title:riemann in 0) [ClassicSimilarity], result of:
    0.6070192 = fieldWeight in 0, product of:
      ...
--
thomas bernhard biography - bio and influence in literature : 0.9936098
--
```

```
0.9936098 = sum of:
  0.42922735 = weight(title:bernhard in 1) [ClassicSimilarity], result of:
    0.42922735 = fieldWeight in 1, product of:
      ...
  0.56438243 = weight(title:influence in 1) [ClassicSimilarity], result of:
    0.56438243 = fieldWeight in 1, product of:
      ...
--
riemann hypothesis - a deep dive into a mathematical mystery : 0.4072008
--
0.4072008 = sum of:
  0.4072008 = weight(title:riemann in 2) [ClassicSimilarity], result of:
    0.4072008 = fieldWeight in 2, product of:
      ...
```

As expected, the ranking respects what's described in the previous section. You can see from the explanation that each term that matched the query contributes according to its weight as they're summed:

```
0.9936098 = sum of:
  0.42922735 = weight(title:bernhard in 1)...
  0.56438243 = weight(title:influence in 1)...
```

On the other hand, the scores aren't exactly the same as when you manually compute TF-IDF weights for terms. The reason is that there are many possible variations of TF-IDF schemes. For example, here Lucene calculates inverse document frequency as

$$\log(N+1)/(\text{df(term)}+1)$$

instead of

$$\log(N/\text{df(term)})$$

Additionally, Lucene doesn't take the logarithm of the term frequency but rather uses the term frequency as it is. Lucene also uses *normalization*, a technique to mitigate the fact that documents with more terms would score too high with respect to short documents (with fewer terms), which can be approximated as `1.0 / Math.sqrt(number-OfTerms))`. Using this normalization technique, calculating the cosine similarity between a query vector and a document vector is equivalent to calculating their scalar product:

```
score(query,document1) = tf-idf(query, bernhard) * tf-idf(document1,bernhard)
    + tf-idf(query, riemann) * tf-idf(document, riemann)
```

Lucene doesn't store vectors. It's enough to be able to compute the TF-IDF for each matching term and combine the results to compute the score.

5.2.3   *Probabilistic models*

You've learned about some VSM theory and how it's applied in practice in Lucene. You've also seen scores being calculated using term statistics. In this section, you'll learn about probabilistic retrieval models, where scores are still calculated on the basis of probabilities. The search engine ranks a document using its probability of relevance with respect to the query.

Probabilities are a powerful tool to address uncertainty. We've discussed how hard it is to bridge the gap between user intent and relevant search results. Probabilistic models try to model ranking by measuring how probable it is that a certain document is relevant with respect to the input query. If you roll a six-sided die, each side has a 1/6 probability of being the result: for example, the probability of rolling a 3 is $P(3) = 0.16$. But in practice, if you roll a die six times, you probably won't get all six different results. Probability is an estimation of how likely a certain event is to occur—this doesn't imply that it will occur exactly that often.

The unconditional probability of rolling any number on a die is 1/6, but what about the probability of rolling two consecutive results that are the same? Such a conditional probability can be expressed as $P(event|condition)$. For the ranking task, you can estimate the probability that a certain document is relevant (with respect to a given query). This is represented as $P(r = 1|x)$, where r is a binary measure of relevance:

$r = 1$: relevant, $r = 0$: not relevant

In a probabilistic retrieval model, you generally rank all documents with respect to a given query by $P(r = 1|x)$. This is best expressed by the *probability ranking principle*: if retrieved documents are ordered by decreasing probability of relevance to the data available, then the system's effectiveness is the best that can be obtained for the data.

One of the most famous and widely adopted probabilistic models is *Okapi BM25*. Briefly, it tries to mitigate two limitations of TF-IDF:

- Limit the impact of term frequency to avoid excessive scoring based on frequently repeated terms.
- Provide a better estimate of the importance of the document frequency of a certain term.

BM25 expresses the conditional probability $P(r = 1|x)$ by means of two probabilities that depend on term frequencies. So BM25 approximates probabilities by calculating probability distribution over term frequencies.

Consider the "bernhard riemann influence" example. In a classic TF-IDF scheme, a high term frequency can lead to a high score. So, if you have a dummy document4 that contains lots of "bernhard" occurrences ("bernhard bernhard bernhard bernhard bernhard bernhard bernhard bernhard bernhard bernhard"), it may score higher than more-relevant documents. If you index it into the previously built index, you get the following outputs with TF-IDF and VSM (`ClassicSimilarity`):

```
riemann bernhard - life and works of bernhard riemann : 1.2888055
bernhard bernhard bernhard bernhard bernhard bernhard ... : 1.2231436
thomas bernhard biography - bio and influence in literature : 1.0464782
riemann hypothesis - a deep dive into a mathematical mystery : 0.47776502
```

As you can see, the dummy document is returned as the second result, which is strange. Additionally, document4's score is almost equal to the first-ranked result: the search engine ranked this dummy document as important, but it isn't. Let's set the `BM25Similarity` in Lucene (the default since version 6) using the same code as for the `ClassicSimilarity` tests:

```
searcher.setSimilarity(new BM25Similarity());
```

With BM25 similarity set, the ranking is as follows:

```
riemann bernhard - life and works of bernhard riemann : 1.6426628
thomas bernhard biography - bio and influence in literature : 1.5724708
bernhard bernhard bernhard bernhard bernhard bernhard ... : 0.9965918
riemann hypothesis - a deep dive into a mathematical mystery : 0.68797445
```

The dummy document is ranked third instead of second. Although this isn't optimal, the score has greatly decreased as compared to the most relevant document. The reason is that BM25 "squashes" the term frequency to keep it below a certain configurable threshold. In this case, BM25 mitigated the impact of the high term frequency for the term "bernhard."

The other good thing about BM25 is that it tries to estimate the probability of terms that appear together in a document. The document frequency of a number of terms in a document is given by the sum of the logs of the probability that each single term appears in that document.

But BM25 also has some limitations:

- Like TF-IDF, BM25 is a bag-of-words model, so it disregards term ordering when ranking.
- Although in general it performs well, BM25 is based on heuristics (functions that reach a fairly good result but aren't guaranteed to work in general) that may not apply well to your data (you may have to adjust those heuristics).
- BM25 performs some approximation and simplification on probability estimation, which causes less-acceptable results in some cases (it doesn't work well with long documents).

Other probabilistic approaches to ranking based on language models are generally better at plain probability estimations, but this doesn't always result in better scoring. In general, BM25 is an okay baseline ranking function.

Now that we've explored some of the most commonly used ranking models for search engines, let's dive into how neural networks can help make those models better and also provide completely new (and better) ranking models.

5.3 Neural information retrieval

So far, we've tackled the problem of effective ranking by looking at terms and their local (per document) and global (per collection) frequencies. If you want to use neural networks to obtain a better ranking function, you need to think in terms of vectors. Actually, this doesn't solely apply to neural networks. You've seen that even the classic VSM treats documents and queries as vectors and measures their similarity using cosine distance. One problem is that the size of such vectors can grow enormously (linearly) with the number of indexed words.

Before neural information retrieval, other techniques were developed to provide more compact (fixed-size) representations of words. These were mainly based on matrix-factorization algorithms such as the *latent semantic indexing* (LSI) algorithm, which is based on *singular value decomposition* (SVD) factorization. In short, in LSI, you create a matrix of terms and documents for each document row: put a 1 in each element where the document contains the corresponding term, and a 0 for all others. Then transform (factorize) this sparse matrix (lots of zeros) with a reduced SVD factorization method, resulting in three (denser) matrixes whose product is a good approximation of the original. Each resulting document row has fixed dimensionality and is no longer sparse. Query vectors can also be transformed using SVD factorized matrixes. (A somewhat similar technique is called *latent Dirichlet allocation* [LDA].) The "juice" here is that no term matching is required; query and document vectors are compared so that the most similar document vectors are ranked first.

Learning good representations of data is one of the tasks deep learning can do best. We'll now look at using such vector representations for ranking. You're already familiar with the algorithm we'll use—word2vec—which learns distributed representations of words. Word vectors are located close to one another when the words they represent appear in similar contexts and, hence, have similar semantics.

5.4 *From word to document vectors*

Let's start building a retrieval system based on vectors generated by word2vec. The goal is to rank documents against queries, but word2vec gives vectors for words, not sequences of words. So the first thing to do is find a way to use these word vectors to represent documents and queries. A query will usually be composed of more than one word, as will indexed documents. For example, let's take the word vectors for each of the terms in the query "bernhard riemann influence" and plot them as shown in figure 5.3.

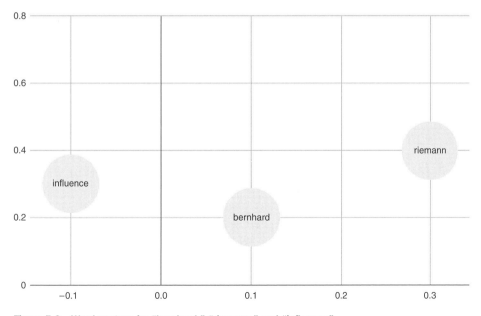

Figure 5.3 Word vectors for "bernhard," "riemann," and "influence"

A simple method to create document vectors from word vectors is to average the word vectors into a single document vector. This is a straightforward mathematical operation: every element at position *j* in each vector is added, and the total is then divided by the number of vectors being averaged (the same as an arithmetic averaging operation). You can do that with DL4J vectors (`INDArrays` objects) as follows:

```
public static INDArray toDenseAverageVector(Word2Vec word2Vec,
    String... terms) {
  return word2Vec.getWordVectorsMean(Arrays.asList(terms));
}
```

The `mean` vector is the result of the averaging operation. In figure 5.4, as expected, the average vector sits at the center of the three word vectors.

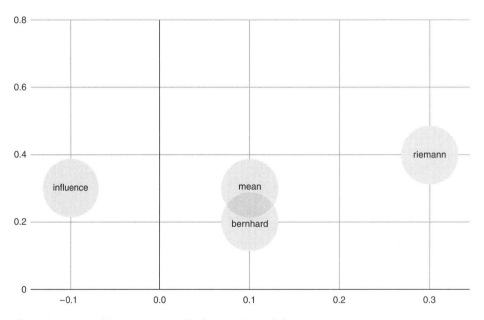

Figure 5.4   Averaging the "bernhard," "riemann," and "influence" word vectors

Note that this technique can be applied to both documents and queries, because they're compositions of words. For each document-query pair, you can calculate the document vectors by averaging the word vectors and then assign the score to each document based on how close their respective averaged word vectors are. This is similar to what you do in the VSM scenario; the big difference is that the values of these document vectors aren't calculated using TF-IDF but come from averaging word2vec vectors. In summary, these dense vectors are less heavy in terms of required memory (and space, if stored to disk) and more informative in terms of semantics.

Let's repeat the earlier experiment but rank documents using averaged word vectors. You first feed word2vec data from the search engine:

```
IndexReader reader = DirectoryReader.open(
    directory);
FieldValuesSentenceIterator iterator = new
    FieldValuesSentenceIterator(reader, "title");
Word2Vec vec = new Word2Vec.Builder()
    .layerSize(3)
    .windowSize(3)
    .tokenizerFactory(new DefaultTokenizerFactory())
    .iterate(iterator)
    .build();
vec.fit();
```

Creates a reader over the search engine document set

Creates a DL4J iterator that can read data from the reader on the title field

Configures word2vec

You're working with a super-small dataset, so you use very small vectors.

Lets word2vec learn word vectors

Once you've extracted the word vectors, you can build query and document vectors:

```
String[] terms = ...
INDArray queryVector = toDenseAverageVector(vec,
    terms);
for (int i = 0; i < hits.scoreDocs.length; i++) {
    ScoreDoc scoreDoc = hits.scoreDocs[i];
    Document doc = searcher.doc(scoreDoc.doc);

    String title = doc.get("title");

    Terms docTerms = reader.getTermVector(scoreDoc.doc,
        "title");

    INDArray denseDocumentVector = VectorizeUtils
        .toDenseAverageVector(docTerms, vec);

    double sim = Transforms.cosineSim(denseQueryVector,
        denseDocumentVector)

    System.out.println(title + " : " + sim);
}
```

Array containing the terms entered in the query ("bernhard," "riemann," and "influence")

Converts the query terms into a query vector by averaging the word vectors of the query terms

For each search result: ignores the score as given by Lucene and transforms the results into document vectors

Gets the document title

Extracts the terms contained in that document (using the IndexReader#getTermVector API)

Converts the document terms into a document vector using the averaging technique shown earlier

Calculates the cosine similarity between the query and document vector and prints it

For the sake of readability, the outputs are shown manually ordered from highest to lowest scores:

```
riemann hypothesis - a deep dive into a
    mathematical mystery : 0.6171551942825317

thomas bernhard biography - bio and influence
    in literature : 0.4961382746696472

bernhard bernhard bernhard bernhard bernhard
    bernhard ... : 0.32834646105766296

riemann bernhard - life and works of bernhard
    riemann : 0.2925628423690796
```

The top-scored document is relevant, regardless of low term frequency.

The second document isn't relevant with respect to user intent.

The dummy document

The (probably) most relevant document has the lowest score.

This is strange: the technique you expected to help you get a better ranking ranked the dummy document better than the most relevant one! The reasons are the following:

- There isn't enough training data available for word2vec to provide word vectors that carefully represent word semantics. Four short documents contain far too few word-context pairs for the word2vec neural network to adjust its hidden layer weights accurately.
- If you pick the document vector of the top-scored document, it will be equal to the word vector for the word "bernhard." The query vector is an average vector of the vectors for "bernhard," "riemann," and "influence"; therefore, these vectors will always be close together in the vector space.

Let's visualize the second statement by plotting the generated document-query vectors in a (reduced) two-dimensional space: see figure 5.5. As expected, document4 and the query embeddings are so close that their labels almost overlap.

One way to improve these results is to make sure the word2vec algorithm has more training data. For example, you can start with an English dump from Wikipedia and index each page's title and content in Lucene. Additionally, you can mitigate the impact of text fragments like the one from document4, which mostly (or only) contains single terms that also appear in the query. A common technique to do so is to smooth the averaged document vectors by using term frequencies. Instead of dividing each word vector by the document length, you divide each word vector by its term frequency according to the following pseudo-code:

```
documentVector(wordA wordB) = wordVector(wordA)/termFreq(wordA) +
    wordVector(wordB)/termFreq(wordB)
```

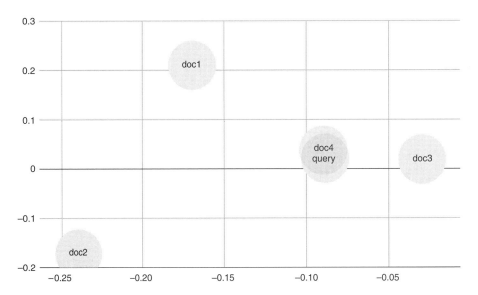

Figure 5.5 Similarity between query and document embeddings

This can be implemented in Lucene and DL4J as follows:

```
public static INDArray toDenseAverageTFVector(Terms docTerms, Terms
    fieldTerms, Word2Vec word2Vec) throws IOException {
  INDArray vector = Nd4j.zeros(word2Vec
    .getLayerSize());                   ⊲────── Initializes all the vector values to zero
  TermsEnum docTermsEnum = docTerms.iterator();  ⊲────── Iterates over all the existing terms of the current doc
  BytesRef term;
  while ((term = docTermsEnum.next()) != null) {
    long termFreq = docTermsEnum.totalTermFreq();  ⊲────── Obtains the term-frequency value for the current term
    INDArray wordVector = word2Vec.getLookupTable().
        vector(term.utf8ToString()).div(termFreq);  ⊲──────
    vector.addi(wordVector);  ⊲──────
  }
  return vector;
}
```

Fetches the next term

Extracts the word embedding for the current term and then divides its values by the term-frequency value

Sums the current vector for the current term with the vector to be returned

When I introduced averaged word vectors, you saw that such document vectors are placed right at the center of their composing word vectors. In figure 5.6, you can see that term-frequency smoothing can help detach the generated document vectors from sitting at the center of the word vectors, nearer to the less-frequent (and hopefully more important) word.

The terms "bernhard" and "riemann" are more frequent than "influence," and the generated document vector `tf` is closer to the `influence` word vector. This has a positive

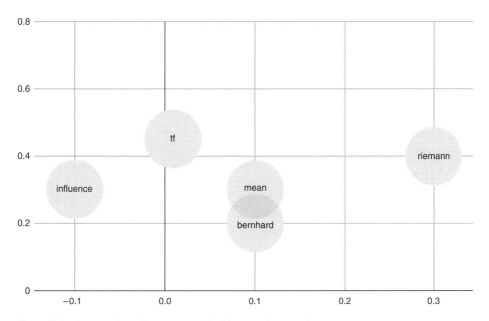

Figure 5.6 Averaged word vector smoothed by term frequencies

impact: documents whose term frequency is low are better ranked but still lie close enough to the query vector:

```
riemann hypothesis - a deep dive into a mathematical
    mystery : 0.6436703205108643
thomas bernhard biography - bio and influence in
    literature : 0.527758002281189
riemann bernhard - life and works of bernhard
    riemann : 0.2937617599964142
bernhard bernhard bernhard bernhard bernhard
    bernhard ...: 0.2569074332714081
```

For the first time, the dummy document receives the lowest score. If you switch from plain term frequencies to TF-IDF as smoothing factors for generating averaged document vectors from word embeddings, you get the following ranking:

```
riemann hypothesis - a deep dive into a mathematical
    mystery : 0.7083401679992676
riemann bernhard - life and works of bernhard
    riemann : 0.4424433362483978
thomas bernhard biography - bio and influence in
    literature : 0.3514146476984024
bernhard bernhard bernhard bernhard bernhard
    bernhard ... : 0.09490833431482315
```

With the TF-IDF–based smoothing (see, for example, figure 5.7), the ranking of documents is the best you can achieve. You got away from strict term weighting–based similarity: the most relevant document has a term frequency of 1 for the term "riemann," whereas the document with the highest term frequency has the lowest score. From a semantic perspective, the most relevant documents are scored higher than the others.

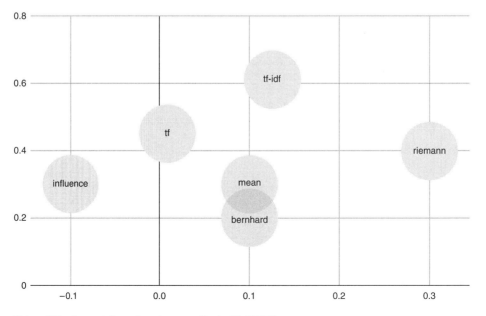

Figure 5.7 Averaged word vector smoothed with TF-IDF

5.5 *Evaluations and comparisons*

Are you happy with this means of ranking documents based on TF-IDF averaged word vectors? In the previous example, you trained word2vec with specific settings: layer size set to 60, skip-gram model, window size set to 6, and so on. The ranking was optimized with respect to a specific query and a set of four documents. Although this is a useful exercise for learning the pros and cons of different approaches, you can't do such fine-grained optimizations for all possible input queries, especially for large knowledge bases. Given that relevance is so difficult to get right, it's good to find ways to automate the evaluation of ranking effectiveness. So before we jump on other ways to address ranking (such as with the help of neural text embeddings), let's quickly introduce some tooling to speed up evaluating ranking functions.

A nice tool for evaluating the effectiveness of Lucene-based search engines is Lucene for Information Retrieval (Lucene4IR). It originated from a collaboration between people from research and industry.[1] A quick tutorial can be found at http://mng.bz/YP7N. Lucene4IR makes it possible to try out different indexing, retrieval, and ranking strategies over standard information retrieval datasets. To try it, you can run Lucene4IR's `IndexerApp`, `RetrievalApp`, and `ExampleStatsApp` in sequence. Doing so will index, search, and record statistics over returned versus relevant results: for example, according to the chosen Lucene configuration (`Similarity`, `Analyzers`, and so on). By default, these apps run on the CACM dataset (http://mng .bz/GWZq) using `BM25Similarity`.

Once you've performed data evaluation with Lucen4IR tools, you can measure precision, recall, and other IR metrics using the `trec_eval` tool (a tool developed to measure the quality of search results on the data from the TREC conference series; http://trec.nist.gov). Here's an example of `trec_eval` terminal output on the CACM dataset using BM25 ranking:

```
./trec_eval ~/lucene4ir/data/cacm/cacm.qrels
    ~/lucene4ir/data/cacm/bm25"results.res
...
num_q                 all  51     ⊲── Number of queries performed
num_ret               all  5067   ⊲── Number of returned results
num_rel               all  793    ⊲── Number of relevant results
num_rel_ret           all  341    ⊲── Number of returned results that are also relevant
map                   all  0.2430 ⊲── Mean average precision
Rprec                 all  0.2634 ⊲── R-precision
P_5                   all  0.3608 │ P_5, P_10, and so on give the precision
P_10                  all  0.2745 │ at 5, 10, and so on retrieved documents.
```

If you change the Lucene `Similarity` parameter in the Lucene4IR configuration file and again run `RetrievalApp` and `ExampleStatsApp`, you can observe how precision, recall, and other measures commonly used in IR change in the dataset. Here's an

---

[1] See Leif Azzopardi et al., "Lucene4IR: Developing Information Retrieval Evaluation Resources using Lucene," *ACM SIGIR Forum* 50, no. 2 (December 2016), http://sigir.org/wp-content/uploads/2017/01/p058.pdf.

example of `trec_eval` terminal output on the CACM dataset using a language model–based ranking (Lucene's `LMJelinekMercerSimilarity`[2]):

```
./trec_eval ~/lucene4ir/data/cacm/cacm.qrels
       ~/lucene4ir/data/cacm/bm25_results.res
...
map               all 0.2292
Rprec             all 0.2552
P_5               all 0.3373
P_10              all 0.2529
```

In this case, `Similarity` was switched to use language models to estimate probabilities of relevance. The results are worse than with BM25: all the metrics have slightly lower values.

The nice thing about using these tools together is that you can evaluate how well your decisions impact the accuracy of search results in a series of quick, easy steps. This doesn't guarantee that you can achieve perfect rankings, but you can use this approach to define the baseline ranking function for your search engine and data. After this short intro to Lucene4IR, you're encouraged to develop your own `Similarity`—for example, based on word2vec—and see whether it makes a difference with respect to `BM25Similarity` and so on.

5.5.1 *Similarity based on averaged word embeddings*

You saw the effectiveness of document embeddings generated using word vectors in the small experiment with the "bernhard riemann influence" sample query. At the same time, in real life, you need better evidence for the effectiveness of a retrieval model. In this section, you'll work on `Similarity` implementations based on averaged word2vec word vectors. You'll then measure their effectiveness on a small dataset using the Lucene4IR project. These measures will give you a sense of how well these ranking models behave in general.

Extending a Lucene `Similarity` correctly is a difficult task that requires some insights into how Lucene works. We'll focus on the relevant bits of the `Similarity` API to use document embeddings to score documents against queries. Let's start by creating a `WordEmbeddingsSimilarity` that creates document embeddings via averaged word embeddings. It requires a trained word2vec model, a smoothing method to average word vectors to combine them in a document vector, and a Lucene field from which to fetch document content:

```
public class WordEmbeddingsSimilarity extends Similarity {

  public WordEmbeddingsSimilarity(Word2Vec word2Vec,
        String fieldName, Smoothing smoothing) {
    this.word2Vec = word2Vec;
    this.fieldName = fieldName;
    this.smoothing = smoothing;
  }
```

---

[2] See Chengxiang Zhai and John Lafferty, "A Study of Smoothing Methods for Language Models Applied to Ad Hoc Information Retrieval," http://mng.bz/zM8a.

The Lucene `Similarity` will implement the following two methods:

```
@Override
public SimWeight computeWeight(float boost,
      CollectionStatistics collectionStats, TermStatistics... termStats) {
  return new EmbeddingsSimWeight(boost, collectionStats, termStats);
}

@Override
public SimScorer simScorer(SimWeight weight,
      LeafReaderContext context) throws IOException {
  return new EmbeddingsSimScorer(weight, context);
}
```

The most important part for this task is to implement the `EmbeddingsSimScorer`, which is responsible for scoring documents:

```
private class EmbeddingsSimScorer extends SimScorer {
  @Override
  public float score(int doc, float freq) throws IOException {
    INDArray denseQueryVector = getQueryVector();          ⊲⌁⌁⌁  Generates the
    INDArray denseDocumentVector = VectorizeUtils                 query vector
      .toDenseAverageVector(reader.getTermVector(doc,
        fieldName), reader.numDocs(),
          word2Vec, smoothing);            ⊲⌁⌁⌁⌁⌁⌁⌁⌁  Generates the
    return (float) Transforms.cosineSim(                  document vector
      denseQueryVector, denseDocumentVector);  ⊲⌁⌁⌁
  }
}
```

Generates the query vector

Generates the document vector

Calculates the cosine similarity between document and query vectors, and uses that as a document score

As you can see, the `score` method does what you did in the previous section, but within the `Similarity` class. The only difference with respect to the previous approach is that the `toDenseAverageVector` utility class also takes a `Smoothing` parameter that specifies how to average word vectors:

```
public static INDArray toDenseAverageVector(Terms docTerms, double n,
    Word2Vec word2Vec, WordEmbeddingsSimilarity.Smoothing smoothing)
        throws IOException {
  INDArray vector = Nd4j.zeros(word2Vec.getLayerSize());
  if (docTerms != null) {
    TermsEnum docTermsEnum = docTerms.iterator();
    BytesRef term;
    while ((term = docTermsEnum.next()) != null) {
      INDArray wordVector = word2Vec.getLookupTable().vector(
        term.utf8ToString());
      if (wordVector != null) {
        double smooth;
        switch (smoothing) {
          case MEAN:
            smooth = docTerms.size();
            break;
          case TF:
            smooth = docTermsEnum.totalTermFreq();
```

```
              break;
          case IDF:
            smooth = docTermsEnum.docFreq();
            break;
          case TF_IDF:
            smooth = VectorizeUtils.tfIdf(n, docTermsEnum.totalTermFreq(),
                docTermsEnum.docFreq());
            break;
          default:
            smooth = VectorizeUtils.tfIdf(n, docTermsEnum.totalTermFreq(),
                docTermsEnum.docFreq());
        }
        vector.addi(wordVector.div(smooth));
      }
    }
  }
  return vector;
}
```

getQueryVector does exactly the same thing, but instead of iterating over docTerms, it iterates over the terms in the query.

The Lucene4IR project comes with tools to run evaluations over the CACM dataset, which you can do using different Similaritys. Following the instructions in the Lucene4IR README (http://mng.bz/0WGx), you can generate statistics to evaluate different rankings. For example, here's the precision over the first five results using different Similaritys:

```
WordEmbeddingsSimilarity:     0.2993
ClassicSimilarity:            0.2784
BM25Similarity:               0.2706
LMJelinekMercerSimilarity:    0.2588
```

These are some interesting numbers. First, VSM with TF-IDF weighting isn't the worst result. The word-embeddings Similarity is 2% better than the others; not bad. But one simple takeaway from this quick evaluation is that the effectiveness of a ranking model can change depending on the data, so you should take care when choosing a model. Theoretical results and evaluations must always be measured against real-life usage of your search engine.

It's also important to decide what to optimize the ranking for. Often, it's difficult to get high precision together with high recall, for example. Let's introduce another metric for evaluating a ranking model's effectiveness: *normalized discounted cumulative gain* (NDCG). NDCG measures the usefulness, or *gain*, of a document based on its position in the results list. The gain is accumulated from the top of the results list to the bottom, so that the gain contributed by each result decreases with ranking. If you evaluate the NDCG of the previous Similaritys over the CACM dataset, the results are even more interesting:

```
WordEmbeddingsSimilarity:     0.3894
BM25Similarity:               0.3805
ClassicSimilarity:            0.3805
LMJelinekMercerSimilarity:    0.3684
```

VSM and BM25 perform exactly the same; the word embeddings–based ranking function got a slightly better NDCG value. So if you're interested in a more precise ranking over the first five results, you should probably choose word embeddings–based rankings, but this evaluation suggests that for an overall higher NDCG, this may not make a significant difference.

Additionally, a good solution that's also supported by recent research can be to mix classic and neural ranking models by using multiple scoring functions at the same time.[3] You can do that by using the `MultiSimilarity` class in Lucene. If you perform the same evaluation but with different flavors of `MultiSimilarity`, you can see that mixing language modeling and word vectors yields the best NDCG value:

```
WV+BM25 :        0.4229
WV+LM :          0.4073
WV+Classic :     0.3973
BM25+LM :        0.3927
Classic+LM :     0.3698
Classic+BM25 :   0.3698
```

Summary

- Classic retrieval models like VSM and BM25 provide good baselines for ranking documents, but they lack semantic understanding of text capabilities.
- Neural information retrieval models aim to provide better semantic understanding capabilities for ranking documents.
- Distributed representations of words (like those generated by word2vec) can be combined to generate document embeddings for queries and documents.
- Averaged word embeddings can be used to generate effective Lucene `Similaritys`, which can achieve good results when evaluated against IR datasets.

---

[3] Dwaipayan Roy et al., "Representing Documents and Queries as Sets of Word Embedded Vectors for Information Retrieval," Neu-IR '16 SIGIR Workshop on Neural Information Retrieval (July 21, 2016, Pisa, Italy), https://arxiv.org/abs/1606.07869.

Document embeddings for rankings and recommendations

This chapter covers
- Generating document embeddings using paragraph vectors
- Using paragraph vectors for ranking
- Retrieving related content
- Improving related-content retrieval with paragraph vectors

In the previous chapter, I introduced you to neural information retrieval models by building a ranking function based on averaged word embeddings. You averaged word embeddings generated by word2vec to obtain a *document embedding*, a dense representation of a sequence of words, that demonstrated high precision in ranking documents according to user intent.

The drawback of common retrieval models such as Vector Space Model with TF-IDF and BM25, however, is that they only look at single terms when ranking documents. This approach can lead to suboptimal results because the context information of those terms is discarded. With this drawback in mind, let's see how you can generate document embeddings that look not just at single words, but at the whole text fragments surrounding those words. A vector representation created from these context-enhanced document embeddings will carry as much semantic information as possible, thus improving the ranking function's precision even more.

Word embeddings are very good for capturing word semantics, but the meaning and deep semantics of text documents don't depend on the meaning of words alone. It would be nice to be able to learn semantics about phrases or longer pieces of text instead of just words. In the previous chapter, you did that by averaging word embeddings. Going forward, you'll discover that you can do better in terms of accuracy. In this chapter, we'll explore a technique for learning document embeddings directly. Using extensions of the word2vec neural network learning algorithms, you can generate document embeddings for text sequences of different granularity (sentences, paragraphs, documents, and so on). You'll experiment with this technique and show how it provides better numbers when used for ranking.

Additionally, you'll learn how to use document embeddings to find related content. *Related content* consists of documents (texts, videos, and so on) that are semantically correlated. When you show a single search result (such as when the user clicks it in a search results web page), it's common to display other content that, for example, deals with similar topics or was created by the same author. Doing so is useful to capture the user's attention and provide them with content they might like but that may not appear on the first search results page.

6.1 *From word to document embeddings*

In this section, I'll introduce an extension of word2vec that aims to learn document embeddings during neural network training. This is different than the previously used method of mixing word vectors (averaging and, eventually, smoothing them, such as with TF-IDF weights) and often gives better results when capturing document semantics.[1] This method, also known as *paragraph vectors*, extends the two word2vec architectures (the continuous-bag-of-words [CBOW] and skip-gram models), incorporating information about the current document in the context.[2] Word2vec performs unsupervised learning of word embeddings by using fragments of texts of a certain size, called the *window*, for training the neural network to either predict the context given a word belonging to that context or predict the word given a context the word belongs to.

Specifically, a CBOW neural network has three layers (see figure 6.1):

- Input layer containing context words
- Hidden layer containing one vector for each word
- Output layer containing the word to predict

---

[1] See the comparisons in Andrew M. Dai, Christopher Olah, and Quoc V. Le, "Document Embedding with Paragraph Vectors," https://arxiv.org/pdf/1507.07998.pdf.

[2] See Quoc Le and Tomas Mikolov, "Distributed Representations of Sentences and Documents," http://cs.stanford.edu/~quocle/paragraph_vector.pdf.

The intuition provided by the paragraph vector–based methods can either decorate or replace the context with a label representing a document, so that the neural network will learn to correlate words and contexts with labels, rather than words with other words.

The CBOW model is expanded so that the input layer also contains the label of the document containing the current text fragment. During training, each text fragment is tagged with a label. Such text fragments can be entire documents or portions of a document, like sections, paragraphs, or sentences. The *value* of the label generally isn't important;[3] a label can be *doc_123456* or *tag-foo-bar* or any kind of machine-generated string. The important thing is that labels should be unique within a document: two

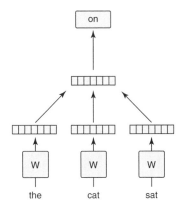

Figure 6.1   Word2vec CBOW model

different text fragments shouldn't be tagged with the same label if they don't belong to the same piece of text.

As you can see in figure 6.2, the architecture of this model is similar to CBOW; it just adds an input label representing the document in the input layer. Consequently, the hidden layer needs to be equipped with a vector for each label, so that at the end of the training, you have a vector representation for each label. The interesting thing about this approach is that it allows you to handle documents of different granularities. You can use labels for either entire documents or smaller parts of them, like paragraphs or sentences. These labels act as a sort of memory that wires contexts to (missing) words; therefore, this method is called the *distributed memory model of paragraph vectors* (PV-DM).

In the case of documents like "riemann hypothesis - a deep dive into a mathematical mystery," it makes sense to use a single label, because the text is relatively short. But for longer documents, like Wikipedia pages, it may be useful to create a label for each paragraph or sentence. Let's pick the first paragraph of Riemann's Wikipedia page: "Georg Friedrich Bernhard Riemann (17 September 1826 – 20 July 1866) was a German mathematician who made contributions to analysis, number theory, and differential geometry. In the field of real analysis, he is mostly known for the first

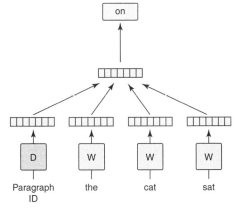

Figure 6.2   Distributed memory model of paragraph vectors

---

[3] Unless you intend to use it in some way other than training, such as using the labels generated by the network as document identifiers when indexing them after training has finished.

rigorous formulation of the integral, the Riemann integral, and his work on Fourier series." You can tag each sentence with a different label and generate a vector representation that will help find similar sentences instead of similar Wikipedia pages.

Paragraph vectors also extend the word2vec skip-gram model with the *distributed-bag-of-words* model (PV-DBOW). The continuous skip-gram model uses a neural network with three layers:

- Input layer with one input word
- Hidden layer containing a vector representation for each word in the vocabulary
- Output layer containing a number of words representing the predicted context with respect to the input word

The DBOW model with paragraph vectors (see figure 6.3) inputs labels instead of words, so the network learns to predict portions of text belonging to the document, paragraph, or sentence having that label.

Both PV-DBOW and PV-DM models can be used to calculate similarities between labeled documents. Just as in word2vec, they achieve surprisingly good results when capturing the document semantics. Let's try using paragraph vectors on the example scenario with the DL4J `ParagraphVectors` implementation:

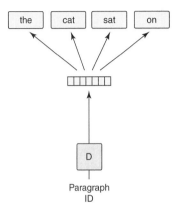

Figure 6.3 Distributed-bag-of-words model with paragraph vectors

Configures paragraph vectors

```
ParagraphVectors paragraphVectors = new ParagraphVectors.Builder()
    .iterate(iterator)
    .layerSize(50)        ←——————— Sets the document embedding dimensions
    .minWordFrequency(7)
    .sequenceLearningAlgorithm(new DM<>())   ←
    .tokenizerFactory(new DefaultTokenizerFactory())
    .build();   ←

paragraphVectors.fit();   ←
```

Selects the chosen paragraph vector model: in this case, PV-DM

Finalizes the configuration

As in word2vec, you can set the minimum frequency threshold for a word to be used during learning.

Performs (unsupervised) learning over the input data

Similar to what you did with word2vec, you can ask the paragraph vector models questions:

- What are the nearest labels to label xyz? This will allow you to find the most-similar documents (because each document is tagged with a label).
- What are the nearest labels, given a new piece of text? This will make it possible to use paragraph vectors on documents or queries that aren't part of the training set.

If you use titles from Wikipedia pages to train paragraph vectors, you can look for Wikipedia pages whose titles are semantically similar to input text. Suppose you want to get information about your next big trip to South America. You can get the top three closest documents to the sentence "Travelling in South America" from the paragraph vector model you just trained:

```
Collection<String> strings = paragraphVectors
    .nearestLabels("Travelling in South America"
    , 3);                          ◁————————————  Gets the labels nearest
for (String s : strings) {                       to the given input string
    int docId = Integer.parseInt(s.substring(4)); ◁———  Each label is in the form
                                                        "doc_"+ documentId, so
    Document document = reader.document(docId);          you only get the document
                                                        identifier part to fetch the
    System.out.println(document.get(fieldName)); ◁———   document from the index.
}
```

Retrieves the Lucene document
having the given ID

Prints the document
title on the console

The output is as follows:

```
Transport in São Tomé and Príncipe   ◁————————  São Tomé and Príncipe (a South
Transport in South Africa                        American republic) information about
Telecommunications in São Tomé and Príncipe ◁—  transport and telecommunications
```

Not very
relevant

If you train paragraph vectors using the entire text of Wikipedia pages, instead of just the title, you get more-relevant results. This is mostly due to the fact that paragraph vectors, like word2vec, learn text representations by looking at the context, and this is more difficult with shorter text (titles) than with longer text (an entire Wikipedia page).

The output when training with the entire text of Wikipedia pages is as follows:

```
Latin America
Crime and violence in Latin America
Overseas Adventure Travel
```

Document embeddings like those generated by paragraph vectors aim to provide a good representation of the semantics of the entire text, in the form of a vector. You can use them in the context of search to address the problem of semantic understanding in ranking. The similarity between such embeddings depends more on the meaning of text and less on simple term matching.

6.2   *Using paragraph vectors in ranking*

Using paragraph vectors in ranking is simple: you can ask the model to either provide the vector for an already-trained label or document, or train a new vector for a new piece of text (such as an unseen document or query). Whereas with word vectors you have to decide how to combine them (you did it at ranking time, but you could have done so at indexing time), paragraph vector–based models make it possible to fetch query and document embeddings easily, to compare and rank them.

Before jumping into using paragraph vectors for ranking, let's take a step back. The previous section talked about using the data indexed in Lucene to train a paragraph vector model. That can be done by implementing a `LabelAwareIterator`: an iterator over document contents that also assigns a label to each Lucene document. You tag each Lucene document with its internal Lucene document identifier, resulting in a label that looks like *doc_1234*:

FieldValuesLabelAwareIterator fetches sequences from an IndexReader (a read view on the search engine).

The content will be fetched from a single field, not from all possible fields in the Lucene document.

```java
public class FieldValuesLabelAwareIterator implements LabelAwareIterator {
  private final IndexReader reader;
  private final String field;
  private int currentId = 0;

  @Override
  public boolean hasNextDocument() {
    return currentId < reader.numDocs();
  }

  @Override
  public LabelledDocument nextDocument() {
    if (!hasNextDocument()) {
      return null;
    }
    try {
      Document document = reader.document(currentId,
        Collections.singleton(field));

      LabelledDocument labelledDocument = new
        LabelledDocument();
      labelledDocument.addLabel("doc_"
        + currentId);
      labelledDocument.setContent(document
        .getField(field).stringValue());
      return labelledDocument;
    } catch (IOException e) {
      throw new RuntimeException(e);
    } finally {
      currentId++;
    }
  }
  ...

}
```

Identifier of the current document being fetched, initialized as 0

If the current identifier is less than the number of documents in the index, there are more documents to read.

Fetches content from the Lucene index

Creates a new LabelledDocument to be used to train DL4J's ParagraphVectors. The internal Lucene identifier is used as the label.

Sets the content of the specified Lucene field into the LabelledDocument

You initialize the iterator for paragraph vectors this way:

```java
IndexReader reader = DirectoryReader.open(writer);
String fieldName = "title";
FieldValuesLabelAwareIterator iterator = new
    FieldValuesLabelAwareIterator(reader, fieldName);
```

Creates an IndexReader

Defines the field to be used

Creates the iterator

```
ParagraphVectors paragraphVectors = new ParagraphVectors.Builder()
    .iterate(iterator)        ◁⎯⎯⎯⎯⎯⎯⎯⎯⎯⎯⎯⎯⎯⎯⎯⎯⎯     Sets the iterator in
    .build();      ◁⎯⎯⎯⎯⎯⎯⎯⎯⎯⎯⎯⎯⎯⎯⎯⎯                ParagraphVectors
                                       Builds a paragraph vectors
paragraphVectors.fit();   ◁⎯⎯⎯⎯⎯⎯⎯     model (still to be trained)
                                       Lets paragraph vectors perform
                                       (unsupervised) learning
```

Once the model has finished training, you can use the paragraph vectors to rescore documents after the retrieval phase:

Creates an IndexSearcher to perform the first query that identifies the result set

Tries to fetch an existing vector representation for the current query. This can fail because you've trained the model over search engine content, not queries.

```
IndexSearcher searcher = new IndexSearcher(reader);

INDArray queryParagraphVector = paragraphVectors
    .getLookupTable().vector(queryString);   ◁⎯⎯
if (queryParagraphVector == null) {              If the query vector doesn't exist, lets the
  queryParagraphVector = paragraphVectors        underlying neural network train and infer
    .inferVector(queryString);   ◁⎯⎯⎯⎯          a vector on that new piece of text (whose
}                                                label will be the entire text of the String)

QueryParser parser = new QueryParser(fieldName, new WhitespaceAnalyzer());
Query query = parser.parse(queryString);
TopDocs hits = searcher.search(query, 10);   ◁⎯⎯⎯⎯   Performs a search
for (int i = 0; i < hits.scoreDocs.length; i++) {
  ScoreDoc scoreDoc = hits.scoreDocs[i];
  Document doc = searcher.doc(scoreDoc.doc);       Builds the label of
                                                   the current doc
  String label = "doc_" + scoreDoc.doc;   ◁⎯⎯⎯⎯

  INDArray documentParagraphVector = paragraphVectors
    .getLookupTable().vector(label);   ◁⎯⎯⎯⎯      Fetches the existing vector
  double score = Transforms.cosineSim(            for the document that has
    queryParagraphVector, documentParagraphVector);   the specified label

  String title = doc.get(fieldName);
  System.out.println(title + " : " + score);   ◁⎯⎯   Prints the results
}                                                      on the console
```

Calculates the score as the cosine similarity between the query and document vector

This code shows how easy it is to fetch a distributed representation for queries and documents without having to work on the word embeddings. For the sake of readability, the results are again shown as scored from best to worst (even though the code doesn't do that). The ranking is very much in line with the actual relevance of the returned documents, and the scores are consistent with the document relevance:

```
riemann hypothesis - a deep dive into a mathematical mystery : 0.77497977
riemann bernhard - life and works of bernhard riemann : 0.76711642
thomas bernhard biography - bio and influence in literature : 0.32464843
bernhard bernhard bernhard bernhard bernhard bernhard ... : 0.03593694
```

The two most relevant documents have high (and very close) scores, and the third has a significantly lower score; that's okay, because it's not relevant. Finally, the dummy document has a score close to zero.

6.2.1 *Paragraph vector–based similarity*

You can introduce a `ParagraphVectorsSimilarity` that uses paragraph vectors to measure the similarity between a query and a document. The interesting part of this similarity is the implementation of the `SimScorer#score` API:

Extracts a paragraph vector for the text of the query. If the query has never been seen before, this will imply performing a training step for the paragraph vector network.

Extracts the paragraph vector for the document with the label equal to its document identifier

```
@Override
public float score(int docId, float freq) throws IOException {
  INDArray denseQueryVector = paragraphVectors
    .inferVector(query);
  String label = "doc_" + docId;
  INDArray documentParagraphVector = paragraphVectors
    .getLookupTable().vector(label);
  if (documentParagraphVector == null) {
    LabelledDocument document = new LabelledDocument();
    document.setLabels(Collections.singletonList(label));
    document.setContent(reader.document(docId).getField(fieldName)
        .stringValue());
    documentParagraphVector = paragraphVectors
        .inferVector(document);
  }
  return (float) Transforms.cosineSim(
    denseQueryVector, documentParagraphVector);
}
```

If a vector with the given label (docId) can't be found, performs a training step over the paragraph vector network to extract the new vector

Calculates the cosine similarity between the query and document paragraph vectors, and uses it as the score for the given document

6.3 *Document embeddings and related content*

As a user, you may have experienced the feeling that a certain search result is *almost* good, but for some reason it isn't good enough. Think about searching for "a book about implementing neural network algorithms" on a retail site. You get the search results: the first is a book titled *Learning to Program Neural Nets*, so you click that result and are taken to a page containing more details about the book. You realize that you like the book's contents. The author is a recognized authority on the subject, but he uses Python as the programming language for his teaching examples, which you don't know well enough. You may wonder, "Is there a similar book, but using Java to teach how to program neural nets?" The retail site may show you a list of similar related books, in the hope that if you don't want to buy the one with examples written in Python, you may instead buy another book with similar contents (which may include a book that has examples in Java).

In this section, you'll see how to provide such related content by finding additional documents in the search engine that are similar not just because they're from the same author or have some words in common, but because there is a more meaningful semantic correlation between two such documents. This should remind you of the semantic-understanding issue we addressed when ranking functions using document embeddings learned with paragraph vectors.

6.3.1   Search, recommendations, and related content

To illustrate how important it is to indicate appropriate related content in a search engine, let's consider the stream of actions a user performs on a video-sharing platform (such as YouTube). The primary (or even only) interface is the search box where users enter a query. Suppose the user types `Lucene tutorial` in the search box and clicks the Search button. A list of search results is shown, and the user eventually picks one they find interesting. From then on, it's common for the user to stop searching and instead click videos in the Related box or column. Typical recommendations for a video entitled "Lucene tutorial" could be videos with titles like "Lucene for beginners," "Intro to search engines," and "Building recommender systems with Lucene." The user can click any of these recommendations; for example, if they learned enough from the "Lucene tutorial" video, they might jump to watching a more advanced video; otherwise, they might want to watch another introductory video, or one introducing search engines, if they realized that additional prior knowledge was required to understand how to use Lucene. This process of consuming retrieved content and then navigating through related content can go on indefinitely. Thus, providing relevant related content is of the utmost importance to best satisfy user needs.

The contents of the Related box can even shift the user's intent toward topics that are far from the initial query. In the previous example, the user wanted to learn how to use Lucene. The search engine provided a related item whose main topic wasn't directly related to Lucene: it was about building a machine learning system for generating recommendations based on Lucene. That's a big switch, from needing information about working with Lucene as a beginner to learning about recommender systems based on Lucene (a more advanced topic).

This brief example also applies to e-commerce websites. The main purpose of such websites is to sell you something. So although you're encouraged to search for the product you (may) need, you're also flooded with lots of "recommended for you" items. These recommendations are based on factors such as these:

- Which products you searched for in the past
- Which topics you search for most
- New products
- Which products you saw (browsed or clicked) recently

One of the main points of this flood of recommendations is *user retention*: an e-commerce site wants to keep you browsing and searching as long as possible, hoping that any of the products they sell will be interesting enough for you to buy it.

This goes beyond buying and selling. Such capabilities are very important for many applications, such as in the field of healthcare: for example, a doctor looking at a patient's medical records would benefit from being able to look at similar medical records from other patients (and their histories) in order to make a better diagnosis. We'll focus now on implementing algorithms for retrieving related or similar documents with respect to an input document, based on their contents. First, we'll look at how to get the search engine to extract related content, and then you'll see how to use different approaches to build document embeddings to overcome some limitations of the first approach; see figure 6.4. We'll also take this chance to discuss how to use paragraph vectors to perform document classification, which is useful in the context of providing semantically relevant suggestions.

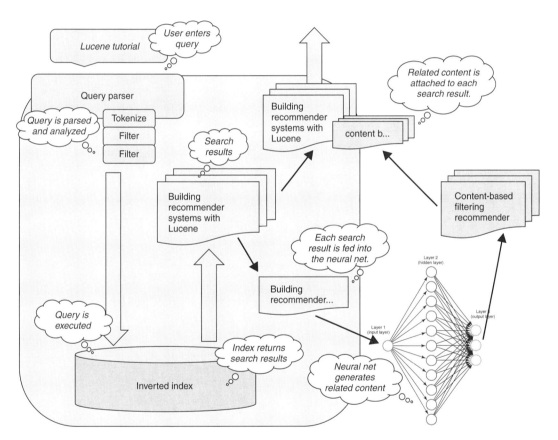

Figure 6.4   **Using neural networks to retrieve related content**

6.3.2   *Using frequent terms to find similar content*

In the previous chapter, you saw how the TF-IDF weighting scheme for ranking relies on term and document frequencies to provide a measure of a document's importance.

The rationale behind TF-IDF ranking is that a document's importance grows with the local frequency and global rarity of its terms, with respect to an input query. Building on these assumptions, you can define an algorithm to find documents that are similar to an input document, solely based on the search engine's retrieval capabilities.

Wikipedia dumps can be a good collection to evaluate the effectiveness of an algorithm for retrieving related content. Each Wikipedia page contains content and useful metadata (title, categories, references, and even some links to related content in the "See also" section). Several available tools can be used to index Wikipedia dumps into Lucene, such as the `lucene-benchmark` module (http://mng.bz/A2Qo). Suppose you've indexed each Wikipedia page with its title and text into two separate Lucene indexes. Given the search results returned by a query, you want to fetch the five most-similar documents to show to the user as related content. To do that, you pick each search result, extract the most important terms from its content (in this case, from the `text` field), and perform another query using the extracted terms (see figure 6.5). The first five resulting documents can be used as related content.

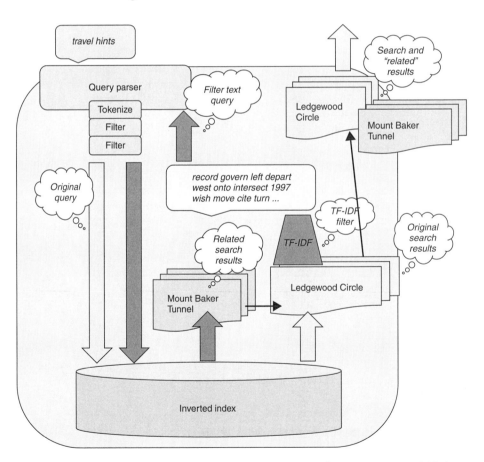

Figure 6.5   Retrieving related content by using a document's most important terms, weighted by TF-IDF scheme

Suppose you run the query "travel hints" and get a search result about a traffic circle in New Jersey called Ledgewood Circle. You take all the terms contained in the Wikipedia page https://en.wikipedia.org/wiki/Ledgewood_Circle and extract those that have at least a term frequency of 2 and a document frequency of 5. This way, you obtain the following list of terms:

```
record govern left depart west onto intersect 1997 wish move cite turn
    township signal 10 lane travel westbound new eastbound us tree 46
    traffic ref
```

You then use these terms as a query to obtain the documents to be used as related content presented to the end user.

Lucene lets you do this using a component called `MoreLikeThis` (MLT, http://mng.bz/ZZlR), which can extract the most important terms from a `Document` and create a `Query` object to be run via the same `IndexSearcher` used to run the original query.

> **Listing 6.1 Searching and getting related content via MLT**

Defines an Analyzer to be used while searching and while extracting terms from search results' content

```
EnglishAnalyzer analyzer = new EnglishAnalyzer();
MoreLikeThis moreLikeThis = new MoreLikeThis(
    reader);
moreLikeThis.setAnalyzer(analyzer);

IndexSearcher searcher = new IndexSearcher(
    reader);

String fieldName = "text";
QueryParser parser = new QueryParser(fieldName,
    analyzer);
Query query = parser.parse("travel hints");

TopDocs hits = searcher.search(query, 10);

for (int i = 0; i < hits.scoreDocs.length; i++) {
    ScoreDoc scoreDoc = hits.scoreDocs[i];
    Document doc = searcher.doc(scoreDoc.doc);

    String title = doc.get("title");
    System.out.println(title + " : " +
        scoreDoc.score);
```

Creates an MLT instance

Specifies the Analyzer to be used by MLT

Creates an IndexSearcher

Defines which field to use when doing the first query and when looking for related content via the MLT-generated query

Executes the query, and returns the top 10 search results

Retrieves the Document object related to the current search result

Prints the current document's title and score

Parses the user-entered query

Creates a QueryParser

```
String text = doc.get(fieldName);
Query simQuery = moreLikeThis.like(fieldName,
    new StringReader(text));

TopDocs related = searcher.search(simQuery, 5);
for (ScoreDoc rd : related.scoreDocs) {
  Document document = reader.document(rd.doc);
  System.out.println("-> " + document.get(
      "title"));
  }
}
```

Extracts the content of the text field from the current Document

Performs the query generated by MLT

Prints the title of the Document found by the Query generated by MLT

Uses MLT to generate a query based on the content of the retrieved Document, by extracting the most important terms (TF-IDF ranking-wise)

No machine learning is involved to extract related content: you use the search engine's capabilities to return related documents containing the most important terms from a search result. Here's some example output for the "travel hints" query and "Ledgewood Circle" search result:

```
Ledgewood Circle : 7.880041
-> Ledgewood Circle
-> Mount Baker Tunnel
-> K-5 (Kansas highway)
-> Interstate 80 in Illinois
-> Modal dispersion
```

The first three related documents (not counting the "Ledgewood Circle" document) are similar to the original document. They all relate to something correlated with traffic circles, such as a tunnel, highway, or interstate. The fourth document, though, is completely unrelated: it deals with fiber optics. Let's dig deeper into why this result was fetched. To do this, you can turn on Lucene's Explanation:

```
Query simQuery = moreLikeThis.like(fieldName, new StringReader(text));
TopDocs related = searcher.search(simQuery, 5);
for (ScoreDoc rd : related.scoreDocs) {
  Document document = reader.document(rd.doc);
  Explanation e = searcher.explain(simQuery, rd.doc);
  System.out.println(document.get("title") + " : " + e);
}
```

Gets the Explanation for the MLT query

The explanation allows you to inspect how the terms signal, 10, travel, and new matched:

```
Modal dispersion :
20.007288 = sum of:
  7.978141 = weight(text:signal in 1972) [BM25Similarity], result of:
    ...
  2.600343 = weight(text:10 in 1972) [BM25Similarity], result of:
    ...
  7.5186286 = weight(text:travel in 1972) [BM25Similarity], result of:
    ...
```

```
1.9101752 = weight(text:new in 1972) [BM25Similarity], result of:
  ...
```

The issue with this approach is that `MoreLikeThis` extracted the most important terms according to TF-IDF weighting. This, as you saw in the previous chapter, has the problem of relying on frequencies. Let's look at these important terms extracted from the "Ledgewood Circle" document text: the terms "record," "govern," "left," "depart," "west," "onto," "intersect," "1997," "wish," "move," and so on don't seem to suggest that the document deals with a traffic circle. If you try to read them as a sentence, you can't derive much sense from it.

The `Explanation` uses the default Lucene `BM25Similarity`. In chapter 5, you saw that you can use different ranking functions and test whether you can get better results. If you adopt the `ClassicSimilarity` (vector-space model with TF-IDF), you get the following:

```
Query simQuery = moreLikeThis.like(fieldName, new StringReader(text));
searcher.setSimilarity(new ClassicSimilarity());       ⟵    Uses ClassicSimilarity
TopDocs related = searcher.search(simQuery, 5);              instead of the default
for (ScoreDoc rd : related.scoreDocs) {                      (only for the similar
  Document document = reader.document(rd.doc);               content search)
  System.out.println(searcher.getSimilarity() +
    " -> " + document.get("title"));
}
```

Here are the results:

```
ClassicSimilarity -> Ledgewood Circle
ClassicSimilarity -> Mount Baker Tunnel
ClassicSimilarity -> Cherry Tree
ClassicSimilarity -> K-5 (Kansas highway)
ClassicSimilarity -> Category:Speech processing
```

They're even worse: both "Cherry Tree" and "Speech processing" are completely unrelated to the original "Ledgewood Circle" document. Let's try using a language model–based similarity, `LMDirichletSimilarity`:[4]

```
Query simQuery = moreLikeThis.like(fieldName, new StringReader(text));
searcher.setSimilarity(
    new LMDirichletSimilarity());
TopDocs related = searcher.search(simQuery, 5);
for (ScoreDoc rd : related.scoreDocs) {
  Document document = reader.document(rd.doc);
  System.out.println(searcher.getSimilarity() +
    " -> " + document.get("title"));
}
```

The results are as follows:

```
LM Dirichlet(2000.000000) -> Ledgewood Circle
LM Dirichlet(2000.000000) -> Mount Baker Tunnel
```

---

[4] See Chengxiang Zhai and John Lafferty, "A Study of Smoothing Methods for Language Models Applied to Ad Hoc Information Retrieval," http://mng.bz/RGVZ.

```
LM Dirichlet(2000.000000) -> K-5 (Kansas highway)
LM Dirichlet(2000.000000) -> Interstate 80 in Illinois
LM Dirichlet(2000.000000) -> Creek Turnpike
```

Interestingly enough, these results all sound good—all of them relate to infrastructures for cars, such as highways or tunnels.

MEASURING THE QUALITY OF RELATED CONTENT USING CATEGORIES

In chapter 5, you learned how important it is to not do single experiments. Although they allow a fine-grained understanding of how retrieval models work in some cases, they can't provide an overall measure of how well such a model works on more data. Because Wikipedia pages come with categories, you can make a first evaluation of the accuracy of related content using them. If documents found by the related-content algorithm (in this case, Lucene's `MoreLikeThis`) fall in any of the original document categories, you can consider them relevant. In real life, you may want to do this evaluation slightly differently: for example, you may also consider a suggested document relevant if its category is a subcategory of the original document category. You can do this (and much more) by building a taxonomy, extracting it from Wikipedia (https://en.wikipedia.org/wiki/Help:Category), or by using a DBpedia project (a crowdsourced effort to build structured information about content in Wikipedia; http://wiki.dbpedia.org). But for the sake of this chapter's experiments, you can define an accuracy measure as the sum of the times a piece of related content shares one or more categories with the original document, divided by the number of related documents retrieved.

Let's use the Wikipedia page for the soccer player Radamel Falcao, which has lots of categories (1986 births, AS Monaco FC players, and so on). Using `BM25Similarity` to rank the MLT-generated `Query` gives the following top five related documents, with the shared category in parentheses (if any):

```
Bacary Sagna (*Expatriate footballers in England*)
Steffen Hagen (*1986 births*)
Andrés Scotti (*Living people*)
Iyseden Christie (*Association football forwards*)
Pelé ()
```

The first four results have a category in common with Radamel Falcao's Wikipedia page, but "Pelè" doesn't. Therefore, the accuracy is 4 (the number of results sharing a category with Radamel Falcao's page) divided by 5 (the number of returned similar results), or 0.8.

To evaluate this algorithm, you can generate a number of random queries and measure the defined average accuracy over the returned related content. Let's generate 100 queries using words that exist in the index (to make sure at least one search result is returned), and then retrieve the 10 most similar documents using paragraph vectors and cosine similarity. For each of these related documents, check whether one of its categories also appears in the search result.

Listing 6.2   Fetching related content and calculating accuracy

Gets the categories associated
with the original Wikipedia   **Creates the related-content**
page returned by a query   **query with MLT**

```
                                                                     Runs the same query with
                                                                     multiple Similarity
int topN = 10;                                                       implementations to evaluate
String[] originalCategories = doc                                    what works best
    .getValues("category");
Query simQuery = moreLikeThis.like(fieldName,          Uses a specific Similarity
    new StringReader(s));                              in the IndexSearcher
for (Similarity similarity : similarities) {
  searcher.setSimilarity(similarity);
  TopDocs related = searcher.search(simQuery,          Performs the related-
    topN);                                             content query
  double acc = 0;              Initializes the
  for (ScoreDoc rd : related.scoreDocs) {    accuracy to zero
    if (rd.doc == scoreDoc.doc) {
      topN--;                                Skips a result if it's equal
      continue;                              to the original document
    }
    Document document = reader.document(rd.doc);    Retrieves the related Document
    String[] categories = document.getValues("category");
    if (categories != null && originalCategories != null) {
      if (find(categories, originalCategories)) {    If any category of the
        acc += 1d;                                   related content is contained
      }                                              in the original Document,
    }                      Divides the accuracy by    increases the accuracy
  }                        the number of returned
  acc /= topN;             related documents
  System.out.println(similarity + " accuracy : " + acc);
}
```

The corresponding output with BM25Similarity, ClassicSimilarity, and LMDirichlet-
Similarity looks like this:

```
BM25(k1=1.2,b=0.75) accuracy : 0.2
ClassicSimilarity accuracy : 0.2
LM Dirichlet(2000.000000) accuracy : 0.1
```

Running this over 100 randomly generated queries and the corresponding 10 top
results gives the following average accuracies:

```
BM25(k1=1.2,b=0.75) average accuracy : 0.09
ClassicSimilarity average accuracy : 0.07
LM Dirichlet(2000.000000) average accuracy : 0.07
```

Given the fact that the best possible accuracy is 1.0, these are low accuracy values. The
best one finds a related document with a matching category only 9% of the time.

Although this is a suboptimal result, it's useful to reason about it and the availabil-
ity of the category information in each document. First, did you choose a good metric
to measure the "aboutness" of the related content retrieved with this approach? Categories attached to Wikipedia pages are usually of good quality, and the "Ledgewood

Circle" page's categories are "Transportation in Morris County" and "Traffic circles in New Jersey." A category like "Traffic circles" would also have been appropriate, but more generic. So the level of detail in the choice of relevant categories attached to such articles can vary and influence the accuracy estimates you calculate. Another thing to analyze is whether the categories are keywords taken from the text. In the case of Wikipedia, they aren't, but in general this may not always be the case. You can think about extending the way you measure accuracy by including not just categories a document belongs to, but also important words or concepts mentioned in the text. For example, the "Ledgewood Circle" page contains a section about a controversy that arose back in the 1990s about a tree planted in the middle of the traffic circle. Such information isn't represented in any way in the categories. If you want to be able to extract concepts discussed on a page, you can add them as additional categories (in this case, it might be a generic "Controversies" category). You can also think of this as tagging each document with a set of generic labels: these can be categories, concepts mentioned in the text, important words, and so on The bottom line is that your accuracy measure is as good as the labels or categories attached to documents. On the other hand, the way you build and use categories can have a significant impact on your evaluations.

Second, did you use the metric appropriately? You extracted the categories of the input document and the related content to see if any category belonged to both. The "Ledgewood Circle" page doesn't have the "Traffic circle" category, but its category "Traffic circles in New Jersey" could be thought of as a subcategory of a more generic "Traffic circle" category. Extending this reasoning to all the categories in Wikipedia, you could imagine building a tree as shown in figure 6.6: the nodes are categories, and the deeper a node is, the more specific and fine-grained its category will be.

In this experiment, you could change the rule for matching categories from "at least one category should be shared between both the input and related content" to "at least one category should be shared between both the input and related content, or one of the categories of a certain document should be a specification of another category in the other document." If you know more about what kinds of relationships exist between categories (and labels in general), you can use that information, too. DBpedia can be used as one such source of information about relationships that exist between pages. Imagine that the algorithm returns the "New Jersey" page as related to "Ledgewood Circle." The main thing they have in common is that Ledgewood Circle is located in the state of New Jersey, specifically in Roxbury Township. If such information is available, it's a great link you can navigate to measure the relevance of related content. For example, you could mark as relevant related documents that have any relation to the input document, or only mark documents relevant when they're linked by any of a subset of existing relations.

The DBpedia project records many such relations between pages from Wikipedia. You can think of it as a graph whose nodes are pages; arcs are relations (with a name). Figure 6.7 shows the relationships between Ledgewood Circle and New Jersey using RelFinder (www.visualdataweb.org/relfinder).

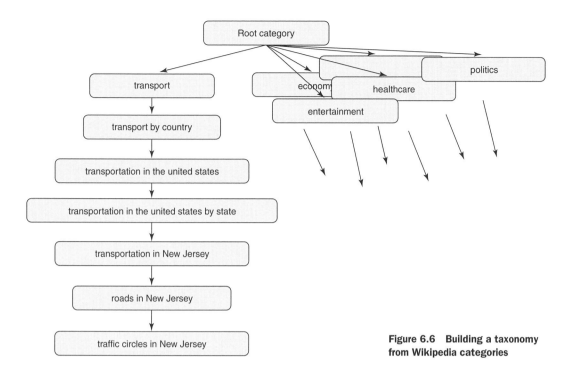

Figure 6.6 Building a taxonomy from Wikipedia categories

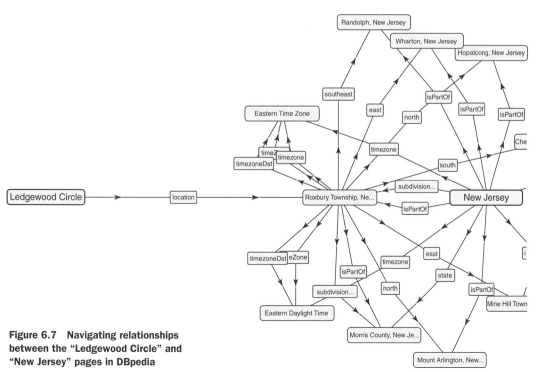

Figure 6.7 Navigating relationships between the "Ledgewood Circle" and "New Jersey" pages in DBpedia

Having a good hierarchical taxonomy for categories is important when you're using them to measure the accuracy of results from `MoreLikeThis` and other related-content algorithms. On the other hand, information about categories and their relations often isn't available in practice; in such cases, methods based on unsupervised learning can help you find out whether two documents are similar. Let's think about algorithms to learn vector representations of text, like word2vec (for words) or paragraph vectors (for sequences of words): when you plot them on a graph, similar words or documents will be located near each other. In that case, you can group the closest vectors together to form *clusters* (there are several ways to do that, but we won't cover them here), and consider related words or documents as belonging to the same cluster. In the next section, we'll look at one of the more straightforward usages of document embeddings: finding similar content.

6.3.3   *Retrieving similar content with paragraph vectors*

A paragraph vector learns a fixed (distributed) vector representation for each sequence of words fed into its neural network architecture. You can feed an entire document into the network, or portions of it, such as sections of an article, paragraphs, or sentences. It's up to you to define the granularity. For example, if you feed the network entire documents, you can ask it to return the most similar document it has already seen. Each ingested document (and generated vector) is identified by a label.

Let's get back to the problem of finding related content for a search engine on Wikipedia pages. In the previous section, we used Lucene's `MoreLikeThis` tool to extract the most important terms and then used them as a query to fetch related content. Unfortunately, the accuracy rates were low, primarily for these reasons:

- The most important terms extracted by `MoreLikeThis` were okay, but could be better.
- If you look at the set of important terms from a document, you may not recognize what kind of document they came from.

Let's look again at our friend the "Ledgewood Circle" page. According to MLT, the most important terms are as follows:

```
record govern left depart west onto intersect 1997 wish move cite turn
    township signal 10 lane travel westbound new eastbound us tree 46
    traffic ref
```

By no means would it be possible to say that these terms come from the "Ledgewood Circle" page, so you can't expect very accurate related-content suggestions. With document embeddings, there's no explicit information you can look at (that's a general problem in deep learning: it's not easy to understand what these black boxes do). A paragraph vector's neural network adjusts each document's vector values during training, as explained in chapter 5.

Let's fetch related content by finding the nearest vectors to the vector representing the input document, using cosine similarity. To do this, you first run a user-entered query—for example, "Ledgewood Circle"—that returns search results. For each such result, you extract its vector representation and look at its nearest neighbors in the embeddings space. This is like navigating on a graph or map that has all documents plotted according to their semantic similarity. You go to the point that represents "Ledgewood Circle," find the nearest points, and see which documents they represent. You'll notice that the "Ledgewood Circle" vector's neighbors will represent documents dealing with traffic and transportation topics; if you instead pick, for example, the vectors of some documents about music, you'll see they'll be located far away from "Ledgewood Circle" and its neighbors in the embedding space (see figure 6.8).

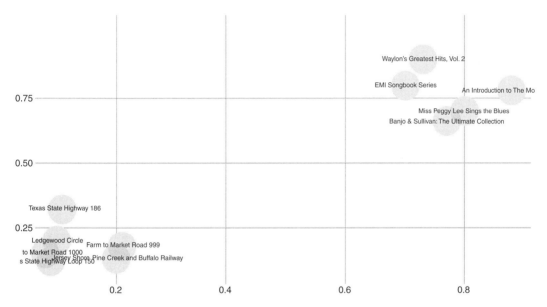

Figure 6.8 **Paragraph vectors for "Ledgewood Circle" and its neighbors, compared with music-related paragraph vectors**

Similarly to what you do for ranking, you first feed the paragraph vector network the indexed data:

```
File dump = new File("/path/to/wikipedia-dump.xml");
WikipediaImport wikipediaImport = new WikipediaImport(dump,
    languageCode, true);
wikipediaImport.importWikipedia(writer, ft);
IndexReader reader = DirectoryReader.open(writer);
FieldValuesLabelAwareIterator iterator = new
    FieldValuesLabelAwareIterator(reader, fieldName);
ParagraphVectors paragraphVectors = new ParagraphVectors.Builder()
  .iterate(iterator)
  .build();
paragraphVectors.fit();
```

Once that's done, you can use DL4J's built-in `nearestLabels` method to find the document vectors closest to the "Ledgewood Circle" vector. Internally, this method uses cosine similarity to measure how close two vectors are:

```
TopDocs hits = searcher.search(query, 10);    ◁── Runs the original query
for (int i = 0; i < hits.scoreDocs.length; i++) {
  ScoreDoc scoreDoc = hits.scoreDocs[i];
  Document doc = searcher.doc(scoreDoc.doc);
  String label = "doc_" + scoreDoc.doc;   ◁── For each result, builds a label
  INDArray labelVector = paragraphVectors
    .getLookupTable().vector(label);   ◁──
  Collection<String> docIds = paragraphVectors
    .nearestLabels(labelVector, topN);  ◁──
  for (String docId : docIds) {
    int docId = Integer.parseInt(docId.substring(4));
    Document document = reader.document(docId);  ◁──
    System.out.println(document.get("title"));
  }
}
```

Fetches the document embedding for the search result

Finds the labels of the nearest vectors to the search result vector

For each nearest vector, parses its label and fetches the corresponding Lucene Document

The results are as follows:

```
Texas State Highway 186
Texas State Highway Loop 150
Farm to Market Road 1000
Jersey Shore, Pine Creek and Buffalo Railway
Farm to Market Road 999
```

Just from looking at this simple example, the results seem to be better than those given by MLT. There are no off-topic results: they all relate to transportation (whereas MLT returned the "Modal dispersion" page, which refers to optics).

To confirm your good feelings, you can do the same thing you did to measure the effectiveness of `MoreLikeThis` by calculating the average accuracy of this method. To make a fair comparison, use the same approach of checking whether any of the search result's categories (such as "Ledgewood Circle") also appear in the related-content categories. Using the same randomly generated queries used when evaluating MLT, paragraph vectors yield the following average accuracy:

```
paragraph vectors average accuracy : 0.37
```

The best average accuracy for MLT was 0.09; 0.37 is much better.

Finding similar documents with close semantics is one of the key advantages of using document embeddings and is also why they're so useful in natural language processing and search. As you've seen, they can be used in various ways, including for ranking and to retrieve similar content. Paragraph vectors aren't the only way you can learn document embeddings, though. You used averaged word embeddings in chapter 5, but researchers keep working on better and more advanced ways of extracting word and document embeddings.

6.3.4 Retrieving similar content with vectors from encoder-decoder models

Chapters 3 and 4 introduced a deep neural network architecture called the *encoder-decoder* (or *sequence-to-sequence* [seq2seq]) model. You may remember that this model consists of an encoder LSTM network and a decoder LSTM network. The encoder transforms an input sequence of words into a fixed-length dense vector as output; this output is the input to the decoder, which turns it back into a sequence of words as the final output (see figure 6.9). You've used such an architecture to produce alternative query representations and to help users type a query. In this case, you're instead interested in using the output of the encoder network, the so-called *thought vector*.

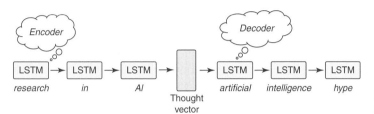

Figure 6.9 Encoder-decoder model

The reason it's called a thought vector is that it's meant to be a compressed representation of the input text sequence, which, when decoded correctly, generates a desirable output sequence. Seq2seq models, as you'll see in the next chapter, are also used for machine translation; they can transform a sentence in an input language into a translated output sequence. You want to extract such thought vectors for the input sequences (documents, sentences, and so on) and use them the same way you used paragraph vectors to measure similarity between documents.

First, you need to hook into the training phase so you can "save" the embeddings as they're generated one step at a time. You place them in a `WeightLookupTable`, which is the entity responsible for holding word vectors in word2vec and paragraph vectors in `ParagraphVectors` objects. With DL4J, you can hook into the training phase with a `TrainingListener` that captures the forward pass as the thought vector is generated by the encoder LSTM. You extract the input vector and transform it back into a sequence by retrieving words one at a time from the original corpus. Then, you extract the thought vector and put the sequence with its thought vector into the `WeightLookupTable`.

Listing 6.3 Extracting thought vectors during encoder-decoder training

```
public class ThoughtVectorsListener implements TrainingListener {
  @Override
  public void onForwardPass(Model model,
      Map<String, INDArray> activations) {
    INDArray input = activations.get(
      inputLayerName);
```

Fetches the network input (a sequence of words transformed into vectors) from the input layer

```
INDArray thoughtVector = activations.get(
    thoughtVectorLayerName);
for (int i = 0; i < input.size(0); i++) {
  for (int j = 0; j < input.size(1); j++) {
    int size = input.size(2);
    String[] words = new String[size];
    for (int s = 0; s < size; s++) {
      words[s] = revDict.get(input.getDouble(i, j, s));
    }
    String sequence = Joiner.on(' ')
        .join(words);
    lookupTable.putVector(sequence, thoughtVector
        .tensorAlongDimension(i, j));
  }
}
}
}
```

Fetches the thought vector from the thought-vector layer

Rebuilds the sequence one word at a time from the input vector

Merges the words together in a sequence (as a String)

Records the thought vector associated with the input text sequence

With these vectors, you can reach the same level of accuracy as paragraph vectors; the difference lies in the fact that you can decide how to influence them. These thought vectors are generated as an intermediate product of encoder and decoder LSTM networks. You can decide what to include in the encoder input and what to include in the decoder output in the training phase. If you put documents belonging to the same category at the edges of the network, the generated thought vectors will learn to output documents whose categories are the same. Therefore, you can achieve much higher accuracy.

If you take the encoder-decoder LSTM defined in chapters 3 and 4 and train it with documents belonging to the same category, you'll get an average accuracy of 0.77. That's much higher than even paragraph vectors!

Summary

- Paragraph vector models provide distributed representations for sentences and documents at configurable granularity (sentence, paragraph, or document).
- Ranking functions based on paragraph vectors can be more effective than old-school statistical models and those based on word embedding because they capture semantics at a sentence or document level.
- Paragraph vectors can also be used to effectively retrieve related content based on document semantics, to decorate search results.
- Thought vectors can be extracted from seq2seq models to retrieve related content based on document semantics, to decorate search results.

Part 3

One step beyond

In part 1 of this book, you got a basic understanding of what search engines and deep neural networks are, how they work, and how they can work together to create smarter search engines. Part 2 dove into the technical details of major deep neural network applications for search engines, mostly using recurrent neural networks and word/document embeddings to give users more relevant results. In this part of the book, we'll tackle more-advanced topics and challenges by extending the applications of neural networks to two new areas: searching text in multiple languages using machine translation (chapter 7), and searching for images using convolutional neural networks (chapter 8). Finally, in chapter 9, we'll look at the thing that makes the biggest difference in production scenarios: performance, whether plain speed when training and predicting, or accuracy of results. You'll see an example of how to tune a neural network model to reach good accuracy in a reasonable training time. In addition, we'll look at how to deal with continuous streams of data for neural search.

Searching across languages

In this chapter, we'll focus on expanding your ability to serve users who speak, read, and write queries in languages other than the language in which documents are written. Specifically, you'll see how to use machine translation to build a search engine that can automatically translate queries so those queries can be used to search and deliver content from multiple languages. We'll spend some time looking at how this translation ability can be useful in various contexts, from common web searches to more specific cases where it's important not to miss search results due to a language barrier. The benefit of being able to automatically translate queries is that your search engines gain the ability to reach more users, without requiring you to store multiple copies of each text document in different languages.

7.1   Serving users who speak multiple languages

Many of the scenarios presented in earlier chapters focused on vertical search engines, or search engines that are specific to an often small, well-defined domain, such as a search engine for movie reviews. In this chapter, which explores the challenge of retrieving useful information for users speaking different languages, there's no better fit than web search, or searching over data from everywhere on the World Wide Web. We use web search on an everyday basis with search engines like Google Search, Bing, and Baidu. Although a lot of online content is written in languages spoken by a huge number of people (like English), there are still many users who need to retrieve information and hope to find that information by using their native language.

You may wonder what the point of this discussion is. If you have a Wikipedia page written in Italian, it will surely be indexed by, for example, Google Search, and you'll be able to search for it by writing a query on Google Search in Italian, as in figure 7.1.

Figure 7.1   Searching for "rete neurale," Italian for "neural network"

Realistically, though, when searching, especially for tech-related topics, it's often expedient to write queries in English. This is because the amount of information available in English, especially for tech topics, often far outweighs the amount written in other languages. A user whose first language is Italian (or Danish, or Chinese, and so on) writes a query in English to maximize the chance of getting as many relevant results as possible. Those results will then include only documents written in English. And the fact is that search results written in English aren't always as helpful to users as results written in their native language. Let me explain by showing what you can do for a query written in English from a user whose native language is Italian. As you can see in figure 7.2, the query written in English also returned a search result in Italian, shown on the right. In cases like this, when a query is performed by a logged-in user, the search engine can look up the user's native language and include results in that language in addition to results that match the original query (in this case, in English).

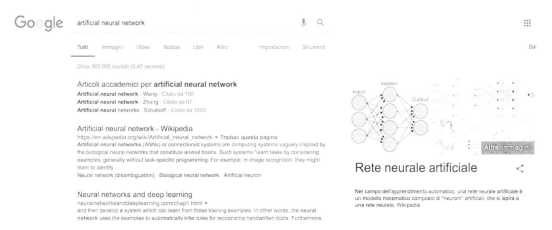

Figure 7.2 Searching for "artificial neural network" and getting results in Italian as well as English

How is this helpful for the user? Think about reading your favorite book in your native language, as opposed to reading it in a language that you studied at school. Even though you may be able to understand the content of the foreign-language version of the book, it may take you extra time and effort, and you may miss some subtle or especially difficult parts. The same applies to documents on the web. The Wikipedia entry for "artificial neural network," for example, exists in many different languages, making it more easily understood by more users. Imagine a search engine that not only shows the English entry (which matches a query written in English), but also highlights the entry written in the native language of the user who entered the query. This search engine better serves the needs of more users.

You can equip your search engine to return both types of results by incorporating *machine translation* (MT) tools into your search engine. With machine translation, a program can translate a sentence from an input language into the corresponding version in a target language. In the rest of this chapter, you'll see how to use MT tools to perform text translation at query time, resulting in improved recall and precision for search engine queries across multiple languages.

7.1.1   Translating documents vs. queries

Imagine having to build a search engine with capabilities similar to the ones briefly outlined in the previous section, for a nonprofit entity that supports refugees around the world with administrative and legal services. A search engine for such an organization would help refugees find appropriate documentation, for example, to fill out asylum requests. Each and every country around the world probably requires different documents and forms to be completed and signed; requirements may also vary depending on the country the applicant comes from. Users of such a platform may speak their native language but not the language of their host country. So if refugees from Iceland are seeking asylum in Brazil, they'll need to retrieve documents that may be written in Portuguese. If users don't know Portuguese, how can they know what to include in the search query for the information they're seeking?

Regardless of the situation, you can assume that users want to be able to retrieve content in their mother tongue whenever possible. There are two straightforward ways to do this using MT:

- Use MT programs to translate queries in order to find matches in more than one language.
- Have content created in one language, and use MT programs to create translated copies of the documents so queries can match the translated versions.

These options aren't mutually exclusive: you can have one or the other or both. What fits best depends on the use case.

Consider customer reviews on sites like Amazon and Airbnb. Such reviews are often written in the reviewer's native language, so for the purpose of easy consumption of search results, it may be good to translate those reviews when they reach the user.

Another good case for translating search results is question-answering systems. Answering questions uses an information retrieval system where the user specifies their intent in the form of a question written in natural language (such as "Who was elected president of U.S.A. in 2009?"). The system replies with an answer: a piece of (hopefully informative) text related to the question (such as "Barack Obama").

On the other hand, for web search, as discussed in the previous section, it may be good to translate the query to get results in different languages, because doing so allows more choices for end users. Once that's done, you need to make an important decision about ranking: how do you rank results that come from the translated query?

In the case of a refugee searching in Icelandic for documents written in Portuguese, if the user searches for "pólitísk hæli" (the Icelandic version of "politic asylum"), the query is translated into Portuguese ("asilo politico"). In such use cases, results from both the original and translated queries are retrieved. For the specific use case of a user who's an asylum seeker, the documents returned from the translated query are more important, because they're the ones the user will need to fill out and submit to the local authorities.

In web search, that may not be always the case. Let's get back to the example of the Wikipedia page for "artificial neural networks." The English version of the page has much more information than the Italian version. Depending on various factors, such as the user's interests and preferred topics, the search engine may decide to rank the translated page lower than the original, because it's less informative. If a deep learning researcher performs a web search for "artificial neural networks," the Italian version of the "artificial neural network" page won't be useful to them, because the amount of information is less, compared to the original English page. If, instead, the user is a newbie on the topic, reading a page in their native language will probably help them grasp the topic. Although a lot depends on the use case, if you decide to use MT in a search engine, it's a good idea to rank the additional results the same as or higher than the "normal" results.

The rest of this chapter focuses on translating queries rather than translating documents; the principles are similar whether translating short or long pieces of text. On the other hand, from a technical perspective, working with very short text (such as a search query) or very long text (such as a long article) is usually more difficult than working with single sentences.

7.1.2 Cross-language search

Let's take a quick look at how to incorporate MT into a search engine to translate user queries. In web search, the MT task is usually performed in the search engine; nothing is said to the user about it. For the other use cases mentioned, users may want to specify the desired language for the search results; an asylum seeker will know the best language for the legal documents they need, but this information may be not available to the search system.

Going forward, I'll assume you have a set of MT tools that can translate from the language of the user query to other languages and that your search engine contains documents in many different languages—a common setup for cross-language information retrieval for web search. The tools for performing MT can be implemented in many different ways; as we go continue through the chapter, you'll see a few different methods of MT. It's common for such tools to be able to translate text from a *source* language to a *target* language. Imagine you have a query written in Icelandic, as mentioned earlier, and you have three models that can translate from Icelandic to English, from English to Icelandic, and from Italian to English, respectively. The search engine needs to be able to choose the right tool for translating the query. If you pick the Italian-to-English tool, then no translation or, even worse, a bad translation may come from the model. This may cause retrieval of unwanted results, which of course is bad. Even when the inappropriate model gives no translation, CPU and memory resources are used, and therefore the attempt may negatively impact performance without giving a useful outcome.

To mitigate such issues, it's a good practice to place a *language detector* program on top of MT models. A language detector receives an input text and outputs the language of the input sequence. You can think of it as a text classifier whose output classes are language codes (en, it, ic, pt, and so on). With the language detector providing the user's query language, you can choose the right MT model to translate the query. The output text from all of the MT models will be sent to the search engine as an additional query together with the original query; you can think of it as using a Boolean OR operator between the original and translated versions of the query (such as "pólitísk hæli OR political asylum"). Figure 7.3 shows an example flow for using MT at query time.

Let's look at how cross-language search can be implemented on top of Apache Lucene. For now, we'll keep the MT part a bit abstract. In the following sections, we'll go over different types of MT models and examine the advantages and weaknesses of each. In particular, we'll focus on why most research and industries have switched

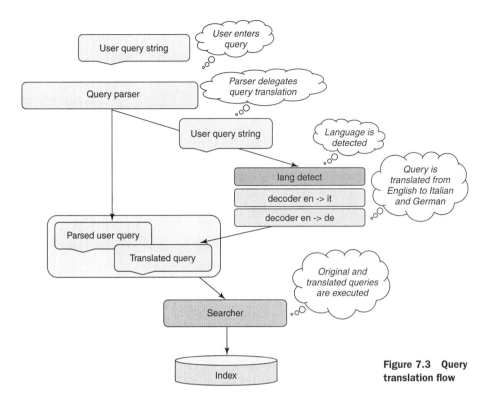

Figure 7.3 Query translation flow

from *statistical machine translation* (based on statistical analysis of probability distributions for words and phrases) to *neural machine translation* based on the use of neural networks.

7.1.3 *Querying in multiple languages on top of Lucene*

Let's continue with the example of asylum seekers. Suppose I'm an Italian refugee in the United States, and I need to fill out some legal documents. I type a query in Italian, looking for documents to enter the United States. Here's what the search engine should do:

```
> q: documenti per entrare negli Stati Uniti  ◁— Input query
> detected language 'ita' for query  ◁— Language detection output
> found 1 translation
> t: documents to enter in the US  ◁— Translated query
> 'documenti per entrare negli ...' parsed as:
  '(text:documenti text:per text:entrare text:negli text:Stati text:Uniti)'
  OR
  '(text:documents text:to text:enter text:in text:the text:US)'
```

**Enhanced query containing both the
original and translated queries
separated by a Boolean OR clause**

As you may guess, the "magic" happens during the parsing of the user-entered query. Here's a simplified sequence of operations performed by the query parser:

1 The query parser reads the input query.
2 The query parser passes the input query to the language detector.
3 The language detector determines the language of the input query.
4 The query parser chooses MT models that can translate the identified language into other languages.
5 Each selected MT model translates the input query into another language.
6 The query parser aggregates the input and the translated text in OR clauses of a Boolean query.

You'll extend a Lucene `QueryParser` whose main method `#parse` transforms a `String` into a Lucene `Query` object.

Listing 7.1 Creating a `BooleanQuery` containing the original query

```
@Override
public Query parse(String query) throws ParseException {

    BooleanQuery.Builder builder = new BooleanQuery
        .Builder();                                          ◁─────────  Creates a Boolean
    builder.add(new BooleanClause(super.parse(query),                   query in Lucene
        BooleanClause.Occur.SHOULD));      ◁─┐
                                             │  Parses the original user query
    ...                                      │  and adds it to the Boolean
}                                            │  query as an OR clause
```

Then the input query language is extracted by a language detector tool. (There are many different ways that can be done; for now, we won't focus on that.) You'll use the `LanguageDetector` tool from the Apache OpenNLP project (http://opennlp.apache.org).

Listing 7.2 Detecting the language of the query

```
Language language = languageDetector.
    predictLanguage(query);           ◁───────────  Performs language detection
String languageCode = language.getLang();    ◁─┐
                                               │  Gets the language code
                                               │  (en, it, and so on)
```

Here you assume you've already loaded the models to perform machine translation, such as in a `Map` whose key is the language code (`en` for English, `it` for Italian, and so on) and whose value is a `Collection` of `TranslatorTools`. For the moment, it doesn't matter how `TranslatorTool` is implemented; we'll focus on that in later sections.

Listing 7.3   Choosing the correct `TranslatorTools`

```
private Map<String,Collection<TranslatorTool>> perLanguageTools;

@Override
public Query parse(String query) throws ParseException {
  ...
  Collection<TranslatorTool> tools =
      perLanguageTools.get(languageString);          ◁─┐ Gets the tools that can
  ...                                                   translate from the detected
}                                                       language into other languages
```

Now that you have the MT tools loaded, you can use them to create additional Boolean clauses to be added to the final query.

Listing 7.4   Translating a query and building a query with the translated text

```
                  for (TranslatorTool tt : tools) {
                    Collection<Translation> translations = tt.          Iterates over all
Translates      ▷    translate(query);                                  possible translations
the input                                                               of the input query
query             for (Translation translation : translations) {    ◁──
                    String translationString = translation.
                ▷    getTranslationString();
                      builder.add(new BooleanClause(super.parse(
                        translationString), BooleanClause.Occur.SHOULD));  ◁──
                  }
                }
                  return builder.build();  ◁──                      Parses the translated
                                                                    query and adds it to
Gets the translation text (each translation                        the Boolean query to
consists of the text and its score,                                 be returned
representing the quality of the translation)    Finalizes the process of
                                                building the Boolean query
```

With this code, you're all set with a query parser that lets you create queries in multiple languages. The missing part is implementing the `TranslatorTool` interface in the best possible way. To do that, we'll take a quick journey into different ways of addressing the MT task. First we'll look at a statistical MT tool, and then we'll move to methods based on neural networks; this will help you understand the main challenges of translating text and how using neural network–based models generally provides better MT models.

7.2   *Statistical machine translation*

Statistical machine translation (SMT) uses statistical approaches to predict what target word or sentence is the most probable translation of an input word or sentence. For example, an SMT program should be able to answer the question, "What's the most probable English translation of the word 'hombre'?" To do that, you train a statistical model over a parallel corpus. A *parallel corpus* is a collection of text fragments (documents, sentences, or even words) where each piece of content comes in two versions:

the source language (such as Spanish) and the target language (such as English). Here's an example:

```
s: a man with a suitcase
t: un hombre con una maleta
```

A *statistical model* is a model that can calculate the probability of source and target text fragments. A correctly trained statistical model for MT will answer the question about the most probable translation for a text fragment by providing the translation together with its probability:

```
hombre -> man (0.333)
```

The probability of a translated text fragment will help you decide whether the translation can be considered good and therefore whether it should be used for search. An SMT model evaluates the probability of many possible translations and only returns the one with the highest probability. If you ask the SMT model to output all the probabilities for the example query "hombre," you'll see high probabilities for good translations and low probabilities for unrelated translations, as in this sample output:

```
man     (0.333)
husband (0.238)
love    (0.123)
...
woman   (0.003)
truck   (0.001)
...
```

Under the hood, the SMT model calculates the probability of each possible translation and records the translation that has the best probability. Such an algorithm looks like this in pseudocode:[1]

```
f = 'hombre'
for (each e in target language)
    p(e|f) = (p(f|e) * p(e)) / p(f)        Calculates the probability of the
                                           current target word given the
                                           source word "hombre"

    if (p(e|f) > pe~)                      If the probability is higher than the current highest
                                           probability, you have a new best translation.
    ⊳ e~ = e

        pe~ = p(e|f)

e~ = best translation, the one with highest probability
pe~ = the probability of the best translation              Records the best
                                                           translation
                                                           probability
Records the best
translation
```

The algorithm isn't complex; the only missing piece is how to calculate probabilities like $p(e)$ and $p(f|e)$. In information theory and statistics, $p(f|e)$ is the conditional probability of e, given f. Generally speaking, you can think of it as the probability of

---

[1] See also Bayes' theorem, https://en.wikipedia.org/wiki/Bayes%27_theorem.

the event *e* occurring as a consequence of event *f*. In this case, "events" are pieces of text! Without going too deep into statistics, you can think of word probabilities relying on counting the frequencies of words. For example, p(man) would be equal to the number of times the word *man* appears in the parallel corpus. Similarly, you can assume p(hombre|man) is equal to the number of times the word *man* appears in a sentence in the target language that's paired with a sentence in Spanish containing *hombre*. Let's look at the following three parallel sentences: two of them contain *man* in the source language and *hombre* in the target sentence; the other contains *man* in the source sentence but not *hombre* in the target:

```
s: a man with a suitcase
t: un hombre con una maleta

s: a man with a ball
t: un hombre con una pelota

s: a working man
t: un senor trabajando
```

In this case, p(hombre|man) equals 2. As another example, in the parallel sentences, p(senor|man) equals 1 because the third parallel sentence contains *man* in the source sentence and *senor* in the target sentence. In summary, *hombre* is translated to *man* because, among the many possible alternatives, *man* is the most frequently used English word when a Spanish sentence contains *hombre*.

You've learned some of the basics of SMT. You'll also get to know some of the challenges that make this task harder than it may seem from this introduction; they're important to know, because neural machine translation is less affected by such problems—part of the rationale behind the current switch from SMT to neural machine translation (NMT).

7.2.1 Alignment

In the previous section, you learned that you can build a statistical model to translate text. This translation happens by estimating probabilities based on the frequency of words. In practice, though, there are other factors at play. For example, the co-occurrence of two words *f* and *e* in two source and target sentences doesn't mean one is the translation of the other. In the previously mentioned sentences, the words *a* and *hombre* co-occur more frequently than *hombre* and *man*:

```
s: a man with a suitcase
t: un hombre con una maleta

s: a man with a ball
t: un hombre con una pelota

s: a working man
t: un senor trabajando
```

So p(hombre|a) = 3, and p(hombre|man) = 2 Does that mean *a* is English for *hombre*? Of course not! This information is important when deciding whether the right translation for *hombre* is *a* or *man*.

But translated words aren't always perfectly aligned. Consider the third parallel sentence: the correct translation for *man* is *senor* in that context. But *man* is in the third position in the source sentence, whereas *senor* is in the second position in the target sentence:

```
s: a working man
t: un senor trabajando
```

The task of dealing with words placed at different positions in source and target sentences is called *word alignment*, and it plays an important role in the effectiveness of SMT. SMT models usually define an *alignment function* that maps, for example, a Spanish target word at position i to an English source word at position j. The mapping for the sentence transforms the positions according to the indices $1 \rightarrow 1, 2 \rightarrow 3, 3 \rightarrow 2$:

```
s: a working man     ◁── "a" and "un" are at the same position.
   ↓        ↙
t: un senor trabajando  ◁── "man" and "senor" are one position apart.
```

Another example where word alignment plays an important role is when there's no one-to-one mapping between words in different languages. This is especially true with languages that don't originate from the same root language. Let's take another example of an English-to-Spanish parallel sentence:

```
s: I live in the USA
t: vivo en Estados Unidos
```

There are two special cases here:

- The words *I live* in English are translated into the single word *vivo* in Spanish.
- The word *USA* in English is translated into the two words *Estados Unidos* in Spanish.

The word-alignment function will need to also take care of these cases:

```
s: I live in the USA
    ↘ ↙        ↙↘
t: vivo en Estados Unidos
```

7.2.2 Phrase-based translation

So far, we've discussed how to translate single words. But, as in many other areas of natural language processing, translating a single word is difficult without knowing the context. Phrase-based translation aims to reduce the amount of error due to the lack of information when translating single words. Generally, performing phrase-based translation requires more data to train a good statistical model, but it can handle longer sentences better, and it's often more accurate than word-based statistical models. All the things you learned for word-based SMT models apply to phrase-based models; the only difference is that the translation units aren't words, but phrases.

When a phrase-based model receives an input text, it breaks the text into phrases. Each phrase is translated independently, and then the per-phrase translations are reordered using a phrase-alignment function. Until the success of neural models for

MT, phrase (and hierarchical) SMT models were the de facto standard for MT and were used in many tools, such as Google Translate.

7.3 *Working with parallel corpora*

As you probably realize, one of the most important aspects of machine learning is having a lot of good-quality data. MT models are usually trained on parallel corpora: (text) datasets provided in two languages so that words, sentences, and so on in the source language can be mapped to words, sentences, and so on in the target language.

A very useful resource for those interested in MT is the Open Parallel Corpus (OPUS, http://opus.nlpl.eu). It provides many parallel resources; you can select the source and target languages, and you'll be shown a list of parallel corpora in different formats. Each parallel corpus is usually provided in different XML formats, or dedicated MT formats like the one from the Moses project (www.statmt.org/moses). Sometimes translation dictionaries with word frequencies are also available.

In this context, let's set up a small tool to parse the Translation Memory eXchange (TMX) format (https://en.wikipedia.org/wiki/Translation_Memory_eXchange). Although the TMX specification isn't new, a lot of the existing parallel corpora are available in TMX format on the OPUS project, so it's useful to be able to work with TMX when you train your first NMT model.

The TMX file format uses one tu XML node per parallel sentence. Each tu node has two tuv child elements: one for the source sentence and one for the target sentence. And each of those nodes has a seg node containing the actual text.

Here's a sample from a TMX file for translating from English to Italian:

```
<?xml version="1.0" encoding="UTF-8" ?>
<tmx version="1.4">
<header creationdate="Wed Jul 30 13:12:22 2014"
        srclang="en"
        adminlang="en"
        o-tmf="unknown"
        segtype="sentence"
        creationtool="Uplug"
        creationtoolversion="unknown"
        datatype="PlainText" />
  <body>
    ...
    <tu>
      <tuv xml:lang="en">
        <seg>
            It contained a bookcase: I soon possessed myself of a volume.
        </seg>
      </tuv>
      <tuv xml:lang="it">
        <seg>
            Vi era una biblioteca e io m'impossessai di un libro.
         </seg>
       </tuv>
    </tu>
```

```
    ...
  </body>
</tmx>
```

In the end, you're interested in getting the contents of the tuv and seg XML nodes. You want to collect parallel sentences where you can obtain the source and target text. To do so, you first create a ParallelSentence class.

Listing 7.5   A class for parallel sentences

```
public class ParallelSentence {

  private final String source;
  private final String target;

  public ParallelSentence(String source, String target) {
    this.source = source;
    this.target = target;
  }

  public String getSource() {
    return source;
  }

  public String getTarget() {
    return target;
  }
}
```

Next, let's create a TMXParser class to extract a Collection of parallel sentences from TMX files.

Listing 7.6   Parsing and iterating through the parallel corpus

```
TMXParser tmxParser = new TMXParser(Paths.get("/path/to/it-en-file.tmx")
    .toFile(), "it", "en");
Collection<ParallelSentence> parse = tmxParser.parse();
for (ParallelSentence ps : parse) {
  String source = ps.getSource();
  String target = ps.getTarget();
  ...
}
```

The TMXParser will look inside all tu, tuv, and seg nodes and build the Collection:

```
    public TMXParser(final File tmxFile, String
      sourceCode, String targetCode) {                ◁──────  Creates a parser on a TMX file, specifying
      ...                                                      the source and target languages
    }

    public Collection<ParallelSentence> parse() throws IOException,
        XMLStreamException {
      try (final InputStream stream = new
          FileInputStream(tmxFile)) {                      Creates an XMLEventReader: a
        final XMLEventReader reader = factory              utility class that emits events every
            .createXMLEventReader(stream);    ◁─────       time it reads XML elements
        while (reader.hasNext()) {  ◁───┐
```

Reads the file ──▷ (points to `FileInputStream(tmxFile)`)

Iterates over each XML event (nodes, attributes, and so on) (points to `while (reader.hasNext()) {`)

```
        final XMLEvent event = reader.nextEvent();
        if (event.isStartElement() && event.asStartElement().getName()
            .getLocalPart().equals("tu")) {    ◁————————— Intercepts tu nodes
          parse(reader);    ◁————————┐
        }                            │ Parses the tu nodes and
      }                              │ reads the contained
    }                                │ parallel sentences
    return parallelSentenceCollection;
  }
```

We won't dig too far into the code for extracting the ParallelSentences, because parsing XML isn't the primary focus here. For the sake of completeness, here's the important part of the parseEvent method:

```
if (event.isEndElement() && event.asEndElement()          ┐ Closing tu element. The
    .getName().getLocalPart().equals("tu")) {    ◁————————┘ ParallelSentence is ready.
  if (source != null && target != null) {
    ParallelSentence sentence = new ParallelSentence(source, target);
    parallelSentenceCollection.add(sentence);
  }
  return;
}
if (event.isStartElement()) {
  final StartElement element = event.asStartElement();
  final String elementName = element.getName().getLocalPart();
  switch (elementName) {
    case, "tuv":                      ◁————————————————┐ Reads the language code
      Iterator attributes = element.getAttributes();   │ from the tuv element
      while(attributes.hasNext()) {
        Attribute next = (Attribute) attributes.next();
        code = next.getValue();
      }
      break;
    case "seg":                       ◁————————————————┐ Reads the text from
      if (sourceCode.equals(code)) {                    │ the seg element
        source = reader.getElementText();
      } else if (targetCode.equals(code)) {
        target = reader.getElementText();
      }
      break;
  }
}
```

Using the generated parallel sentences, you can train an MT model—either statistical, as described in the previous section, or neural, as you'll see next.

7.4 *Neural machine translation*

With all that background about SMT and parallel corpora, you're now ready to learn about why and how neural networks are used in the context of MT applied to search. Imagine you're an engineer who has the task of building a search engine for a non-profit organization that helps refugees from all around the world gather information about required legal documentation for each country. You need MT models for as many language pairs as possible (for example, Spanish to English, Swahili to English, English to Spanish, and so on). Training statistical models based on explicit probability estimation, like the word- or phrase-based SMT models discussed earlier, would be time-consuming because of the amount of manual work such an approach usually takes. For example, word alignment would require a lot of work for each of the language pairs.

When the first NMT models were introduced, one of their most intriguing features was that they didn't require much tuning. When Ilya Sutskever presented the work he and his coauthors did on an encoder-decoder architecture for NMT,[2] he stated, "We use minimum innovation for maximum results."[3] That turned out to be one of the best qualities of this type of model.

This approach uses a deep, long short-term memory (LSTM) network whose output is a big vector, the *thought vector* mentioned in chapter 3, and then feeds the sequence (and the thought vector) to another decoder LSTM that generates the translated sequence. Over time, different "flavors" of NMT models have been proposed, but the main idea of using an encoder-decoder network was a milestone: it was the first model fully based on neural networks to beat SMT models in an MT task.

These models are flexible for mapping sequences to sequences in different domains, not just for MT. For example, you used seq2seq encoder-decoder models to perform query expansion in chapter 3, and thought vectors to retrieve related content in chapter 6. Now we'll go a bit deeper into how such models work and how the sequences flow into and out of them.

7.4.1 Encoder-decoder models

At a high level, the encoder LSTM reads and encodes a sequence of the source text into a fixed-length vector, the thought vector. A decoder LSTM then outputs a translated version of the source sentence from the encoded vector. The encoder–decoder system is trained to maximize the probability of a correct translation, given a source sentence. So, to some extent, these encoder-decoder networks, like many other deep learning–based models, are a statistical model! The difference with respect to "traditional" SMT is that NMT models learn to maximize the correctness of a generated translation via neural networks, and they do so in an end-to-end fashion. For example, there's no need for dedicated tools for word alignment; an encoder-decoder network only needs a huge collection of source/target sentence pairs.

The key features of encoder-decoder models are as follows:

- They're easy to set up and understand—the model is intuitive.
- They can handle variable-length input and output sequences.
- They produce input sequence embeddings that can be used in different ways.

---

[2] Ilya Sutskever, Oriol Vinyals, and Quoc V. Le, "Sequence to Sequence Learning with Neural Networks," September 10, 2014, https://arxiv.org/abs/1409.3215.

[3] "NIPS: Oral Session 4 - Ilya Sutskever," Microsoft Research, August 18, 2016, https://www.youtube.com/watch?v=-uyXE7dY5H0.

- They can be used for seq2seq mapping tasks in various domains.
- They're an end-to-end tool, as just explained.

Let's break down the graph shown in figure 7.4 to better understand what's in each part of the model and how the parts work together. The encoder is made up of a recurrent neural network (RNN), usually an LSTM or another alternative like gated recurrent units (GRUs[4]), which we don't expand on here. Remember that the main difference between a feed-forward network and an RNN is that the latter has recurrent layers that make it possible to easily work with unbounded sequences of inputs while keeping the size of the input layer fixed. The encoder RNN is usually deep, so it has more than one hidden recurrent layer. Just as you saw when we introduced RNNs in chapter 3, you can add more hidden layers if the translation quality is poor even when a lot of training data is provided. In general, between two and

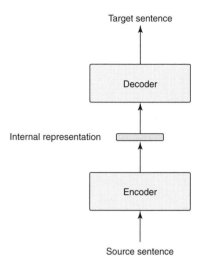

Figure 7.4   An encoder-decoder model

five recurrent layers is enough for training sets on the order of magnitude of tens of gigabytes. The output of the encoder network is the thought vector, which corresponds to the last time step of the last hidden layer of the encoder network. For instance, if the encoder has four hidden layers, the last time step of the fourth layer will represent the thought vector.

For simplicity, let's consider translating a sentence with four words, written by an Italian user who's looking for information about entering the UK with an Italian identity card. The source sentence could be something like "carta id per gb." The encoder network is fed one word of the sentence at each time step. After four time steps, the encoder network has been fed all four words in the input sentence, as shown in figure 7.5.

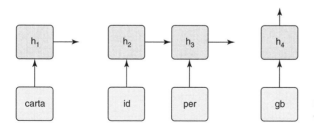

Figure 7.5   An encoder network with four hidden recurrent layers

---

[4]   See the well-known paper by Kyunghyun Cho et al., "Learning Phrase Representations Using RNN Encoder-Decoder for Statistical Machine Translation," June 3, 2014, https://arxiv.org/abs/1406.1078.

NOTE In practice, the input sequence is often reversed, because it turns out the neural network usually gives better results that way.

When you learned about word2vec in chapter 2, you saw that words are often transformed into one-hot-encoded vectors to be used in a neural network. Word embeddings were an output of the word2vec algorithm. The encoder network does something similar, using an *embedding layer*. You transform the input words into one-hot-encoded vectors, and the network's input layer has a dimension equal to the size of the vocabulary of words in the collection of source sentences. Remember that a one-hot-encoded vector for a certain word, such as *gb*, is a vector with a single 1 for the vector index assigned to that word, and 0 in all the remaining positions. Before the recurrent layer, the one-hot-encoded vector is transformed into a word embedding of a layer with a lower dimension than the input layer. This layer is the embedding layer, and its output is a vector representation of the word (a word embedding) similar to the one obtained using word2vec.

Looking closer at the encoder network layers, you see a stack similar to that shown in figure 7.6. This input layer consists of 10 neurons, which implies that the source language contains only 10 words; in reality, the input layer may contain tens of thousands of neurons. The embedding layer reduces the input word size and generates a vector whose values aren't just 0s and 1s, but real values. The embedding layer output vector is then passed over to the recurrent layers.

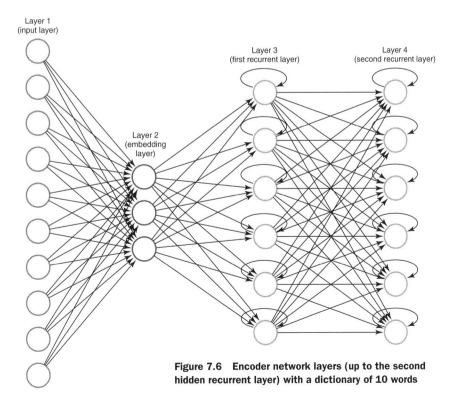

Figure 7.6 Encoder network layers (up to the second hidden recurrent layer) with a dictionary of 10 words

After processing the last word in the input sequence, a special token (such as <EOS>: end of sentence) is passed to the network to signal that the input is finished and decoding should start. This makes it easier to handle variable-length input sequences, because decoding won't start until the <EOS> token is received.

The decoding part mirrors the encoding part. The only difference is that the decoder (see figure 7.7) receives both the fixed-length vector and one source word at each time step.

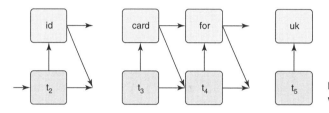

Figure 7.7   A decoder network with four hidden recurrent layers

No embedding layer is used in the decoder. The probability values in the output layer of the decoder network are used to sample a word from the dictionary at each time step. Let's look now at an encoder-decoder LSTM with DL4J in action.

7.4.2   *Encoder-decoder for MT in DL4J*

DL4J lets you declare the architecture of your neural network via a *computational graph*. This is a common paradigm in the deep learning framework; similar patterns are used in other popular deep learning tools such as TensorFlow, Keras, and others. With a computational graph for a neural network, you can declare which layers exist and how they're connected to one another.

Let's consider the encoder network layers defined in the previous section. You have an input layer, an embedding layer, and two recurrent (LSTM) layers (shown as visualized by the DL4J UI in figure 7.8). The encoder network computational graph is as follows:

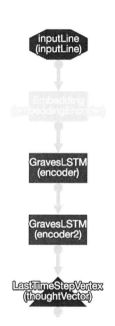

Figure 7.8   Encoder layers

```
ComputationGraphConfiguration.GraphBuilder graphBuilder =
      builder.graphBuilder()
  ...
  .addInputs("inputLine", ...)
  .setInputTypes(InputType.
      recurrent(dict.size()), ...)    ◁── Specifies an input type for an RNN
  .addLayer("embeddingEncoder",
      new EmbeddingLayer.Builder()    ◁── Creates an embedding layer
          .nIn(dict.size())      ◁── The embedding layer expects a number of inputs
                                       equal to the size of the word dictionary.
```

```
              ▷    .nOut(EMBEDDING_WIDTH)
Output               .build(),
embedding        "inputLine"          ◁──── Embedding layer input
vector width  .addLayer("encoder",        ◁──── Adds the first encoder layer
                  new GravesLSTM.Builder()    ◁───
                      .nIn(EMBEDDING_WIDTH)          The first layer of the
                      .nOut(HIDDEN_LAYER_WIDTH)      encoder is an LSTM layer.
                      .activation(Activation.TANH)  ◁───
                      .build(),                          Uses a tanh function in the
                  "embeddingEncoder")      ◁───          LSTM layers
              .addLayer("encoder2",  ◁───          The encoder layer takes inputs from
                  new GravesLSTM.Builder()           the embeddingEncoder layer.
                      .nIn(HIDDEN_LAYER_WIDTH)       Adds the second layer of the
                      .nOut(HIDDEN_LAYER_WIDTH)      encoder (another LSTM layer)
                      .activation(Activation.TANH)
                      .build(),
                  "encoder");    ◁───     The encoder2 layer takes inputs
              ...                          from the encoder layer.
```

**Figure 7.9
Decoder layers**

The decoder part contains two LSTM layers and an output layer (see figure 7.9). Translated words are sampled from the output values generated by the softmax function on the output layer:

```
...
.addLayer("decoder",
    new GravesLSTM.Builder()            ◁───
        .nIn(dict.size() + HIDDEN_LAYER_WIDTH)
        .nOut(HIDDEN_LAYER_WIDTH)              The decoder recurrent
        .activation(Activation.TANH)          layers are also based
        .build(),                             on LSTMs.
    "merge")
.addLayer("decoder2",
    new GravesLSTM.Builder()     ◁───
        .nIn(HIDDEN_LAYER_WIDTH)
        .nOut(HIDDEN_LAYER_WIDTH)
        .activation(Activation.TANH)
        .build(),
    "decoder")
.addLayer("output",
    new RnnOutputLayer.Builder()   ◁──── Normal RNN output layer
        .nIn(HIDDEN_LAYER_WIDTH)
        .nOut(dict.size())
        .activation(Activation.SOFTMAX)   ◁───
        .lossFunction(LossFunctions.            The output is a probability
                                                distribution generated by
                                                the softmax activation.
```

```
         LossFunction.MCXENT)
      .build(),
   "decoder2")
.setOutputs("output");
```
◁——— **The cost function to be used is multiclass cross entropy.**

At this point, you may think you're finished, but you're still missing the glue that connects the encoder with the decoder. This consists of the following:

- The thought vector layer, which captures the distributed representation of the source word used by the decoder to generate the correct translated word
- A side input used by the decoder to keep track of the words it generates

The graph will look slightly more complex than you may expect, because the decoding side of the neural network uses both the thought vector and the outputs it generates as well, at each time step. The decoder network starts generating translated words as soon as it receives a special word (such as *go*) on a dedicated input. At that time step, the decoder fetches both the value from the thought vector generated by the encoder and this special word, and generates its first decoded word. In the next time step, it uses the just-generated decoded word as new input, together with the thought vector value, to generate the subsequent word—and so forth,

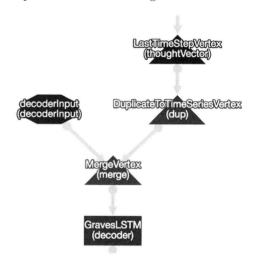

Figure 7.10   Connecting layers

until it generates a special word (such as EOS) that stops the decoding.

In summary, the thought vector layer is fed the last time step of the final recurrent (LSTM) layer of the encoder network and used as input to the decoder together with a word at each decoding time step, as illustrated in figure 7.10. The complete model looks like figure 7.11.

The connections between the encoder and the decoder, shown in figure 7.10, are implemented by the following code:

```
.addVertex("thoughtVector", new LastTimeStepVertex(
    "inputLine"), "encoder2")      ◁———
.addVertex("dup", new DuplicateToTimeSeriesVertex(
    "decoderInput"), "thoughtVector") ◁—
.addVertex("merge", new MergeVertex(), "decoderInput"
——▷ , "dup")
```

Only the last time step of the encoder output is recorded in the thought vector.

Creates a new time-series input for the decoder, initialized with the values from the thought vector

Prepares the decoder to receive merged inputs from the thought vector and the decoder side input

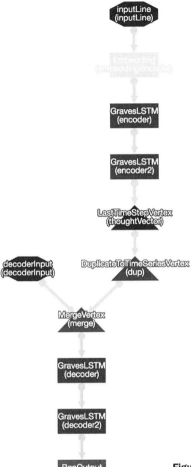

Figure 7.11   Encoder-decoder model with two LSTMs layers per side

With this computational graph built, you're ready to train the network with a parallel corpus. In order to do so, you build a `ParallelCorpusProcessor` that processes the parallel corpus: for example, in the form of a TMX file downloaded from the OPUS project. This processor extracts the source and target sentences and builds the dictionary of words. Then it will be used to provide the input and output sequences required for training the encoder-decoder model:

TMX file containing the parallel corpus

Parses the TMX file and extracts source and target sentences based on the language codes (for example, "it" for the source, "en" for the target)

```
File tmxFile = new File("/path/to/file.tmx");
ParallelCorpusProcessor corpusProcessor = new
    ParallelCorpusProcessor(tmxFile, "it", "en");
corpusProcessor.process();
```

Processes the corpus

```
Map<String, Double> dictionary =
    corpusProcessor.getDict();     ⟵————— Retrieves the corpus dictionary
Collection<ParallelSentence> sentences =
    corpusProcessor.getSentences();   ⟵————— Retrieves the parallel sentences
```

The dictionary is now used to set up the network: the dictionary size defines the number of inputs (for one-hot-encoded vectors). In this case, the dictionary is a Map whose keys are the words and whose value is a number used to identify each word when feeding it into the embedding layer. The sentences and the dictionary are needed to build an iterator over the parallel sentences. A DataSetIterator over the parallel corpus is then used to train the network across different epochs (an *epoch* of training is a full round of training on all the available training examples from the training set):

Builds the network using the computational graph

Builds the iterator over the parallel corpus

```
ComputationalGraph graph = createGraph(dictionary.
 ⟶  getSize());

ParallelCorpusIterator parallelCorpusIterator = new
    ParallelCorpusIterator(corpusProcessor);   ⟵
for (int epoch = 0; epoch < EPOCHS; epoch++) {                    Iterates over
  while (parallelCorpusIterator.hasNext()) {   ⟵————————        the corpus
    MultiDataSet multiDataSet = parallelCorpusIterator
        .next();        ⟵
    graph.fit(multiDataSet); ⟵
  }                    Trains the network over        Extracts a batch of input
}                       the current batch              and output sequences
```

The network now begins to learn to generate English sequences from Italian sequences. Figure 7.12 shows the network error decreasing.

The translation performed by the network consists of a feed-forward pass for all the words in the input sequence across the encoder and decoder networks. The encoder network implements the TranslatorTool API, and the output method performs the feed-forward pass on the neural network. That gives the translated version of the source sentence:

```
@Override
public Collection<Translation> translate(String text) {
  double score = 0d;
  String string = Joiner.on(' ').join(output(text, score));
  Translation translation = new Translation(string, score);
  return Collections.singletonList(translation);
}
```

The output method transforms the text sequence into a vector and then passes it along the encoder and decoder networks. The text vector is fed into the network using the word indexes generated by the ParallelCorpusProcessor. So you transform a String into a List<Double>, which is the ordered list of word indexes corresponding to each token in the source sequence:

```
Collection<String> tokens = corpusProcessor.tokenizeLine(text);
List<Double> rowIn = corpusProcessor.wordsToIndexes(tokens);
```

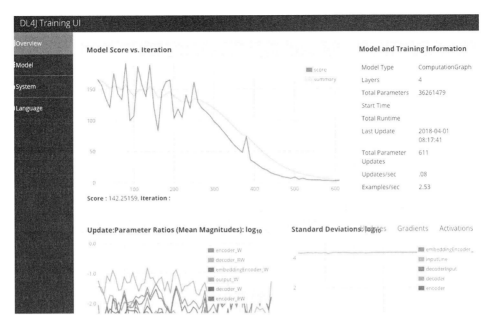

Figure 7.12 Encoder-decoder network training

Now you prepare the actual vectors to be used as input to both the encoder (the input vector) and the decoder (the decode vector), and perform separate feed-forward passes for the encoder and decoder networks. The encoder feed-forward pass is as follows:

```
net.rnnClearPreviousState();
Collections.reverse(rowIn);
Double[] array = rowIn.toArray(new Double[0]);
INDArray input = Nd4j.create(ArrayUtils.toPrimitive(array),
    new int[] {1, 1, rowIn.size()});
int size = corpusProcessor.getDict().size();
double[] decodeArr = new double[size];
decodeArr[2] = 1;
INDArray decode = Nd4j.create(decodeArr, new int[] {1, size, 1});
net.feedForward(new INDArray[] {input, decode}, false, false);
```

The decoder feed-forward pass is slightly more complex because it expects to use the thought vector generated by the encoder pass *and* the source sequence token vectors. So, at each time step, the decoder performs a translation, given the thought vector and a source sentence token vector:

```
Collection<String> result = new LinkedList<>();
GravesLSTM decoder = (GravesLSTM) net.getLayer("decoder");
Layer output = net.getLayer("output");
GraphVertex mergeVertex = net.getVertex("merge");
INDArray thoughtVector = mergeVertex.getInputs()[1];
for (int row = 0; row < rowIn.size(); row++) {
```

```
    mergeVertex.setInputs(decode, thoughtVector);
    INDArray merged = mergeVertex.doForward(false);
    INDArray activateDec = decoder.rnnTimeStep(merged);
    INDArray out = output.activate(activateDec, false);
    double idx = sampleFrom(output);
    result.add(corpusProcessor.getRevDict().get(idx));
    double[] newDecodeArr = new double[size];
    newDecodeArr[idx] = 1;
    decode = Nd4j.create(newDecodeArr, new int[] {1, size, 1});
}
return result;
```

Finally everything is set to start translating queries using the encoder-decoder network. (In practice, you'd perform the training phase outside of the search workflow.) Once training is finished, the model is persisted to disk and then loaded by the query parser defined at the beginning of this chapter:

```
ComputationGraph net ...
File networkFile = new File("/path/to/file2save");
ModelSerializer.writeModel(net, networkFile, true);
```

The query parser is created using the encoder-decoder network for Italian sentences (and the language detector tool):

```
File modelFile = new File("/path/to/file2save");
ComputationGraph net = ModelSerializer.restoreComputationGraph(modelFile);
net.init();
TranslatorTool mtNetwork = new MTNetwork(modelFile);

Map<String, Collection<TranslatorTool>> mappings = new HashMap<>();
mappings.put("ita", Collections.singleton(mtNetwork));
LanguageDetector languageDetector = new LanguageDetectorME(new
    LanguageDetectorModel(new FileInputStream("/path/to/langdetect.bin")));
MTQueryParser MTQueryParser = new MTQueryParser("text",
    new StandardAnalyzer(), languageDetector, mappings);
```

The query parser's internal logging will tell you how it's translating incoming queries. Suppose an Italian user wants to know whether their identity card is valid in the UK. Their query, written in Italian, is translated to English as follows using the encoder-decoder network:

```
> q: validità della carta d'identità in UK
> detected language 'ita' for query 'validità della carta d'identità in UK'
> found 1 translation
> t: identity card validity in the UK
> 'validità della carta d'identità in UK' was parsed as:
 '(text:validità text:della text:carta text:identità text:in text:UK)'
 OR
 '(text:identity text:card text:validity text:in text:the text:UK)'
```

This wraps up the end-to-end solution for machine translation based on an encoder-decoder model using LSTM networks. Many MT production systems use such models or extensions of them. One of the key advantages of using NMT is that it generally results in accurate translations, given enough training data—but such models can require significant computational resources when training. In the next section, we'll examine another approach to implementing MT programs that uses word and document embeddings (word2vec, paragraph vectors, and so on). When compared with models like the one implemented in this section, it may not be able to achieve the same level of accuracy, but it requires far less computational resources and therefore may be a good compromise.

7.5 Word and document embeddings for multiple languages

Previous chapters used word embeddings (dense vectors representing words' semantics), in particular the word2vec model, both to generate synonyms to enrich the text of documents to be indexed, and to define a ranking function that better captures the relevance of search results. In chapter 6, you saw a paragraph vector algorithm that learns dense vectors of sequences of text (entire documents or portions of them, such as paragraphs or sentences), and you used it to recommend similar content and create another (yet more powerful) ranking function. Now you'll see each of those neural network algorithms applied to the task of translating text.

7.5.1 Linear projected monolingual embeddings

One of the key aspects of the word vectors generated by the word2vec model is that when such vectors are plotted as points in a vector space, words with similar meanings are placed close to one another. Soon after the publication of the paper that introduced word2vec, the same researchers wondered what would happen to word embeddings if they came from the same data but were translated. Would there be any relation between the word vectors for a piece of English text and the same text written in Spanish? They discovered that there were significant geometric similarities in the relations that hold between the same words in different languages. For example, the distribution of numbers and animals in English and Spanish is similar if their respective word vectors are plotted, as you can see in figure 7.13.

These visual and geometric similarities suggested that a function that can transform a word vector from the English embedding space into a word vector from the Spanish embedding space would be a good candidate for translating words. Such a function is called a *linear projection* because it's sufficient to multiply the source vector (for an English word) by a certain *translation vector* to project the source word into a target word (in Spanish). Let's assume you have a small vector with two dimensions <0.1, 0.2> for the English word *cat* from the word2vec model of the English text (in practice, this will never happen; real-life dimensions for word embeddings are usually in the order of hundreds or thousands). You can learn a transformation matrix that will approximate the source vector for *cat* in the corresponding vector <0.07, 0.22> of the word *gato* in the Spanish embedding space. A transformation matrix multiplies its weights by the input vector and outputs a projected vector.

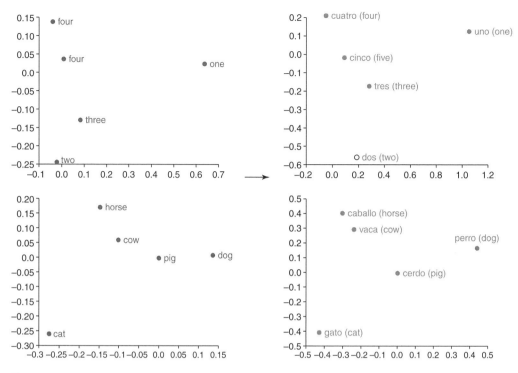

Figure 7.13   English and Spanish embeddings from the paper "Exploiting Similarities among Languages for Machine Translation" by Mikolov et al.

To make this more practical, let's set this up in DL4J using the same English-to-Italian parallel corpus used for the encoder-decoder. You'll get a parallel corpus and build two independent word2vec models, one for the source language and one for the target language.

> **Listing 7.7   Building two independent word2vec models**

```
Collection<ParallelSentence> parallelSentences = new
    TMXParser(tmxFile, source, target).parse();    ⟵── Parses the parallel corpus file

Collection<String> sources = new LinkedList<>();    | Creates two separate collections
Collection<String> targets = new LinkedList<>();    | for source and target sentences
for (ParallelSentence sentence : parallelSentences) {
    sources.add(sentence.getSource());
    targets.add(sentence.getTarget());
}

int layerSize = 100;
Word2Vec sourceWord2Vec = new Word2Vec.Builder()    ⟵── Trains two word2vec models:
        .iterate(new CollectionSentenceIterator(sources))     one from the source
        .tokenizerFactory(new DefaultTokenizerFactory())      sentences and one from the
        .layerSize(layerSize)    ⟵── The embedding dimensions, equal to the size
        .build();                    of the hidden layer of the word2vec model,
sourceWord2Vec.fit();                must be consistent across the two models.
```

```
Word2Vec targetWord2vec = new Word2Vec.Builder()
        .iterate(new CollectionSentenceIterator(targets))
        .tokenizerFactory(new DefaultTokenizerFactory())
        .layerSize(layerSize)    ⊲
        .build();
targetWord2vec.fit();
```

Trains two word2vec models: one from the source sentences and one from the target sentences

The embedding dimensions, equal to the size of the hidden layer of the word2vec model, must be consistent across the two models.

In this case, you also need extra information about word translations, not just raw source and target text. You need to be able to say which Italian word is the translation of each English word in the parallel corpus. You can obtain this information either from a dictionary (containing information such as *cat = gato*) or from a word-aligned corpus, where positional information about the source and target words is available for each parallel sentence. In the OPUS portal, it's easy to find dictionary files with one word translation per line:

```
...
Transferring trasferimento
Transformation Trasformazione
Transient transitori
...
```

You can parse the dictionary with the following line of code:

```
List<String> strings = FileUtils.readLines(dictionaryFile,
    Charset.forName("utf-8"));
int dictionaryLength = strings.size() - 1;
```

At this point, you've learned word embeddings for both the English sentences and the Italian ones. The next step is to build a translation matrix. To do this, you need to put the word embeddings for English and Italian into two separate matrixes. Each matrix contains a row for each word, and each row consists of the embedding relative to the given word. From those matrixes, you learn the projection matrix.

Listing 7.8 Putting embeddings from each word2vec model in a separate matrix

```
INDArray sourceVectors = Nd4j.zeros(dictionaryLength, layerSize);
INDArray targetVectors = Nd4j.zeros(dictionaryLength, layerSize);
int count = 0;
for (String line : strings) {
    String[] pair = line.split(" ");
    String sourceWord = pair[0];
    String targetWord = pair[1];
    if (sourceWord2Vec.hasWord(sourceWord) &&
            targetWord2Vec.hasWord(targetWord)) {
        sourceVectors.putRow(count, sourceWord2Vec
            .getWordVectorMatrix(sourceWord));
        targetVectors.putRow(count, targetWord2Vec
            .getWordVectorMatrix(targetWord));
        count++;
    }
}
```

With the two matrixes in place, the projection matrix can be learned using various methods. The goal is to minimize the distance between each target word vector and its corresponding source word vector multiplied by the transformation matrix. This example uses an algorithm for linear regression called *normal equation*. We'll skip the details; the key point is that this approach finds the combination of values in the projection matrix that will give the best translation results.

Listing 7.9   Finding the projection matrix

```
INDArray pseudoInverseSourceMatrix = InvertMatrix.pinvert(
    sourceVectors, false);          ◁——————————— Inverts the source vectors matrix
INDArray projectionMatrix = pseudoInverseSourceMatrix.mmul(
    targetVectors).transpose();     ◁——————————— Calculates the translation matrix
```

This ends the training phase. All of this is now encapsulated in a `TranslatorTool` called `LinearProjectionMTEmbeddings`. The training steps can be performed either in a constructor or in a dedicated method (such as `LinearProjectionMTEmbeddings#train`).

From this point on, you can use the two word2vec models in conjunction with the projection matrix to translate words. For each source word, you check that you have a word embedding for it and then multiply that vector by the projection matrix. Such a candidate vector represents the approximation of the target word vector. Finally, you look for the nearest neighbor of the candidate vector in the target embedding space: the word associated with the resulting vector is the translation you're looking for.

Listing 7.10   Decoding a source word into a target word

```
public List<Translation> decodeWord(int n, String sourceWord) {
    if (sourceWord2Vec.hasWord(sourceWord)) {        ◁—— Checks whether the source
        INDArray sourceWordVector = sourceWord2Vec          word2vec model has a word
            .getWordVectorMatrix(sourceWord);               vector for the source word
        INDArray targetVector = sourceWordVector
            .mmul(projectionMatrix.transpose());     ◁—— Multiplies the source vector
        Collection<String> strings = targetWord2Vec          by the projection matrix
            .wordsNearest(targetVector, n);
        List<Translation> translations = new ArrayList<>(strings.size());
        for (String s : strings) {
            Translation t = new Translation(s,
                targetWord2Vec.similarity(s,
                sourceWord));    ◁———————
            translations.add(t);
            log.info("added translation {} for {}", t, sourceWord);
        }
        return translations;
    } else {
        return Collections.emptyList();
    }
}
```

Retrieves the word embedding

Finds the candidate nearest-neighbor words

Adds the translations to the final result, including a score based on the distance between the source and target words

You can perform a word-by-word translation on longer text sequences by extracting tokens from the input text sequence and applying the decodeWord method to each source word.

Listing 7.11   Translating text using `LinearProjectionMTEmbeddings`

```
public Collection<Translation> translate(String text) {
    StringBuilder stringBuilder = new StringBuilder();
    double score = 0;
    List<String> tokens = tokenizerFactory.create(
        text).getTokens();
    for (String t : tokens) {
        if (stringBuilder.length() > 0) {
            stringBuilder.append(' ');
        }
        List<Translation> translations = decodeWord(
            1, t);
        Translation translation = translations.get(0);
        score += translation.getScore();
        stringBuilder.append(translation);
    }
    String string = stringBuilder.toString();
    Translation translation = new Translation(string,
        score / (double) tokens.size());
    log.info("{} translated into {}", text, translation);
    return Collections.singletonList(translation);
}
```

- Splits the input text into tokens (words)
- Translates one word at a time and gets exactly one translation each
- Accumulates the translation score
- Accumulates the translated words in a StringBuilder
- Generates the resulting translation with the translated text and score

You're finally ready to run some test translations.

Listing 7.12   Testing `LinearProjectionMTEmbeddings`

```
String[] ts = new String[]{"disease", "cure",
    "current", "latest", "day", "delivery", "destroy",
     "design", "enoxacine", "other", "validity",
    "other ingredients", "absorption profile",
    "container must not be refilled"};
File tmxFile = new File("en-it_emea.tmx");
File dictionaryFile = new File("en-it_emea.dic");
LinearProjectionMTEmbeddings lpe = new
    LinearProjectionMTEmbeddings(tmxFile,
    dictionaryFile, "en", "it");
for (String t : ts) {
  Collection<TranslatorTool.Translation> translations =
      linearProjectionMTEmbeddings.transalate(t);
  System.out.println(t + " -> " + translations);
}
```

- Test input words and sentences
- Parallel corpus file
- Parallel dictionary file
- Trains the models and projection matrix for the LinearProjectionMTEmbeddings
- For each input text, returns the top translation

You can expect good results, especially for translations of single words. This approach performs each translation in isolation, without using the surrounding words, so there's room for improvement. In the following output, I've manually added an accuracy tag to each translation (in pointy brackets), to help readers who don't know Italian:

```
disease -> malattia <PERFECT>
cure -> curativa <AVERAGE>
current -> stanti <BAD>
day -> giorno <PERFECT>
destroy -> distruggere <PERFECT>
design -> disegno <PERFECT>
enoxacine -> tioridazina <BAD>
other -> altri <PERFECT>
validity -> affinare <BAD>
other ingredients -> altri eccipienti <PERFECT>
absorption profile -> assorbimento profilo <GOOD>
container must not be refilled -> sterile deve non essere usarla <BAD>
```

The outputs are okay although not perfect; you'd expect a properly trained encoder-decoder model to work better than this, but the amount of time and computational resources required are typically so much lower with linear projected machine translation embeddings that people working with low-resource systems may be willing to accept the compromise. In addition, word2vec models can be reused in other contexts. For example, you can use these projected embeddings for machine translation to make search more effective, and you can also use word2vec models in ranking or synonym expansion. You can select which word2vec model to use at search time, using a language detection tool like the one you used for query expansion.

Summary

- Machine translation can be useful in the context of search to improve the user experience for users who speak various languages.
- Statistical models can achieve good translation accuracy, but the amount of pair tuning required for each language is nontrivial.
- Neural machine translation models provide ways to learn to translate sequences of text into different languages in a less articulated yet more powerful way.

Content-based image search

8

This chapter covers

- Searching for images based on their content
- Working with convolutional neural networks
- Using query by example to search for similar images

Traditionally, most users use search engines by writing text queries and consuming (reading) text results. For that reason, most of this book is focused on showing you ways neural networks can help users search through text documents. So far, you've seen how to

- Use word2vec to generate synonyms from the data ingested into the search engine, which makes it easier for users to find documents they may otherwise miss
- Expand search queries under the hood via recurrent neural networks (RNNs), giving the search engine the ability to express a query in more ways without asking the user to write all of them
- Rank text search results using word and document embeddings, thus providing more-relevant search results to end users
- Translate text queries with the seq2seq model to improve how the search engine works with text written in multiple languages and better serve users speaking different languages

But users increasingly expect search engines to be "smarter" and to be able to handle more than just written text queries. Users want search engines to search the web using voice, as with the built-in microphone on a smartphone, and to return not just text documents, but also relevant images, videos, and other formats. In addition to web search, it's becoming the norm for other types of search engines to index images and videos as well as text. A newspaper website, for instance, consists of more than text articles: on the homepage of any newspaper, you'll find multimedia content in addition to text. Therefore, a search engine for these websites needs to index images and video as well as text.

For some time now, databases have indexed images using *metadata*: written information about an image, such as its title or a description of its contents, that's attached to the image. Traditional information retrieval techniques, as well as the newer approaches described in this book, use metadata tags to help users find the pictures they're looking for. But manually crafting and inputting descriptions and tags for every image you need to index is tedious, time consuming, and prone to subjective error—one indexer's couch, after all, may be another indexer's sofa. Wouldn't it be nice if you could index images and make them searchable just as they are, without any manual intervention?

In this chapter, we'll look at how to do just that: outfit a search engine with image search that allows users to search through images based on their contents rather than based on text descriptions of their contents. To build this kind of image search, we'll use convolutional neural networks, which are a special type of deep neural network.

A search engine for images works by indexing image features. When we talk about machine learning, a *feature* represents semantically relevant data that we want to capture in order to solve a particular task. More concretely, when dealing with images, an image feature can be represented by specific image points or regions (for example, high-contrast regions, shapes, edges, and so on). I'll start by touching on the traditional ways of extracting important semantics from images, because we can use these techniques as a guide to the challenges of extracting features from images. This is a key step, because the extracted features can then be used to compare images, make and answer queries, and perform other tasks that a search engine needs to do.

Then I'll show you a different and better way to extract image features using deep neural networks, which requires less manual work and no handcrafted feature extractors. Finally, we'll look into how to incorporate the extracted features in a search engine, while also taking into account performance based on the time and space required to manage this type of image search.

> **NOTE** In this chapter, images are discussed rather than videos, for simplicity's sake. A video is essentially a sequence of images with attached audio bits, so you can certainly apply the approaches in this chapter to a video search scenario as well as an image search scenario.

8.1 Image contents and search

Back in chapter 1, I gave a brief introduction to one of deep learning's most promising aspects: representation learning. *Representation learning* is the task of taking input data (for example, images) and automatically extracting features that make it easy for a program to resolve a particular problem (such as recognizing which objects are shown in an image, how similar two images are, and so on). A good representation of a certain image should be expressive, meaning it should ideally provide information about different aspects of the image (objects contained, light, exposure, and so on) while also making it easy to compare single aspects (for example, you may want to determine whether two images contain a butterfly by comparing such learned representations). At a high level, learning an image representation using a deep neural network commonly follows the simple flow shown in figure 8.1, where pixels are converted to edges, edges to shapes, and shapes to objects.

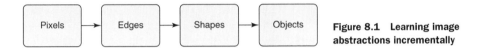

Figure 8.1   Learning image abstractions incrementally

Let's consider an image stored on the hard disk of a computer and see what such a binary representation tells us about its contents. Can you quickly open an image file as you would a text file, and immediately recognize what the image shows? The answer is no. If you look at the raw contents (for example, using the Linux `cat` command) of the file of an image showing, say, a butterfly, you see nothing that can tell you about its contents:

```
$ cat butterfly.jpg
????m,ExifII*
            ???(2?;??i?h%??*?1HH2018:07:01
    08:37:38&??6??>"?'??0?2???0230?F?Z??
n?v?
~?  ?
??|?
?)2?*4?5.*5?9??59?0100??p????)??)??)?????0?1?
```

The image file shows a butterfly when opened with the proper program: you can use tools to "view" images, but a computer isn't able to automatically recognize what the image contains or tell you if it's a picture of an old lady, a wild animal in a landscape, or whatever else it might be. The binary content representation of an image isn't good for telling you that there's a butterfly in it.

Deep learning (DL), however, *can* help you learn a representation that, when used properly, can tell you more about image contents. In this case, a deep neural network could tell you that the image features a butterfly. A DL algorithm usually accomplishes this by learning more and more information at each deep layer. For instance, in the first layers, it learns edges, at successive layers it learns shapes, and in the final layers it learns objects (like a butterfly, or a portion of one) so that it can tell what an image contains. Additionally, this information from all the layers is often encoded in a dense vector representation for each image. Later in this chapter, we'll unpack this quick overview of the process, and you'll finally meet deep neural networks that can learn image representations.

If you've ever tried to create a postcard by using an image (royalty-free, of course) available on the internet, then you may have experienced problems when searching for images relevant to a specific topic of interest. Let's say, for instance, that you bought a model car for your nephew or niece, and you want to print a postcard of a car to use as a card that you can write on and send to him or her. So you go to a search engine for images—perhaps Google Images or Adobe Stock—and type something like "sports car" in the query box. The important thing to understand about this process is that users look for images that contain a particular object or a specific feature. For example, you may want a "red sports car" or a "vintage sports car." Search engines for images often use a mechanism called *query by example* (QBE) where you upload or take a picture to be used as your input query. The search engine then returns images similar to the one that is input.

Let's freeze our running query for a moment and look at how this QBE process works. We'll start by thinking about how images are produced: how a digital camera or a graphics app creates and stores a picture. Snap a picture with a camera, and a file is stored somewhere that contains binary data (0s and 1s). You can think of this image stored in a computer as a grid with a certain width and height, where each cell in the grid is called a *pixel* and each pixel has a certain color. A colored pixel can be represented in different ways, and several color models are used to describe colors. For the sake of simplicity, we'll pick the most common scheme, *RGB* (Red, Green, Blue), in which each color is made by a mixture of some red, some green, and some blue. Each of those three colors has a range of values from 0 to 255, indicating the amount of red, green, and blue to be used in each combination (there's not just *one* red). Each such value can then be represented with 8 binary values ($2^8 = 256$) and thus contains all the possible ranges from 0 to 255. So an RGB image has a grid whose pixels are made from binary values representing their colors.[1] For example, the color *red* is R:255, G:0, B:0; *blue* is R:0, G:0, B:255, and so on.

With this in mind, let's unfreeze our query. How can you match a query for "sports car" when images are just series of bits? In the following sections, you'll see a few different ways you can make queries and images match, and learn some techniques for finding the particular sports car you want.

---

[1] Although in practice images can have lots of different formats and color schemes, the core problem is that images are usually stored as plain binaries, optionally with metadata that usually doesn't tell anything about their contents.

8.2 A look back: Text-based image retrieval

Users naturally tend to think about images in terms of what objects they contain (like sports cars), rather than their RGB values. But shapes and colors are better for specifying the information need, as in the thing they're looking for, whether it's a red sports car, a Formula 1 sports car, or some other kind.

A less-smart but common approach to mitigating the problem of matching text queries with binary images is to add metadata to images during indexing. You're indexing images, but each one has a relevant text caption or description. This allows you to do a normal search with a text query; the search will return images that have metadata text attached to them that matches the query. Conceptually, this isn't much different from a regular full-text search, except the search results are images instead of document titles or excerpts.

Using the sports car query, let's assume there are four images that can match that query. During indexing, you can ingest both the image data and a small caption describing each image; see figure 8.2. The image data is used to return the actual image content to the end user (in the search results list), and the text description of the image is indexed to match queries and images (as you'll see in the next section, in figure 8.3).

Figure 8.2   Manually captioned sports car images

If you search for "sports car," the search engine will return all the images shown in figure 8.2. If you search for "black sports car," only two of them will appear in the results list (recall that using double quotes in a query forces matches on the entire phrase "black sports car" rather on the single words "black," "sports," and "car").

This approach can be performed in Lucene in a straightforward way. You store the image binary as it is but index a manually entered description of the image (the description won't be returned with the search results):

```
byte[] bytes = ...              ⊲──┐  Obtains the image
String description = ...     ⊲──────    content as a byte[]
Document doc = new Document();            Writes an image
                                          description as a String

doc.add(new StoredField("binary", bytes)); ⊲──────   Adds the image binary
                                                      content as a stored field

doc.add(new TextField("description", description, Field.Store.NO));  ⊲──────

writer.addDocument(doc);  ⊲─────                      Adds the image
                          Indexes the image           description as a text field
writer.commit();  ⊲───┐   document
Commits the index changes
```

At search time, a simple text query can be used:

```
DirectoryReader reader = DirectoryReader
    .open(writer);  ⊲──────
                            Opens an IndexReader over the
IndexSearcher searcher = new    index containing the images
    IndexSearcher(reader);   ⊲──────
                                           Creates an IndexSearcher
TopDocs topDocs = searcher.search(new PhraseQuery(   to run the query
    "description", "black", "sports", "car"), 3); ⊲
for (ScoreDoc sd : topDocs.scoreDocs) {              Runs a query for
    Document document = reader.document(sd.doc);  ⊲   "black sports car"
                                                      on the caption field
    IndexableField binary = document.getField(   Fetches each
            ⊳ "binary");                          matching document
Retrieves the
"binary" field    BytesRef imageBinary = binary.binaryValue(); ⊲
    ...                                         Retrieves the actual image as a
}                                               binary and does something with it
```

This approach can work for a small number of images. But it's very common to have data of a size in the order of magnitude of millions or billions of documents. Even a small online shop that makes postcards will probably have hundreds or thousands of images. In many cases, it isn't possible to ask people to undertake the (not very pleasant) task of looking at each and every image and coming up with good descriptive text. And, sometimes, such text isn't good enough for all search cases. (In production systems, it isn't uncommon to have issues like "Why isn't the query 'black sports car' returning the black fluorescent sports car? Please change the description so that it can match such a query.") In summary, this approach doesn't scale, and it's only as good as the quality of the descriptions: poor descriptions lead to irrelevant search results.

8.3 Understanding images

As I said, an image can be described in various ways, and the most common is to specify the people, objects, animals, and other recognizable objects it contains: for example, "This is a picture of a man." Additionally, you can mention descriptive details, such as "This image shows a tall man." As you can see in figure 8.3, however, such brief descriptions are prone to ambiguity. The ambiguity comes from the simple fact that one object or entity can be described in many different ways.

Figure 8.3   Some images described as "tall man"

All three images in the figure certainly fit the description of a "tall man" that might be used as a text query. The image in the middle, however, is different from the others. Yes, it's a picture of a tall man, but it's also a picture of a player from the Houston Rockets NBA basketball team. So other phrases, including "basketball player," "houston rockets player," and "basketball player wearing a 35 numbered jersey" describe that image as well. It's impossible for a human tasked with the job of writing short metatags to think of every possible way an image can be described.

In the same vein, a description like "basketball player wearing a 35 numbered jersey" would perfectly fit not only the center image in figure 8.3, but also the images in figure 8.4, which are of entirely different players and teams. In this case, the user may be looking for one kind of image and get an entirely different kind, even though both have the same descriptive metatag and would appear in the search results.

Figure 8.4   Some images described as "basketball player wearing a 35 numbered jersey"

These simple examples teach you that text is extremely prone to mismatches, because a single entity (a person, an animal, an object, and so on) can be described in many different ways. This makes the quality of search results dependent on

- The way the user defines queries
- The way documents are written

You've already seen such problems in the context of search—that's one of the reasons why we use synonyms, query expansion, and so on. The search engine should be smart enough to be able to enhance queries and indexed documents.

In contrast, images, visually speaking, are generally less affected by this kind of ambiguity. Let's take the first image described as "tall man" and imagine you find images that are visually similar to it, as in figure 8.5.

Figure 8.5   Some visually similar images

An input image allows for a better definition of what's in the image, regardless of the different ways it can be textually described. At the same time, it's easy to say whether an image is *not* similar to the input one: for example, the basketball player image from figure 8.3 is clearly different from the images in figure 8.5, in terms of both the color and type of clothing the man is wearing.

Using sample images instead of text as input queries (also known as *querying by example*) is very common in image search platforms where systems try to extract semantic information from the images for accurate retrieval rather than having text metadata describe each image. Users express their query intent by means of a visual query. Just as with text queries, the quality of the query has an impact on the relevance of the results. Thinking in terms of text for a second may help: the query "red car" can return results ranging from a toy car to a Formula 1 race car, as long as it's red. If instead the query is "red sports car" or "Formula 1 red race car," then the range of possibly relevant results will be less broad and less vague. The same applies to visual queries and search results: the more accurate the query (the visual description of the information needed), the better the search results. With images, what makes the difference isn't the user's ability to write a "good" query—instead, the algorithm responsible for extracting the information to be indexed and searching for images is most significant.

Capturing objects and their features (color, light, shape, and so on) in an image, for example, is one of the challenges in this area.

Now you have all the pieces you need to start looking at some algorithms to extract information from images and represent them in a way that makes it possible to run queries that return meaningful results.

8.3.1 Image representations

The biggest challenge at this point is how to describe images in a way that makes it possible to find similar images. In the example, you want to create a postcard to accompany a gift. It would be great if you could take a picture of the gift with a camera and use that as a query to the image search engine. That way, the postcard will have a nice-looking picture that somehow suggests what's inside the gift box when you give it to the recipient.

Although images are made up of pixels, it isn't possible to perform a plain pixel comparison. Pixel values alone don't provide enough information about what's in an image. One problem is that a pixel represents only a very tiny portion of the image, and it gives no information about its context. A red pixel may be part of a red apple or a red car: there's no way to determine which one it comes from by looking at pixels alone. Even if pixels alone gave useful global information about an image, a large, high-quality image these days may contain millions of pixels, so performing a pixel-by-pixel comparison wouldn't be computationally efficient. Additionally, even two pictures of the same object taken with the same camera in the exact same conditions (light, exposure, and so on), but taken from two slightly different angles, will probably generate very different binary images, pixel-wise.

In this case, you want to take a picture of your gift—a red model sports car—while you're at home, without caring about lighting conditions and the exact angle you shoot the photo from. For example, you might take a picture like the one in figure 8.6. And you want the image search engine to return a nice picture of an actual red sports car, preferably the very same car model, as in figure 8.7.

Figure 8.6   The red toy sports car you want to give as a gift

Figure 8.7   A red sports car photo like the one you want retrieved by the search engine, based on the picture of a toy

To overcome the problem of pixels providing poor information, the most widely used technique to create searchable images is to extract *visual features* from them and index those features instead of "just" the pixels. These visual features promise to provide information that can be used to look for the contents of an image. Features are usually represented by sets of numbers or vectors.

> **NOTE**   You'll see in the next section what this means, when we look at a couple of feature extraction techniques. Understanding how feature extraction works with non-neural network–based methods is useful to set the basis for the kind of semantics they can convey and how different (and less human readable) they are with respect to features extracted by DL techniques. As you'll learn later in this chapter, the amount of engineering effort spent on DL techniques is much less than is required to design an accurate algorithm for feature extraction. Also important is the fact that at the time of writing, DL-based feature extraction beats every handcrafted feature extraction algorithm.

The search engine must be able to work with such features to find similar images in the QBE scenario. It will extract features from the images at indexing time and from the example query image at query time. So feature extraction is important for understanding what's in the image; but another important aspect is how to efficiently compare features of different images. Feature-indexing techniques will impact the amount of disk space required to store such inverted indexes; fast search algorithms for features are required to efficiently retrieve images at search time.

Visual features can be of different types:

- They can refer to *global features* like the colors used across the image, identified textures, or global or average values for RGB and other color models (CMYK, HSV, and so on).

- They can refer to *local features* (extracted from portions of the image) like edges, corners, or other interesting key points in image cells (as in methods like scale-invariant feature transform, speeded-up robust features, difference of Gaussians, and so on, discussed later in the chapter).

- They can be learned end to end as semantic abstractions that are close to the human cognition process, thanks to the use of deep neural networks.

The first two types are often referred to as *handcrafted* features because the respective algorithms have been designed and tuned for the purpose based on heuristics. Many DL-based models for image representations feed the network layers with image pixels (inputs to the neural network) and learn to classify images (the network output classes); during training, the neural network *learns* features automatically—this is the third type of features.

Let's now look at some methods to extract both local and global handcrafted features. Then we'll focus on DL-based feature learning for images.

8.3.2 Feature extraction

Many cameras allow you to review a picture as soon as it's taken. Some also provide information about the amount of color contained in the picture for each of the three RGB channels (red, green, blue). Let's take as an example a picture of a butterfly, shown in figure 8.8. The camera used to take that picture provides its color histogram, shown in figure 8.9.

Figure 8.8   A picture of a butterfly

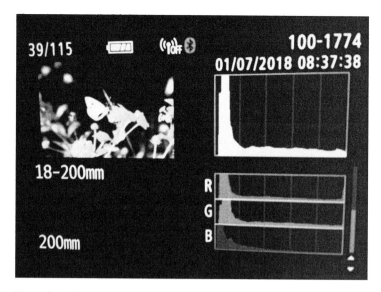

Figure 8.9   Color histogram for the butterfly picture

A color histogram is a representation of the distribution of the three color channels' possible values (for example, from 0 to 255) among the pixels. For example, if a certain pixel has a red channel value of 4 and another pixel has the same value, the color histogram for the red channel for that image will have a size of 2 for the value 4 (two pixels have a red channel value of 4). This process, applied to all the channels and pixels in a certain image, produces three red, green, and blue graphs like those shown in figure 8.9. The color histogram is an example of a very simple, intuitive global feature that can be used to describe an image. We'll look next at global and local feature extractors.

GLOBAL FEATURES

Instead of indexing images by manually tagging them with captions or descriptions, you can index the image binaries accompanied by their extracted features, as in figure 8.10. To do so, you can use the open source library Lucene Image Retrieval (LIRE, licensed under the GNU GPL 2 license) to extract the color histogram from an image. LIRE provides a lot of useful tools for working with images, which are Lucene friendly. (At the time of writing, it doesn't yet support any DL-based methods to extract image features.) Here's an example:

```
File file = new File(imgPath);        ⟵┐ The image file       Creates a color
                                                                histogram object
SimpleColorHistogram simpleColorHistogram = new SimpleColorHistogram();  ⟵┘

BufferedImage bufferedImage = ImageIO.read(file);  ⟵┐ Reads the image
                                                      from the file
simpleColorHistogram.extract(bufferedImage);

    double[] features = simpleColorHistogram.getFeatureVector();  ⟵┐

Extracts the color histogram                    Extracts the color histogram
from the image                                  feature vectors as a double array
```

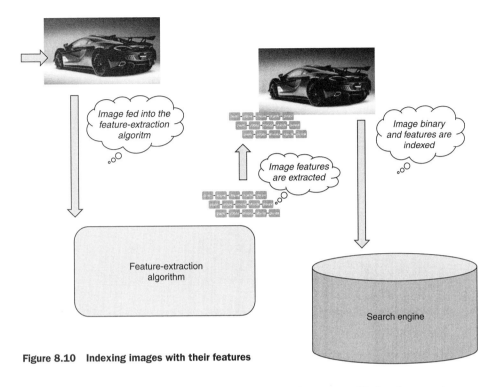

Figure 8.10 Indexing images with their features

Such a global representation of images has the advantage of being human interpretable and usually efficient in terms of performance. But if you think for a moment of the fact that the color histogram image representation is bound to the color distribution over the image (disregarding position), it's not hard to realize that two different images with the same subject (such as a butterfly) may have very different color distributions. Consider the butterfly image shown earlier, in figure 8.8, and another image of a butterfly, shown in figure 8.11.

Although the butterfly is the primary subject in both images, they have different color schemes: as you can see in electronic versions of this book, in figure 8.8, the main colors are yellow and green; whereas in figure 8.11, the main colors are red, blue, and yellow. Comparisons of images based on histograms are mostly based on color distributions. The images' histograms look very different (see figure 8.12), so the images won't be considered similar by the search engine. Remember at this point that you aren't running a search yet—you're analyzing the histogram feature and trying to understand what kind of information it can give you.

The color histogram scheme is just one of many possible ways to extract global features, but in general they suffer from the problem that it's difficult to capture image details. For example, the first butterfly image doesn't just contain a butterfly: there are also flowers and leaves. Such entities aren't captured by the color histogram; roughly speaking, such histograms tell you, "There's a certain amount of light green, another

Figure 8.11   **Another picture of a butterfly**

Figure 8.12   **Comparing histograms of two butterfly images**

amount of yellow, a small portion of white, some black, and so on." One situation where global features can work well is duplicate image detection, where the searcher is looking for an image very similar to, if not exactly the same as, the one at hand.

One detail that would help immensely is distinguishing background regions of a photo from the central image. We'd like the representations of the two butterfly images to somehow understand that the regions containing the butterfly are more important than the background portions.

LOCAL FEATURES

In contrast to global features, local features can more accurately capture details of portions of images. So if you want to make a program detect potentially interesting objects (for example, a butterfly) in an image, a common approach is to start by splitting that image into smaller cells, and then look in those cells for relevant shapes or objects. Let's see how this works in figure 8.13, using the same butterfly picture, but now split into smaller cells.

Figure 8.13 Splitting an image into smaller cells

Once the image is split into smaller parts (such as squares), the task of extracting local features consists of two steps:

1 Find interesting points (rather than objects).
2 Encode interesting points with respect to the local region into a descriptor that can be used later to match interesting regions.

But what does *interesting* mean in this context? You're looking for points that delimit or center regions of the image that contain objects. The final goal is still to have a way to find objects and represent them using features that are comparable. Given two images containing butterflies, you want features that carry this information in both. Each image is usually represented as a feature vector—a number of features—so that if you compute the distance (for example, the cosine distance) between image feature vectors, images containing the same or similar objects should be close (have a low distance value).

Typical kinds of local features include human-understandable visual features like edges and corners. But in practice, local feature–extraction techniques like *scale-invariant feature transform* (SIFT) and *speeded-up robust features* (SURF) are used.

SIFT

Finding edges is a relatively simple task that can be solved using mathematical tools like Fourier, Laplace, or Gabor transforms; the SIFT and SURF algorithms are more complex but also more powerful. With SIFT, for example, it's possible to recognize important regions in an image so that an object and a rotated version of the same object produce the same or similar local features. This means that with SIFT-based features, images that contain the same rotated objects can be recognized as similar.

We won't dive into the details of SIFT, because that's not part of the focus of this book; but briefly, it uses a *filter* called *Laplacian of Gaussian* to recognize interesting points in an image. You can think of a filter as a mask applied to the image. A Laplacian of Gaussian filter produces an image where edges and other key points are highlighted, and most other points are no longer visible. The filter is applied to a preprocessed version of the image, so the resulting image is represented in a scale-invariant manner. After the application of such a filter, the interesting points are made orientation invariant by recording the orientation of each interesting point, so each time it's compared with other points, the orientation component is integrated in each calculation or comparison operation. Finally, all the found local features are encoded in a single comparable descriptor/feature vector.

Local features are representations of portions of an image. A single image is associated with several local features. But you need a single representation of an image so that:

- The final image representation contains information about all the interesting local points.
- Efficient comparison can be performed at query time (one feature vector versus many feature vectors).

To do that, local features need to be aggregated into a single representation (the feature vector). A common approach is to aggregate local features using the *bag-of-visual-words* (BOVW) model. You may recall the bag-of-words model from earlier in the book: in such a model, a document is represented as a vector whose size is equal to the number of words in all the existing documents. Each position in the vector is tied to a certain word: if the value is 1 (or any value larger than zero: for example, calculated using term frequency–inverse document frequency [TF-IDF]), then the related document contains that word; otherwise, the value is 0.

Recall the sample bag-of-words representations for some documents in chapter 5, shown in table 8.1.

Table 8.1 Bag-of-words representations

Terms	bernhard	bio	dive	hypothesis	in	influence	into	life	mathematical	riemann
doc1	1.28	0.0	0.0	0.0	0.0	0.0	0.0	1.0	0.0	1.28
doc2	1.0	1.0	0.0	0.0	1.0	1.0	0.0	0.0	0.0	0.0

In the BOVW model, each value of the vector is greater than zero if the image has the local feature corresponding to that position. So instead of the word "bernhard" or "bio" in the text case, the BOVW model will have "local-feature1," "local-feature2," and so on. Each image is represented according the same principle, but using clustered local features instead of words; see table 8.2.

Table 8.2 Bag-of-visual-words representations

Features	local-feature1	local-feature2	local-feature3	local-feature4	local-feature5
image1	0.3	0.0	0.0	0.4	0.0
image2	0.5	0.7	0.0	0.8	1.0

Using local feature extractors, like SIFT, each image comes with a number of descriptors that may vary depending on image quality, image size, and other factors.

The BOVW model involves an additional preprocessing step to identify a fixed number of local features. Let's assume that for a dataset of images, SIFT extracts local features for each image, but some have tens and others hundreds of features. To create a shared vocabulary of local features, all the local features are collected together, and a clustering algorithm such as k-means is performed over them to extract n centroids. The centroids are the words for the BOVW model.

If you look at a clear sky on a dark night, you'll see many different stars. Each star can be considered a cluster point: a local feature. Now imagine that the brightest stars in the sky have more stars near them (in reality, the brightness of a star depends on distance, size, age, radioactivity, and other factors). Under those conditions, the brightest stars are the cluster centroids; you can use them to represent all the points with some approximation. So instead of billions of stars (local features), you consider only tens or hundreds of stars: the circled centroids. That's what clustering algorithms do (see figure 8.14).

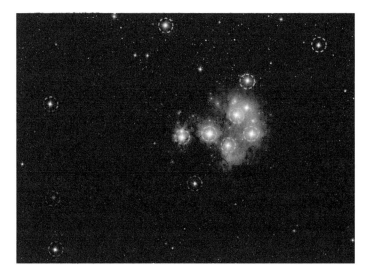

Figure 8.14   Stars, clusters, and centroids

It's now possible to use LIRE to create image feature vectors using a BOVW model. First, you extract local features with SIFT and generate a vocabulary of visual words using a clustering algorithm like k-means:

```
for (String imgPath : imgPaths) {    ⟵— Iterates over all the images
    File file = new File(imgPath);
    SiftExtractor siftExtractor = new
        SiftExtractor();    ⟵············
    BufferedImage bufferedImage = ImageIO
        .read(file);
    siftExtractor.extract(bufferedImage);    ⟵·········
    List<LocalFeature> localFeatures = siftExtractor
        .getFeatures();
    for (LocalFeature lf : localFeatures) {
        kMeans.addFeature(lf.getFeatureVector());    ⟵····
    }
}
for (int k = 0; k < 15; k++) {
    kMeans.clusteringStep();
}
Cluster[] clusters = kMeans.getClusters();    ⟵— Extracts the generated clusters
```

Creates a local feature extractor based on the SIFT algorithm

Reads the image contents

Performs the SIFT algorithm on the given image

Extracts all the SIFT local features

Adds all the SIFT features for the current image as points for clustering

Performs k-means clustering for a predefined number of steps

This code computes all the visual words as a fixed number of clusters. With the visual vocabulary in place, the local features of each image are compared with the cluster centroids to calculate the final value of each visual word. This task is performed by the

BOVW model, which calculates the Euclidean distance between SIFT features and cluster centroids:

```
for (String imgPath : imgPaths) {    ⟵──── Iterates again over all the images
    File file = new File(imgPath);
    SiftExtractor siftExtractor = new SiftExtractor();
    BufferedImage bufferedImage = ImageIO.read(file);
    siftExtractor.extract(bufferedImage);
    List<LocalFeature> localFeatures = siftExtractor
        .getFeatures();    ⟵────────────────────────
    BOVW bovw = new BOVW();
    bovw.createVectorRepresentation(localFeatures
        , clusters);    ⟵──
    double[] featureVector = bovw
        .getVectorRepresentation();    ⟵──
}
```

Creates a BOVW instance ──▷

Extracts the SIFT local features again. SIFT features can be temporarily cached per image in a map to avoid computing them twice.

Computes a single vector representation for the current image, given local SIFT features and centroids

Extracts feature vectors

This code gives a single feature-vector representation for each image that you can use in image searches.

In the examples, global feature extraction uses a simple color histogram extractor, and local feature extraction uses SIFT in conjunction with BOVW. These are just some of several algorithms that can be used to perform explicit feature extraction. For example, for global feature extraction, alternatives include the fuzzy-color approach, which is a bit more flexible. For local feature extraction, SURF (mentioned earlier) is a variant of SIFT that's more robust and usually better in terms of speed.

The main advantage of the color histogram feature extractor is its simplicity and intuitiveness; the main advantage of SIFT, SURF, and other local feature extractors is that they perform well for identifying objects in smaller portions of an image in a scale- and rotation-invariant way. In practice, a production system needs an approach that gives the best guarantees in terms of accuracy, speed, engineering effort, and maintenance required to make the entire system work. Once you have a feature vector of a fixed dimension representing an image, the indexing and search strategies make the most difference in terms of speed, as you'll see later in this chapter. Regarding engineering effort, maintenance, and accuracy, the global and local feature extractors discussed so far have been overtaken by DL architectures. The central point is that features aren't manually extracted but rather are learned through a deep neural network.

In the next section, you'll see how that makes feature extraction a straightforward end-to-end learning process, from pixels to feature vectors. Such DL-generated features are also typically better in terms of a semantic understanding of visual objects.

8.4 Deep learning for image representation

So far in this chapter, we've extracted features from images. Learning representations of data is what has made DL so successful in recent years. Computer vision was the first field where DL outperformed previous state-of-the-art approaches; in computer vision, computers are tasked with recognizing objects in images or videos. This can be used in a variety of applications, from retina scans, to identify driving violations (such as identifying vehicles overtaking where it's not permitted), optical character recognition, and so on. The technology's success is driving DL researchers and engineers to work on increasingly difficult tasks such as, for example, driverless cars.

Some famous results of DL applied to images include LeNet (http://yann .lecun.com/exdb/lenet), a neural network that can recognize handwritten and machine-printed digits; and AlexNet (http://mng.bz/6j4y), a neural network that can recognize objects in an image. AlexNet is particularly interesting for the image search scenario, because it was able to categorize (assign a category to) a certain image among 1,000 different very fine-grained categories. For example, it can differentiate between very similar dogs of different canine breeds, as shown in figure 8.15.

EntleBucher   Appenzeller

Figure 8.15   Image of dogs classified by AlexNet

Both LeNet and AlexNet use a special kind of feed-forward (artificial) neural network called a *convolutional neural network* (CNN or ConvNet). In recent years, CNNs have been applied not just to images and videos but also to sound and text; they're very flexible and can be used for a variety of tasks.

At the beginning of this chapter, I mentioned that you can use DL to find increasingly abstract structures in images. Researchers have discovered that this is what CNNs do during the training phase. As the number of layers grows, layers closer to the input learn raw features like edges and corners, while layers placed toward the end of the deep neural network learn features that represent shapes and objects. Going forward, you'll learn the architecture of CNNs, how to train them and set them up, and finally, how to extract features for image search (as in figure 8.16).

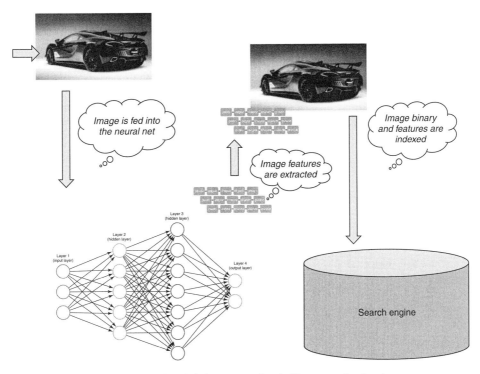

Figure 8.16 Indexing images with their features, extracted by a neural network

8.4.1 *Convolutional neural networks*

Despite their names, the connection between artificial neural networks and how the human brain works isn't obvious. Most common neural network architectures have a fixed architecture: often neurons are fully connected, whereas the neurons in the brain don't have such fixed (and simple) structures. CNNs were originally inspired by how the visual cortex in the human brain works: dedicated cells take care of certain portions of the image, passing the information to other cells that elaborate the information in a flow similar to the one you're going to see for a CNN. A fundamental difference in how CNNs work with respect to other types of neural networks is that they don't handle *flat signal* inputs (for example, dense, one-hot-encoded vectors).

When we looked at creating a color histogram for an image, I mentioned that images are commonly represented using RGB: a single pixel is described by three different values for the red, green, and blue channels. If you extend that to an entire image, with many different pixels, you'll have a representation for an image of width X and height Y consisting of three different matrixes for each of the three RGB components, each with Y rows and X columns. For example, an image 3×3 pixels in size would have 3 matrixes with 9 values each. An RGB code of R:31, G:39, and B:201 would generate the color shown in figure 8.17 (visible in the e-book).

If you imagine such a value placed in the first element of the second row of the 3×3 image, the RGB matrixes might look as shown in tables 8.3–8.5 (the bold values represent the pixel in figure 8.17).

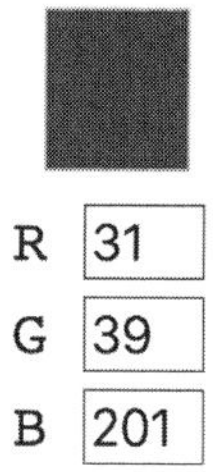

R 31

G 39

B 201

Figure 8.17
Sample RGB pixel value

Table 8.3   Red channel

0	4	0
31	8	3
1	12	39

Table 8.4   Blue channel

10	40	31
39	0	0
87	101	18

Table 8.5   Green channel

37	46	1
201	8	53
0	0	10

Instead of a single matrix of words or character vectors, a neural network needs to handle three matrixes for each input image, one per color channel. This poses severe performance issues when you're handling images with conventional feed-forward, fully connected neural networks. Very small images of size 100×100 would need $100 * 100 * 3 = 30,000$ learnable weights just for the first layer. With a medium-sized image (1024×768), the first layer would need more than 2,000,000 parameters ($1024 * 768 * 3 = 2,359,296$)!

CNNs solve the problem of handling by training over large inputs, adopting a lightweight design in layers and neuron connections. Fewer connections means fewer weights to be learned by the network. And fewer weights makes learning less computationally complex and also faster. Not all neurons in this type of layer are always connected to neurons in the preceding layer; such neurons have a *receptive field* of a certain configurable size that defines the local region of the input matrixes they're

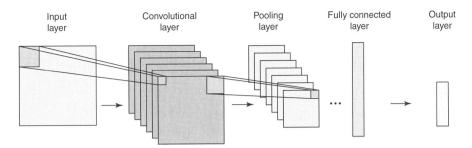

Figure 8.18 Building blocks (and flow) of CNNs

connected to. Therefore, some neurons aren't connected to the entire input region and hence don't have an attached weight. Such layers called *convolutional layers* and are the main building block of CNNs (together with *pooling layers*; see figure 8.18).

Back when I briefly introduced the SIFT feature extractor, I mentioned the Laplacian of Gaussian (LoG) filter, which identifies the interesting points in an image. Convolutional layers have that same responsibility; but in contrast with the LoG filter, which is fixed, convolutional filters are *learned* during the network training phase to best adapt to the images in the training set (see figure 8.19).

Convolutional layers have a configurable depth (4, in figure 8.19), a number of filters, and some other configuration hyperparameters. The layer's filters contain the parameters (weights) that are learned by the network via backpropagation during training. You can think of each filter as a small window over the entire image that

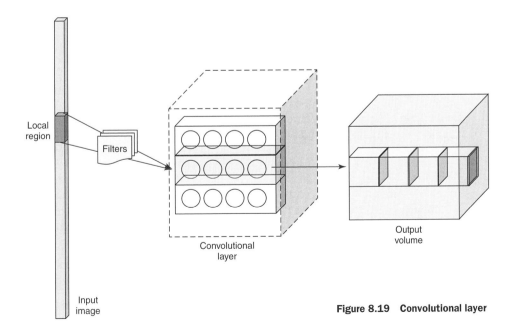

Figure 8.19 Convolutional layer

changes the input pixels it's currently "seeing"; the filter is slid over the entire image so that it's applied to all of the input values. This sliding filtering is the convolution operation that gives the name to this type of layer (and to the network).

A 5×5 filter has 25 weights, so it sees 25 pixels at a time. Mathematically speaking, the filter computes the dot product between the 25 values of the pixels and the 25 weights of the filter. Suppose a convolutional layer receives a $100 \times 100 \times 3$ input image (also called an *input volume* because it has 3 dimensions). If the layer has 10 filters, the output is a volume of $100 \times 100 \times 10$ values. The 10 generated 100×100 matrixes (1 for each filter) are called *activation maps*.

When the filter slides over the input values, it moves one value/pixel at a time. But sometimes, the filter can slide two or three values at a time (for example, on the width axis) to reduce the number of generated outputs. This parameter for the move size is generally called `stride`. Sliding one value at a time is `stride = 1`, sliding by two values means `stride = 2`, and so on.

CNNs also reduce the computational burden of training with large input volumes by adopting a way to control the number of weights to be learned. Imagine all the neurons in figure 8.19 having a certain depth (for example, `depth = 2`). Then they will share the same weights. This technique is called *parameter sharing*.

In the end, the primary differences between convolutional layers and normal fully connected neural network layers is that convolutional neurons are only connected to a local region of the input, and some neurons in a convolutional layer share parameters.

POOLING LAYERS

A pooling layer's responsibility is to downsample the input volume: it reduces the input size while trying to maintain the most important information. This has the advantage of reducing the computational complexity and the number of parameters to be learned for successive layers (for example, other convolutional layers). Pooling layers aren't associated with weights to be learned; they look at portions of the input volume and extract one or more values, depending on the chosen function. Common functions are `max` and `average`.

Like convolutional layers, pooling layers have a configurable receptive field size and `stride`. For example, a pooling layer with a receptive field size of 2 and `stride` of 2 with a `max` function will take four values from the input volume and output the maximum value from those input values.

CNN TRAINING

You've learned about the main building blocks of CNNs. Let's stack them together to create an actual CNN and see how such a network is trained. Remember that the main goal is to extract feature vectors that capture the notion of semantically similar images.

A typical CNN architecture usually involves at least one (or more) convolutional layers, followed by

- A dense, fully connected layer to hold the feature vectors for the images
- An output layer containing class scores for each of the classes an image can be tagged with

A CNN is usually trained in a supervised way using training examples whose input is an image and whose expected outputs are a set of classes the image belongs to.

Let's look at a known dataset that has been used a lot in computer vision research. The CIFAR dataset (www.cs.toronto.edu/~kriz/cifar.html) contains thousands of images labeled with 10 categories (see figure 8.20). Images from the CIFAR dataset are color images, each of which is 32×32 pixels (very small). The first layer will therefore receive inputs of $32 * 32 * 3 = 3{,}072$ values.

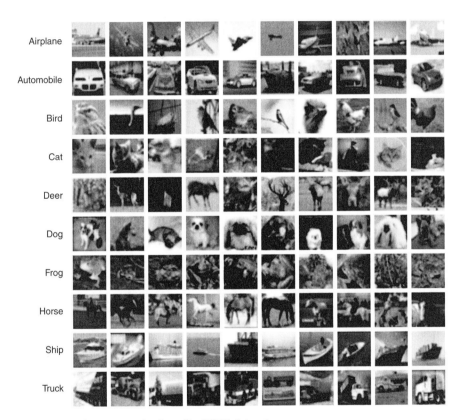

Figure 8.20 Some examples from the CIFAR dataset

Let's create a simple CNN with two convolution + pooling layers, one dense layer, and the output layer; see figure 8.21. You expect the network to produce an evaluation of the likelihood that the input image belongs to any of the 10 categories; figure 8.22 shows some example output (the image was generated using the ConvNetJS CIFAR-10 demo at https://cs.stanford.edu/people/karpathy/convnetjs/demo/cifar10.html).

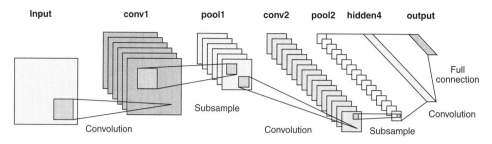

Figure 8.21   A simple CNN with two convolution + pooling layers

Figure 8.22   Testing a CNN on the CIFAR dataset

As you can see, during CNN training, no feature engineering has to be performed; the feature vectors can be drained from the final dense layer, end to end. You "just" need lots of images with labels!

This architecture is a simple example of a CNN. Many things can be changed in the fundamental design and in the many hyperparameters. For example, adding more convolutional layers has been shown to improve accuracy. The size of the receptive field and the depth of convolutional layers or pooling operations (max, average, and so on) are all powerful aspects that can be tweaked to improve accuracy.

SETTING UP A CNN IN DL4J

The CNN from the previous section can easily be implemented in Deeplearning4j. DL4J comes with a utility class to iterate and train over the CIFAR dataset, so let's use that to train the CNN.

Listing 8.1   Setting up a CNN for CIFAR in DL4J

```
int height = 32;    ⬅── Height of input images

int width = 32;     ⬅── Width of input images

int channels = 3;   ⬅── Number of image channels to be used

int numSamples = 50000;    ⬅──┐  Number of training examples to
                               │  drain from the CIFAR dataset
int batchSize = 100;    ──────┘
```

Size of the mini-batch

```
int epochs = 10;  ⟵── Number of epochs to train the network

MultiLayerNetwork model = getSimpleCifarCNN();  ⟵
CifarDataSetIterator dsi = new CifarDataSetIterator(        Sets up the network
    batchSize, numSamples, new int[] {height, width,       architecture
    channels}, false, true);  ⟵
                              Creates an iterator over
for (int i = 0; i < epochs; ++i) {    the CIFAR dataset
  model.fit(dsi);  ⟵───────────────────────── Trains the network
}
cf.saveModel(model, "simpleCifarModel.json");  ⟵── Saves the model for later use
```

The model architecture is defined by the `getSimpleCifarCNN` method, which is shown next and in figure 8.23.

Listing 8.2 Configuring the CNN

```
public MultiLayerNetwork getSimpleCifarCNN() {
  MultiLayerConfiguration conf = new NeuralNetConfiguration.Builder()
      .list()
      .layer(0, new ConvolutionLayer.Builder(
          new int[]{4, 4}, new int[]{1, 1},
          new int[]{0, 0}).name("cnn1")
        ⟶ .convolutionMode(ConvolutionMode.Same)
          .nIn(3).nOut(64).weightInit(WeightInit.XAVIER_UNIFORM).activation(
            Activation.RELU)
      .layer(1, new SubsamplingLayer.Builder(
          PoolingType.MAX, new int[]{2,2})
          .name("maxpool1").build())  ⟵── First pooling layer

      .layer(2, new ConvolutionLayer.Builder(
          new int[]{4,4}, new int[] {1,1},
          new int[]{0,0}).name("cnn2")
        ⟶ .convolutionMode(ConvolutionMode.Same)
          .nOut(96).weightInit(WeightInit.XAVIER_UNIFORM)
          .activation(Activation.RELU).build())
      .layer(3, new SubsamplingLayer.Builder(
          PoolingType.MAX, new int[]{2,2}).name(
          "maxpool2").build())  ⟵─────────── Second pooling layer

      .layer(4, new DenseLayer.Builder().name(
          "ffn1").nOut(1024).build())  ⟵
                                          Dense layer (the one
      .layer(5, new OutputLayer.Builder(LossFunctions    from which you'll
        ⟶ .LossFunction.NEGATIVELOGLIKELIHOOD)           extract features)
```

First convolution layer *(label for layer 0)*

Second convolution layer *(label for layer 2)*

Output layer *(label for layer 5)*

```
    .name("output").nOut(numLabels).activation(Activation.SOFTMAX).build())
      .backprop(true).pretrain(false)
      .setInputType(InputType.convolutional(height, width, channels))
      .build();

  MultiLayerNetwork model = new MultiLayerNetwork(conf);
  model.init();
  return model;
}
```

Once the CNN has finished training, you're ready to use the network outputs.

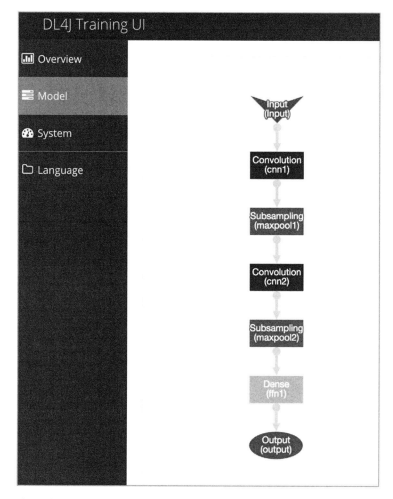

Figure 8.23 Resulting model from the DL4J UI

Think back to the color histogram or BOVW models—you obtained a feature vector for each image. A CNN gives you more than that: the dense layer close to the output layer contains the feature vectors you can use to compare images, and you also have a trained CNN that you can use to tag new images.

After training has finished, if you want to index the feature vectors learned for each image by the convolutional neural network, you have to iterate again over the image dataset, perform a feed-forward computation for each image, and extract the feature vectors generated by the CNN.

Listing 8.3 Extracting feature vectors

Obtains the iterator over the images to be processed

```
DataSetIterator iterator = ...
while (iterator.hasNext()) {      ⟵──── Iterates over the dataset

    DataSet batch = iterator.next(batchSize);  ⟵──── Iterates over each batch
    for (int k = 0; k < batchSize; k++) {

        DataSet dataSet = batch.get(k);  ⟵───┐
                                             │  Iterates over each image
                                             │  from the current batch
        List<INDArray> activations = model.
            feedForward(dataSet.getFeatureMatrix(),
            false);       ⟵──────────────┐
                                         │  Performs a feed-forward pass,
                                         │  without training, with the
        INDArray imageRepresentation = activations │  current image (pixels as input)
            .get(activations.size() - 2);  ⟵───┐
                                               │  Extracts the image representation
                                               │  stored in the dense layer before the
        INDArray classification = activations.get(  │  final output layer
            activations.size() - 1);  ⟵───┐
        ...   ⟵──┐                         │  Extracts the classification
    }            │  Processes (stores) the image │  scores for the current image
}                │  feature-vector representation
```

You're now ready to learn how you can efficiently index and search the feature vectors extracted by a CNN (although this applies generally for any feature vector).

8.4.2 Image search

Let's return to the example from the beginning of the chapter: given a picture taken with your smartphone camera, you want to find a professional picture to use as a card with a gift. You need to do the following:

1 Feed the input image to the CNN.
2 Extract the generated feature vectors.
3 Use the feature vectors to make a query to find similar images in the search engine.

You saw how to perform the first two steps in the previous section. In this section, you'll learn how to perform the query efficiently.

An obvious way to perform the query would be to perform a comparison between the input-image feature vectors and the feature vectors of all the images stored in the search engine. Imagine extracting the feature vectors from a CNN like the one in the previous section, and putting them on a graph: the points represent similar images that are close to one another. This is the same line of thought we applied to word and document embeddings. So you can compute the distance between the feature vector from the input image and the feature vectors of all the other images and, for example, return the top 10 images that have the least-distant feature vectors. From a computational perspective, this approach won't scale, because the time taken to perform a query grows linearly with the number of images in the search engine. In real life, such nearest-neighbor algorithms are often approximated: they perform better, but at the cost of accuracy. Such an approximated nearest-neighbor search algorithm may not return the exact closest items with respect to the input image, but it will still return close neighbors, much more quickly.

In Lucene, you can use the (experimental) `FloatPointNearestNeighbor` class, which provides an approximate nearest-neighbor function, or implement an approximate nearest-neighbor search using *locality-sensitive hashing* (LSH). `FloatPointNearest-Neighbor` is more expensive at search time, with no additional space footprint on the index; LSH increases the size of the index, because it requires you to store more than just the feature vectors, but it's faster at search time. We'll start by using the `Float-PointNearestNeighbor` class, and then look at LSH.

USING FLOATPOINTNEARESTNEIGHBOR

To use `FloatPointNearestNeighbor`, you need to extract the CNN feature vectors and index them in Lucene as points. Recent Lucene versions have support for *n*-dimensional points (another way to see a vector) based on the *k*-d tree algorithm (https://en .wikipedia.org/wiki/K-d_tree). So the feature vector you extract from the CNN is indexed using a dedicated field type called `FloatPoint`.

Listing 8.4   Indexing a feature vector as a point

```
List<INDArray> activations = cnnModel.feedForward(currentImage, false);
INDArray imageRepresentation = activations
    .get(activations.size() - 2);      ⊲──────────────────── Obtains the feature vector
float[] aFloat = imageRepresentation.data()                 generated by the CNN
    ⊳ .asFloat();
doc.add(new FloatPoint("features", floats));  ⊲───────── Indexes the feature vector
                                                          as a Lucene FloatPoint
Converts it to a float array
```

Unfortunately, as of Lucene 7, `FloatPoints` can index points whose dimension is at most 8. Feature vectors are usually much bigger than that: for example, our example CNN for CIFAR generates feature vectors whose dimension is 1,024. You'll need to reduce the `float[]` used to instantiate `FloatPoint` from having 1,024 values to holding at most 8.

You can try to reduce the number of dimensions in vectors while retaining the most important information; this technique is also called *dimensionality reduction*. There are various dimensionality reduction algorithms, and we'll look at one that you can also reuse in other scenarios.

A common dimensionality reduction algorithm is *principal component analysis* (PCA). As the name suggests, PCA identifies the most important features from a feature-vector set and throws away the others. The feature vectors extracted from the CNNs have 1,024 values each. You want to use PCA to merge each feature vector's 1,024 values into at most 8 different values. With PCA, you transform a point/vector on a graph that has 1,024 coordinates into a point/vector on a graph that has 8 coordinates.

Intuitively, a PCA algorithm goes through the values of each feature in each vector to find the features whose values differ the most (have the highest variance). Such features are considered the most important. PCA doesn't discard the others; rather, it builds new features from them, to avoid losing information. The features with the highest variance have more weight when building out the new features. PCA will combine the 1,024-sized feature vectors extracted from the CNN into 8 new features, so that you can index each feature vector as a Lucene point.

PCA can be implemented in several ways; because you're dealing with vectors, you could stack them together in a big matrix and use matrix factorization algorithms, such as non-negative matrix factorization, truncated singular value decomposition, and others. For the sake of feature-vector indexing, we won't go into details about how such PCA algorithms work, because they're out of the scope of this book. DL4J provides tools to implement PCA, so we'll use them instead.

CIFAR has about 50,000 images of 1,024 dimensions each, so you have a huge matrix with 50,000 rows (the number of feature vectors) and 1,024 columns (the feature vectors dimension). You want to reduce that to a $50,000 \times 8$ matrix.

Listing 8.5 Building the image feature-vectors matrix

```
CifarDataSetIterator iterator ...
INDArray weights = Nd4j.zeros(50000, 1024);      ◁─── Creates the weights matrix
while (iterator.hasNext()) {
  DataSet batch = iterator.next(batchSize);      ◁──────┐ Iterates over the
  for (int k = 0; k < batchSize; k++) {                 │ entire (CIFAR) dataset
    DataSet dataSet = batch.get(k);
    List<INDArray> activations = model
        .feedForward(dataSet.getFeatureMatrix(),
        false);         ◁····························· Performs feed-forward on the CNN
    INDArray imageRepresentation = activations
        .get(activations.size() - 2);       ◁──────┐ Extracts feature
    float[] aFloat = imageRepresentation.data().asFloat();  │ vectors from the
    weights.putRow(idx, Nd4j.create(aFloat));   ◁────┘ dense layer
  }
}                                              Stores the feature vectors
                                               in the weights matrix
```

With the entire feature-vectors matrix built, you can run PCA and obtain vectors that are small enough to be indexed as `FloatPoints` in Lucene. Note that because this matrix is so big, it may take a while (for example, several minutes on a modern laptop) for PCA to complete.

Listing 8.6 Reducing the vector dimensions to 8

```
int d = 8;         ◁───────────────────── Target-vector size
INDArray reduced = PCA.pca(weights, d, true);   ◁──────┐ Performs PCA on the
                                                        │ weights matrix
```

Although this should work well, you can generate smaller feature vectors of better quality by borrowing a technique for compressing word embeddings from the paper

"Simple and Effective Dimensionality Reduction for Word Embeddings"[2] and use it for image vectors, too. This technique is based on the combination of PCA and a postprocessing algorithm to highlight which features of an embedding are "stronger" than the others. The postprocessing algorithm for stronger embeddings is described in the paper "All-but-the-Top: Simple and Effective Postprocessing for Word Representations."[3] You can implement the postprocessing in DL4J as follows.

Listing 8.7   Postprocessing for stronger embeddings

Removes the mean values from each embedding in the weights matrix

Performs PCA on the resulting weights matrix

```
private INDArray postProcess(INDArray weights, int d) {
    INDArray meanWeights = weights.sub(weights.meanNumber());
    INDArray pca = PCA.pca(meanWeights, d, true);
    for (int j = 0; j < weights.rows(); j++) {
        INDArray v = meanWeights.getRow(j);
        for (int s = 0; s < d; s++) {
            INDArray u = pca.getColumn(s);
            INDArray mul = u.mmul(v).transpose().mmul(u);
            v.subi(mul.transpose());
        }
    }
    return weights;
}
```

Emphasizes each vector's specific values

Subtracts the principal component values for each vector

Returns the modified weights matrix

The entire algorithm for this modified version of dimensionality reduction for embeddings performs postprocessing on the weights matrix, followed by PCA, and again followed by postprocessing on the reduced weights matrix.

Listing 8.8   Dimensionality reduction with postprocessing of embeddings

```
int d = 8;
INDArray x = postProcess(weights, d);

INDArray pcaX = PCA.pca(x, d, true);

INDArray reduced = postProcess(pcaX, d);
```

Postprocesses the original feature-vector values

Performs PCA to obtain eight-dimensional feature vectors

Postprocesses the reduced feature-vector values

You can now iterate over the weights matrix and index each row as a `FloatPoint` in Lucene.

Listing 8.9   Indexing feature vectors

```
IndexWriter writer = new IndexWriter(directory, config);

for (int k = 0; k < reduced.rows(); k++) {
    Document doc = new Document();
```

Creates an IndexWriter

Iterates over the rows of the reduced weights matrix

---

[2]   By Vikas Raunak, https://arxiv.org/abs/1708.03629.
[3]   By Jiaqi Mu, Suma Bhat, and Pramod Viswanath, https://arxiv.org/abs/1702.01417.

```
    doc.add(new FloatPoint("features", reduced.getRow(k)
    .toFloatVector()));   ◁
```
Indexes the vector as a FloatPoint

```
    doc.add(new TextField("label", ..., Field.Store.YES));   ◁
```
Indexes the label related to the current vector

```
    writer.addDocument(doc);   ◁── Indexes the document
}
writer.commit();   ◁── Commits changes
```

Now that you have images indexed by means of their feature vectors, you can query by an example image and find the most similar images in the search engine. So, to run some tests, you get a random indexed image, extract its feature vectors, and then perform a search using the `FloatPointNearestNeighbor` class.

Listing 8.10 Nearest-neighbor search

Gets the document associated with the randomly generated ID

Extracts the input-image features, and performs a nearest-neighbor search returning the top three results

```
int rowId = random.nextInt(reader.numDocs());
Document document = reader.document(rowId);   ◁
TopFieldDocs docs = FloatPointNearestNeighbor.nearest(searcher,
    "features", 3, reduced.getRow(rowId).toFloatVector());   ◁
ScoreDoc[] scoreDocs = docs.scoreDocs;
System.out.println("query image of a : " + document.get("label"));
for (ScoreDoc sd : scoreDocs) {   ◁────────────── Iterates over the search results
    System.out.println("-->" + sd.doc + " : " +
    reader.document(sd.doc).getField("label").stringValue());
}
```

For example, you expect the nearest neighbors of images of dogs to be labeled as dogs as well. Here's some sample output:

```
query image of a : dog
--> 67 : dog
--> 644 : dog
--> 101 : cat

query image of a : automobile
--> 2 : automobile
--> 578 : automobile
--> 311 : truck

query image of a : deer
--> 124 : deer
--> 713 : dog
--> 838 : deer

query image of a : airplane
--> 412 : airplane
--> 370 : airplane
--> 239 : ship

query image of a : cat
--> 16 : cat
--> 854 : cat
--> 71 : cat
```

You've completed the flow from extracting features, to indexing, and finally to searching through images. I mentioned that you can improve the search performance by adopting an algorithm called *locality-sensitive hashing*; the next section introduces it and looks at one possible implementation in Lucene.

8.4.3   *Locality-sensitive hashing*

The simplest possible implementation of a *k*-nearest-neighbor algorithm goes through all the existing images in the search engine and compares the input-image feature vector with each indexed-image feature vector, keeping the *k*-closest ones only. Those are the input-nearest neighbors—the search results. This is what we implemented in the previous section.

Recall the earlier example of stars and clustering: if you plot the image feature vectors on a graph and apply a clustering algorithm, you obtain clusters and centroids. Each image belongs to a cluster, and each cluster has a centroid, which is the center of the cluster. Instead of comparing the input-image feature vectors to all the vectors from all the images, you can compare them against only the centroids' feature vectors. The number of clusters is usually much smaller than the number of points (vectors), so this speeds up the comparison. Once you've found the nearest cluster, you can decide whether to stop and keep all the other vectors belonging to the cluster as nearest neighbors, or perform a second round of nearest-neighbor search against the other feature vectors belonging to the nearest cluster.

This basic idea can be implemented in a number of ways. Of course, you can run a k-means clustering algorithm over the feature vectors, and index the centroids with a special label (for example, adding a dedicated field that only centroids have) so that during search, an initial query is performed to fetch the centroids. With the centroids available, one or two executions of an exact or approximate nearest-neighbor algorithm can be performed (first over the centroids, and then over the nearest cluster points).

One problem with this is a cluster needs to be maintained and kept up to date; as new images are indexed, the cluster and, consequently, the centroids may change. This might require you to have to run the clustering algorithm several times. The same applies to the dimensionality reduction algorithm required to index small vectors.

A lighter-weight but nice approach is to use hash functions and hash tables to find near-duplicates. Hash functions are just one way that deterministic functions can always transform an input into the same output. (It isn't possible to recover the input value from the output value.) The reason to choose hash functions for this task is that they're very good at detecting near-duplicates. When two values produce the same output, they cause a *hash collision*. When a hash function is applied to several different inputs, and you want to quickly retrieve those inputs, they can be collected in a hash table. The nice thing about hash tables is that you can retrieve an item via hashing; rather than you having to look for it by scrolling through all the items, the hash function tells you its position in the hash table.

With LSH, input-image feature vectors are passed through several different hash functions so that similar items map to the same *buckets* (hash tables). Internally, the purpose of LSH is to maximize the probability of a hash collision for two similar items. When an input image is fed to LSH, it passes its feature vectors through several hash functions, and the bucket where the input-image feature vectors end up says what images the input image needs to be compared with. This operation is just as quick as hashing functions, which are usually fast. Additionally, by using special types of hash functions, you can usually map similar inputs into the same buckets.

In Lucene, you implement this approach by creating a dedicated `Analyzer`. The LSH `Analyzer` you're going to build will perform some steps to produce hash values or buckets that are stored in the index, just like plain text. So although you can use `FloatPoint` fields to work with feature vectors as points in the vector space, you can also use Lucene's text capabilities for LSH. You store hash values generated by LSH as plain tokens.

The LSH algorithm will create hashes for portions of a feature vector, as well as for the entire feature vector. This is done to maximize the probability of matching. First you tokenize the feature vector and extract each feature with its position. For example, from the feature vector `<0.1, 0.2, 0.3, 0.4, 0.5>`, you'll obtain the following tokens: 0.1 (position 0), 0.2 (position 1), 0.3 (position 2), 0.4 (position 3), 0.5 (position 4). You can incorporate the position of each token in the token text so that the hash function applied to the token text is calculated based on the position of each token. The entire feature vector is also kept.

Then you'll create ngrams of each individual token: you don't make hashes of the entire vector or single features, but rather of the entire vector and portions of it. For example, the bigram of the feature vector `<0.1, 0.2, 0.3, 0.4, 0.5>` is `0.1_0.2`, `0.2_0.3`, `0.3_0.4`, `0.4_0.5`.

Finally, you'll apply LSH by using Lucene's built-in `MinHash` filter. The `MinHash` filter applies several hash functions to the terms, generating the corresponding hash values.

Listing 8.11 The `LSHAnalyzer` class

```
public class LSHAnalyzer extends Analyzer {                    Tokenizes the features
  ...                                                          of the feature vector
    @Override
    protected TokenStreamComponents createComponents(String fieldName) {
      Tokenizer source = new FeatureVectorsTokenizer();   <─
      TokenFilter featurePos = new FeaturePositionTokenFilter(source);  <─
      ShingleFilter shingleFilter = new ShingleFilter
        (featurePos, min, max);                      Attaches the position
          shingleFilter.setTokenSeparator(" ");    information to each token
      shingleFilter.setOutputUnigrams(false);
      shingleFilter.setOutputUnigramsIfNoShingles(false);
      TokenStream filter = new MinHashFilter(shingleFilter, hashCount,
        bucketCount, hashSetSize, bucketCount > 1);   <─── Applies the LSH filter
      return new TokenStreamComponents(source, filter);
    }
  ...
}
```

Creates feature ngrams *(margin annotation pointing to the ShingleFilter lines)*

To use LSH, you need to use this analyzer (as you've seen in other parts of this book) at both indexing and search time over the field where you index feature vectors. Note that with LSH, you don't need to reduce the feature vectors as you did in the previous section: the feature vectors can be kept as they are (for example, 1,024 values) and passed to LSHAnalyzer, which creates the feature-vector hash values.

As you did before, you configure the LSHAnalyzer to be used for the field that will host the hash values.

Listing 8.12   Configuring `LSHAnalyzer` for the "lsh" field

Creates a map to contain
per-field analyzers

```
Map<String, Analyzer> mappings = new HashMap<>();

mappings.put("lsh", new LSHAnalyzer());

Analyzer perFieldAnalyzer = new PerFieldAnalyzerWrapper(new
    WhitespaceAnalyzer(), mappings);

IndexWriterConfig config = new IndexWriterConfig(perFieldAnalyzer);

IndexWriter writer = new IndexWriter(directory, config);
```

Whenever a Document
has a field named "lsh",
uses LSHAnalyzer

Creates a per-field Analyzer

**Creates the indexing configuration
with the defined Analyzers**

**Creates the IndexWriter to
index Lucene documents**

Once you've set up the indexing configuration, you can proceed to index feature vectors. Assuming you extracted feature vectors for each image in a matrix (for example, called `weights`) where each row has 1,024 columns (the feature values), you can index each row in a field called `lsh` that's processed by LSHAnalyzer.

Listing 8.13   Index feature vectors in an LSH field

Iterates over the images by their labels
(for example, "dog," "deer," "car," and
so on for the CIFAR dataset)

```
int k = 0;
for (String sl : stringLabels) {
  Document doc = new Document();
  float[] fv = weights.getRow(k).toFloatVector();

  String fvString = toString(fv);

  doc.add(new TextField("label", sl, Field.Store.YES));

  doc.add(new TextField("lsh", fvString, Field.Store.YES));

  writer.addDocument(doc);
  k++;
}
writer.commit();
```

Gets the feature
vector from the
weights matrix

Converts the feature-
vector float[] to a String

**Indexes the
current
image label**

Indexes the
current image
feature vector in
the "lsh" field

Indexes the document

Persists changes on disk

To query for similar images using LSH, you retrieve the feature vector of the query image, extract its token hashes, and run a simple text query using those hashes.

Listing 8.14 Querying using `LSHAnalyzer`

Gets the query-image
feature-vector String

Creates the LSHAnalyzer

Gets the token hashes
of the feature vector
using the LSHAnalyzer

```
String fvString = reader.document(docId).get("lsh");

Analyzer analyzer = new LSHAnalyzer();

Collection<String> tokens = getTokens(analyzer, "lsh", fvString);

BooleanQuery.Builder booleanQuery = new BooleanQuery.Builder();

for (String token : tokens) {
    booleanQuery.add(new ConstantScoreQuery(new TermQuery(new Term(
    fieldName, token))), BooleanClause.Occur.SHOULD);
}
Query lshQuery = booleanQuery.build();

TopDocs topDocs = searcher.search(lshQuery, 3);
```

Creates a
Boolean query

For each token hash,
creates a term query
(with a constant score)

Finalizes query creation

Runs the LSH query, and
takes the three top results

With LSH, you can generally get similar candidates faster than you could by querying using a nearest-neighbor search, at the cost of more index space being occupied by the feature-vector terms produced by `LSHAnalyzer`. The speed benefits of LSH are especially clear when the number of images in the index is very large. In addition, reducing the feature-vector dimensions to a small value (such as 8, as in the previous section) can sometimes be very computationally expensive; LSH doesn't require such preprocessing of feature vectors, so it may be a better choice than nearest-neighbor in such scenarios, regardless of the query time.

8.5 Working with unlabeled images

In this section, we'll touch the case where you have a set of unlabeled images and you can't create a training set where each image is tagged with the proper classes (like deer, automobile, ship, track, and so on in the CIFAR dataset).

This can be your own set of images you want to be able to search for. As you've seen in the previous sections, you need to have a vector representation for each image to search for it based on its contents. But if your images don't have labels, you can't generate their feature vectors leveraging the CNN architecture seen in the previous sections.

To overcome this problem, you'll use a type of neural network whose task is to learn to encode the input data, usually with a lower dimensionality than the original one, and then reconstruct that. Such neural networks, called *autoencoders*, are typically built so that one part of the network encodes the input into a vector (also known as *latent representation*) with a fixed size, and then this vector is transformed back again in the original input data, which is also used as the target output. Such autoencoders can be used, for example, to transform an image vector into an eight-dimensional vector to allow indexing it as a Lucene `FloatPoint`. The part of the autoencoder that transforms the input data into another vector with a desired dimensionality (in our case, it may be eight), is called the *encoder*. The part of the network that transforms the latent representation back into the original data is called the *decoder*. Most commonly, the structure of the encoder and the decoder is the same, just mirrored, as you can see in the example of an autoencoder in figure 8.24.

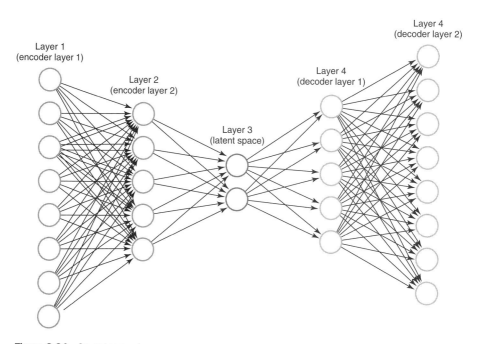

Figure 8.24   An autoencoder

There are many "variations" of autoencoders. For the case of generating a compact latent representation of large image vectors, you'll use a *variational autoencoder* (or VAE). A variational autoencoder generates latent representations that follow a unit Gaussian distribution.

To test the usage of an autoencoder with unlabeled data, you'll still use the CIFAR dataset, but you won't use the classes attached to each image to train the network. You'll instead use them to evaluate whether the search results are good after training has finished. But the important part of this approach is that you'll have a way to generate a dense vector representation, like a feature vector, for your images, even when they're not labeled.

Let's build a VAE in DL4J with a latent representation of size 8 and two hidden layers for both encoder and decoder. The first hidden layer will have 256 neurons, and the second one will have 128 neurons.

Listing 8.15 Variational autoencoder configuration

```
int height = 32;
int width = 32;
int numSamples = 2000;

MultiLayerConfiguration conf = new NeuralNetConfiguration.Builder()
    .list()
    .layer(0, new VariationalAutoencoder.Builder()          ⊲─── Uses the VAE-specific
            .activation(Activation.SOFTSIGN)                         builder class
            .encoderLayerSizes(256, 128)
            .decoderLayerSizes(256, 128)                    ⊲─── Defines each hidden
            .pzxActivationFunction(Activation.IDENTITY)           layer size for the decoder
            .reconstructionDistribution(
                new BernoulliReconstructionDistribution(
                    Activation.SIGMOID.getActivationFunction())))
            .numSamples(numSamples)
            .nIn(height * width)   ⊲─── The size of the input data
            .nOut(8)   ⊲──────────── The size of the latent representation
            .build())
    .pretrain(true).backprop(false).build();

MultiLayerNetwork model = new MultiLayerNetwork(conf);
model.init();
```

Defines each hidden layer size for the encoder → `.encoderLayerSizes(256, 128)`

You want to use the CIFAR images to train the VAE; however, as discussed in previous sections, images are composed of multiple channels. In the case of CIFAR, each image is associated with three matrixes of size 32 × 32. Even if you use one single channel, the autoencoder expects a vector, not a matrix. To fix that, you have to reshape a 32 × 32 matrix into a 1024-sized vector, which can be done by a *reshaping* operation, as shown in the following code. For simplicity, we assume using grayscale CIFAR images, so only one channel instead of three.

Listing 8.16 Reshaping CIFAR images for ingestion in the variational autoencoder

```
int channels = 1;
int batchSize = 128;
CifarDataSetIterator dsi = new CifarDataSetIterator(
    batchSize, numSamples, new int[] {height, width,
    channels}, preProcessCifar, true);   ⊲─── Reads the CIFAR dataset

Collection<DataSet> reshapedData = new
    LinkedList<>();                ⊲─────────┐  Stores the reshaped data
while (dsi.hasNext()) {   ⊲──────────────────┤  into a Collection to be used
  DataSet batch = dsi.next(batchSize);        │  for training the VAE
  for (int k = 0; k < batchSize; k++) {      ⊲─── Iterates through the images
    DataSet current = batch.get(k);
    DataSet dataSet = current.reshape(1, height *
        width);   ⊲────────────────┐
    reshapedData.add(dataSet);   ⊲─┤  Reshapes the image
  }                                   from 32 × 32 to 1
}
dsi.reset();
```

Adds the reshaped image to the Collection

Once images have been reshaped, you can feed them into the VAE for training.

Listing 8.17   Pretraining the variational autoencoder

```
int epochs = 3;
DataSetIterator trainingSet = new
    ListDataSetIterator<>(reshapedData);
model.pretrain(trainingSet, epochs);
```

Converts the Collection into a DL4J DataSetIterator

Trains the VAE for a number of epochs

As soon as training has finished, you can finally index each image latent representation into a Lucene index. For the sake of a simpler evaluation, you can also index the labels of each image into the search engine. This way, you can compare the labels of the query image with the labels of the resulting images.

Listing 8.18   Indexing image vectors extracted from VAE

```
VariationalAutoencoder vae = model.getLayer(0);

trainingSet.reset();
List<float[]> featureList = new LinkedList<>();
while (trainingSet.hasNext()) {
  DataSet batch = trainingSet.next(batchSize);
  for (int k = 0; k < batchSize; k++) {
    DataSet dataSet = batch.get(k);
    INDArray labels = dataSet.getLabels();
    String label = cifarLabels.get(labels.argMax(1)
        .maxNumber().intValue());

    INDArray latentSpaceValues = vae.activate(dataSet
        .getFeatures(), false, LayerWorkspaceMgr
        .noWorkspaces());
    float[] aFloat = latentSpaceValues.data().asFloat();
    Document doc = new Document();
    doc.add(new FloatPoint("features", aFloat));
    doc.add(new TextField("label", label, Field.Store.YES));
    writer.addDocument(doc);
    featureList.add(aFloat);
  }
}
writer.commit();
```

Gets the VAE to extract image vectors

Iterates through the CIFAR images

Gets the label attached to the current image

Makes the VAE perform a feed-forward pass with the current reshaped image as input

Stores the extracted features for each image into a List so you can use them later for querying

Indexes the document with its image vector and its label

With all the images indexed with their latent representation and label, you can use Lucene's `FloatPointNearestNeighbor` to perform a nearest-neighbor search. To see whether the results are good without looking at each and every query and the resulting image data, you can check if the query and each resulting image share the same label.

Listing 8.19   Querying by image using nearest-neighbor

```
DirectoryReader reader = DirectoryReader.open(writer);
IndexSearcher searcher = new IndexSearcher(reader);

Random r = new Random();
```

```
for (int counter = 0; counter < 10; counter++) {
    int idx = r.nextInt(reader.numDocs() - 1);          ⟵── Picks a random number
    Document document = reader.document(idx);           ⟵
    TopFieldDocs docs = FloatPointNearestNeighbor            Fetches a Document
        .nearest(searcher, "features", 2, featureList       with the random
        .get(idx));                                     ⟵   number as its
                                                            document identifier
    ScoreDoc[] scoreDocs = docs.scoreDocs;
    System.out.println("query image of a : " +          Performs a nearest-neighbor
        document.get("label"));                         search using the image
                                                        vector associated with the
    for (ScoreDoc sd : scoreDocs) {                     document identifier
        System.out.println("-->" + sd.doc +" : " +
            reader.document(sd.doc).getField("label")
            .stringValue());                ⟵           Prints the resulting
    }                                                   image document
    counter++;                                          identifier and label
}
```

Prints the query image label →

We expect query and result images to share the same label most of the times. You can check that in the following output:

```
query image of a : automobile
-->277 : automobile
-->1253 : automobile
query image of a : airplane
-->5250 : airplane
-->1750 : ship
query image of a : deer
-->7315 : deer
-->1261 : bird
query image of a : automobile
-->9983 : automobile
-->4239 : automobile
query image of a : airplane
-->6838 : airplane
-->4999 : airplane
```

As expected, most of the results share the label with the query. Note that you can also use the locality-sensitive hashing technique described in the previous section instead of nearest-neighbor search.

Summary

- Searching through binary content like images requires learning a representation that can capture visual semantics that can be compared across images.
- Traditional techniques for feature extraction have limits and require significant engineering effort.
- Convolutional neural networks are at the core of the recent rise of DL, because they can learn image-representation abstractions (edges, shapes, and objects) incrementally during network training.
- CNNs can be used to extract feature vectors from images that can be used to search for similar images.

- Locality-sensitive hashing techniques can be used as an alternative to the nearest-neighbor approach for image search based on feature vectors.
- Autoencoders can help extract image vectors if your images aren't labeled.

A peek at performance

This chapter covers

- Setting up DL models in production
- Optimizing performance and deployment
- Getting real-life neural search systems to work with data streams

After reading the previous eight chapters, you hopefully have gained a broad understanding of deep learning and how it can improve search. At this point, you should be ready to make the most out of DL when setting up successful search engine systems for your users. Along the way, however, you may have wondered about applying these ideas to real-world production systems:

- How are these approaches applied in practice in a production scenario?
- Will adding these DL algorithms have a serious impact on the time and space constraints of your systems?
- How big is that impact, and which parts or processes (such as searching versus indexing) will be affected?

In this chapter, I'll address these practical concerns and discuss the considerations you'll need to think about as you apply DL and neural networks to your search engine. We'll look at the performance bits when search engines and neural networks work side by side, and I'll provide some example-driven suggestions for applying these DL techniques in practice.

The previous chapters explored several different search problems DL can help solve. If you think about the application of the word2vec model for synonym expansion (chapter 2) or recurrent neural networks to expand queries (chapter 3), you may recall that data flows in and out of neural networks and in and out of search engines. We can consider a search engine and a neural network as two separate components in a real-world software architecture. A neural network needs to be trained to predict accurate outputs. At the same time, a search engine must ingest data so that users can search for it. To use DL to produce more-effective search results, we need the neural network to be effective. These are somewhat conflicting requirements that bring up a few logistical questions:

- Should training happen before indexing?
- Or should indexing happen first?
- Can you combine those data-feeding tasks?
- How do you handle updates to the data?

We'll answer some of these questions as we look at the considerations you need to take into account when launching real-world deployments of search engines using neural networks.

9.1   *Performance and the promises of deep learning*

New DL architectures are published continuously to solve more and more complex tasks. We've looked at some of them in this book: for example, generating text (chapters 3 and 4), translating text from one language into another (chapter 7), classifying and representing images based on their contents (chapter 8), and more. Not just entire models, but also new types of activation functions, cost functions, backpropagation algorithm optimizations, weight-initialization schemes, and others are constantly being researched and published.

The DL concepts introduced in this book apply to recent-past, current, and (hopefully) newer neural network architectures. If you're responsible for a search engine infrastructure, you'll probably look for approaches that researchers have demonstrated work best for a specific task (also known as *state of the art*). For example, think about machine translation or image search: at the time of writing, the state of the art for machine translation is represented by sequence-to-sequence models, such as encoder-decoder networks with attention.[1] So you'd want to implement those state-of-the-art models, and you'd expect them to give you good results like those you can read about in the related research papers. In those cases, the first challenge is to reproduce

---

[1] See this recent research that even discards RNNs: Ashish Vaswani et al., "Attention Is All You Need," http://mng.bz/nQZK.

the model described in the paper and then to make it work effectively on your data and infrastructure. To do so,

- The neural network must provide accurate results.
- The neural network must provide results quickly.
- The software and hardware must be adequate for the computational load, in terms of time and space (and, remember, training is costly).

In the next section, we'll run through the entire process of implementing a neural network model to solve a specific task and see what common steps you may have to take along the way to solve these challenges.

9.1.1 *From model design to production*

In chapter 8, you saw convolutional neural networks in action, classifying images. Once training was finished, you used the network to extract feature vectors to be indexed and searched by the search engine. But we didn't consider the accuracy of the neural network classifications. Let's now track some numbers for accuracy, training, and prediction times on the road to building a good neural network model to use in conjunction with a search engine. We'll return to the CIFAR dataset we used in chapter 8 and see how to gradually adjust the neural network model to improve accuracy while keeping reasonable training timings; we'll go through it step by step, as you would in your own project.

Indexing is usually costly with real-world data. CIFAR is only a few tens of thousands of images, but many live deployments have to index hundreds of thousands, millions, or billions of images or documents. If you index 100 million images with their feature vectors, you don't want to have to repeat the process as you might need to if the feature vectors don't accurately reflect the image contents, so the user experience isn't great. So you'll usually run a few experiments and evaluations before indexing feature vectors.

Let's start with a convolutional neural network (CNN) similar to one of the first CNN-based architectures that achieved good results for categorizing images: the LeNet architecture (http://yann.lecun.com/exdb/lenet). This is a simple CNN similar to the one you set up in chapter 8, but with slightly different configuration parameters for convolution depth, receptive-field size, stride, and dense-layer dimensionality (see figure 9.1).

The model contains two sequences of convolutional layers followed by a max pooling layer and a fully connected layer. The filters are size 5×5, the first convolutional layer's depth is 28, and the second convolutional layer's depth is 10. The dense layer is size 500. The max pooling layers have `stride` equal to 2.

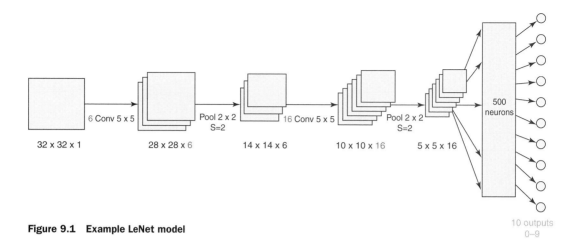

Figure 9.1   Example LeNet model

Listing 9.1   LeNet type of model

```
MultiLayerConfiguration conf = new NeuralNetConfiguration.Builder()
    .list()
    .layer(0, new ConvolutionLayer.Builder(new int[]{5, 5}, new int[]{1, 1}
        , new int[]{0, 0}).convolutionMode(ConvolutionMode.Same)
        .nIn(3).nOut(28).activation(Activation.RELU).build())
    .layer(1, new SubsamplingLayer.Builder(PoolingType.MAX,
        new int[]{2,2}).build())
    .layer(2, new ConvolutionLayer.Builder(new int[]{5,5}, new int[] {1,1},
        new int[] {0,0}).convolutionMode(ConvolutionMode.Same)
        .nOut(10).activation(Activation.RELU).build())
    .layer(3, new SubsamplingLayer.Builder(PoolingType.MAX,
        new int[]{2,2}).build())
    .layer(4, new DenseLayer.Builder().nOut(500).build())
    .layer(5, new OutputLayer.Builder(LossFunctions.LossFunction
        .NEGATIVELOGLIKELIHOOD)
        .nOut(numLabels).activation(Activation.SOFTMAX).build())
    .backprop(true)
    .pretrain(false)
    .setInputType(InputType.convolutional(height, width, channels))
    .build();
```

This model is old, so you shouldn't expect it to perform too well, but it's a good practice to start with a small model and see how far it gets.

You'll train over 2,000 examples from the CIFAR dataset at first, to get some quick feedback about how good the model parameters are. If the model begins to diverge too soon, you can avoid loading huge training sets before discovering it.

Listing 9.2   Training over 2,000 samples from CIFAR

```
int height = 32;
int width = 32;
int channels = 3;
```

```
int numSamples = 2000;
int batchSize = 100;
boolean preProcessCifar = false;
CifarDataSetIterator dsi = new CifarDataSetIterator(batchSize, numSamples,
    new int[] {height, width, channels}, preProcessCifar, true);

MultiLayerNetwork model = new MultiLayerNetwork(conf);
model.init();
for (int i = 0; i < epochs; ++i) {
  model.fit(dsi);
}
```

You use only 2,000 random samples from the CIFAR dataset.

MODEL EVALUATION

To monitor how well the neural network learns to categorize the images, you'll monitor the training process with the DL4J UI. In the best possible case, you'd see the score steadily decrease towards 0, but in this case, as shown in figure 9.2, it decreases very slowly without ever reaching a point close to 0. Recall that the score is a measure of the amount of error the neural network commits when trying to predict the classes for each input image. So, with these stats, you don't expect it to perform very well.

To evaluate the accuracy of predictions for a machine learning model, it's always a good practice to separate a collection of data used for training (the training set) from a collection of data to be used for testing the quality of a model (the test set). During training, the model may *overfit* the data and therefore give good accuracy on the training set while being unable to generalize well over slightly different data, so using a test set helps in finding out how well a model can work on data that it hasn't previously trained with.

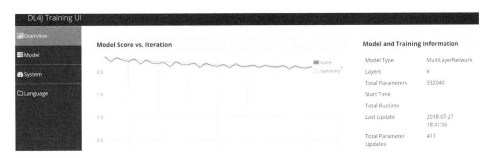

Figure 9.2   LeNet training

A separate iterator over a different set of images can be created and passed to DL4J tools for evaluation.

Listing 9.3   Model evaluation with DL4J

```
CifarDataSetIterator cifarEvaluationData = new
    CifarDataSetIterator(batchSize, 1000, new int[] {
    height, width, channels}, preProcessCifar, false);
```

Creates a test set iterator

```
Evaluation eval = new Evaluation(cifarEval
    .getLabels());

while(cifarEvaluationData.hasNext()) {

  DataSet testDS = cifarEvaluationData.next(
    batchSize);

  INDArray output = model.output(testDS
    .getFeatureMatrix());

  eval.eval(testDS.getLabels(), output);
}
System.out.println(eval.stats());
```

Instantiates the DL4J
evaluation tool

Iterates over the
test dataset

Fetches the next mini-batch of data
(100 examples, in this case)

Performs prediction
over the current batch

Performs evaluation using the
actual output and the CIFAR
output labels

Prints the statistics on
the standard output

The evaluation stats include metrics like accuracy, precision, recall F1 score, and confusion matrix (the *F1 score* is a measure whose value ranges between 0 and 1 and which takes into account precision and recall):

```
=======================Evaluation Metrics=======================
 # of classes:    10
 Accuracy:        0.2310
 Precision:       0.2207
 Recall:          0.2255
 F1 Score:        0.2133
Precision, recall & F1: macro-averaged (equally weighted avg. of 10 classes)

=======================Confusion Matrix=======================
   0  1  2  3  4  5  6  7  8  9
\\------------------------------
 31  9  4 10  2  3  6  3 26  9 | 0 = airplane
  6 19  0  7  6  6  4  0 16 25 | 1 = automobile
 18  8  6 14  8  6 15  4 12  9 | 2 = bird
 11 14  1 28 14  5  8  6  3 13 | 3 = cat
  8  5  3 14 15  5 15  7  5 13 | 4 = deer
  9  5  5 21 18  8  8  1  3  8 | 5 = dog
  8  9  7 12 21  4 29  7  5 10 | 6 = frog
 11 11  8 13  8  4  6 10 11 20 | 7 = horse
 18  6  1  9  4  1  2  2 47 16 | 8 = ship
 12 12  2  8  6  3  2  3 23 38 | 9 = truck
```

In the confusion matrix, you can see that for the class airplane in the first row, 31 samples have been correctly assigned to the airplane class, but about the same number of predictions (26) were assigned the incorrect class ship for an airplane image. Ideally, a confusion matrix will contain high values on the right diagonal and low values everywhere else.

Changing the numSamples value to 5000 and performing training and evaluation again, you expect better results:

```
=======================Evaluation Metrics=======================
 # of classes:    10
 Accuracy:        0.3100
 Precision:       0.3017
```

```
Recall:              0.3061
F1 Score:            0.3010
Precision, recall & F1: macro-averaged (equally weighted avg. of 10 classes)

========================Confusion Matrix========================
    0   1   2   3   4   5   6   7   8   9
\\------------------------------
   38   2   6   3   5   1   1   9  25  13 | 0 = airplane
    4  34   3   2   4   4   6   4  14  14 | 1 = automobile
   15   4  12   7  15   9  16   8  10   4 | 2 = bird
    7   4   4  26  16  11  15  13   1   6 | 3 = cat
    4   2  10   9  24   7  13   5   8   8 | 4 = deer
    7   5   5  19   9  14  11   7   3   6 | 5 = dog
    3   8  10   9  22   5  40  12   1   2 | 6 = frog
    4   8   6  13  12   2   9  29   2  17 | 7 = horse
   17   5   2   8   4   2   0   4  51  13 | 8 = ship
    7  13   3   4   4   3   2  10  21  42 | 9 = truck
```

The F1 score went up by 9% (0.30 versus 0.21), which is a big step forward, but getting good results only about 30% of the time wouldn't be appropriate in production.

You may recall that neural network training uses the backpropagation algorithm (eventually with variations, depending on the specific architecture, such as backpropagation through time for recurrent neural networks). The backpropagation algorithm aims to reduce the prediction error committed by the network by adjusting the weights so that the overall error rate decreases. At some point, the algorithm will find a set of weights (such as the weights attached to connections between neurons in different layers) with the lowest possible error, but this may take a long time, depending on features of the data used for training:

- *Diversity in training examples*—Some text is written in formal language, and other text is written in slang. Or some images are pictures taken during daylight, and others were taken at night.
- *Noise in the training examples*—Some text has typos or grammatical errors. Or some images are of poor quality or contain watermarks or other types of noise that makes training more difficult.

The ability of neural network training to converge to a good set of weights also depends a great deal on the tuning parameters, such as the *learning rate*. I already mentioned this, but it's worth repeating that this is a fundamental aspect to get right. A learning rate that's too high will make training fail, and a learning rate that's too low will make training take too long to converge to a good set of weights.

Figure 9.3 shows the training loss of the same neural network but with different learning rates. You can clearly see that both learning rates converge over time to the same set of weights. Learning begins at time t0; let's consider what will happen if you stop training at time t1 or t2. If you stop training after a small number of iterations (before time t1), you'll exclude the high learning rate, because it will make the loss increase instead of decrease. If you stop training at time t2, you'll instead discard the low learning rate, because it will keep the same score as the high learning rate, or

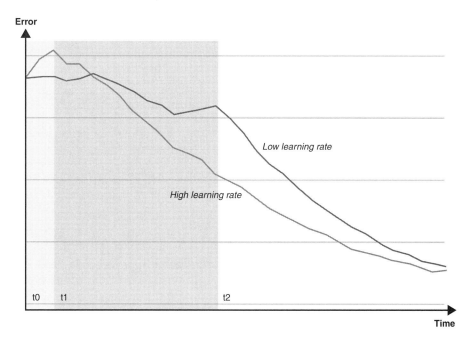

Figure 9.3   Loss plotted for the same neural networks but trained with different learning rates

begin to increase. It's therefore a good idea to come up with a few possible architectures with reasonable parameter settings and run some experiments.

In DL4J `Updater` implementations, you can set the learning rate for your neural network.

Listing 9.4   Setting the learning rate

```
MultiLayerConfiguration conf = new NeuralNetConfiguration.Builder()
    .updater(new Sgd(0.01))    ◁
    ...                            Sets the learning
    .build();                      rate to 0.01
```

ADDING MORE WEIGHTS

Using more weights to be learned is likely to cause training to take more time and resources; a common mistake is to add layers or increase the size of layers as much as possible. But adding layers can help when the network doesn't have enough training power to fit over lots of different training examples, such as when the number of weights is far less than the number of examples, and the neural network is having a hard time converging to a good set of weights (perhaps the score doesn't go below a certain value).

The code defined in the previous sections trained a relatively lightweight CNN with 5,000 examples. Let's see what happens if you make the convolutional layers deeper (depth of 96 and 256, respectively). The training time for 5,000 examples increases from 10 minutes to 1 hour, with the following evaluation stats:

```
========================Evaluation Metrics========================
# of classes:    10
Accuracy:        0.3011
Precision:       0.3211
Recall:          0.2843
F1 Score:        0.3016
```

In this case, it wasn't worth adding more power to the network.

Working with deep neural networks in production requires some experience, but it isn't magic. The number of weights to be learned is an important factor: the number of data points in the training set should always be less than the number of weights. Possible consequences of not following this rule are overfitting and difficulties in converging.

Let's do some reasoning about the data. You have tiny images of 32 × 32 pixels. CNNs learn features over time with convolutional layers while downsampling with pooling layers. Maybe it would help to give the initial convolution layer a few more weights but give the pooling layer a `stride` value of 2 instead of 1. You expect training the network to achieve slightly better results in less time:

```
========================Evaluation Metrics========================
# of classes:    10
Accuracy:        0.3170
Precision:       0.3069
Recall:          0.3297
F1 Score:        0.3316
```

Training finishes in 5 minutes instead of 7, thanks to the change to the pooling layer, and the result quality also improved. This may not seem like much, but it would make a real difference when training over the entire dataset.

TRAINING WITH MORE DATA

So far, you've performed experiments with only a few examples from the CIFAR dataset. To better understand how well the CNN model can work, you need to train it with more data.

You have more than 50,000 images in CIFAR: you should split the dataset in such a way that most of it is used for training, but many images are available to perform evaluation.

Before using the full dataset, it's important to note the time taken by training with respect to the available hardware and requirements of a production scenario. The first iteration of training for 10 epochs with 2,000 images took 3 minutes on a normal laptop; 5,000 images training for 10 epochs took 7 minutes. These are acceptable times for experiments where you want quick feedback, but training over the full dataset for several epochs may take hours—time that would be better used if you knew in advance what to change.

Now, let's run the current settings over 50,000 images for training and 10,000 for evaluation. You expect better evaluation metric results and a lower score at the end of training:

```
========================Evaluation Metrics========================
# of classes:     10
 Accuracy:         0.4263
 Precision:        0.4213
 Recall:           0.4263
 F1 Score:         0.4131
Precision, recall & F1: macro-averaged (equally weighted avg. of 10 classes)

========================Confusion Matrix========================
    0   1   2   3   4   5   6   7   8   9
\\----------------------------------------
 459  60  39  40  14  24  41  49 191  83 | 0 = airplane
  29 592   3  30   3  12  47  34  50 200 | 1 = automobile
  92  50 123  81 165  89 229  97  46  28 | 2 = bird
  19  34  40 247  48 200 216 103  19  74 | 3 = cat
  44  21  58  83 284  60 263 128  33  26 | 4 = deer
  11  22  69 189  63 337 158 100  29  22 | 5 = dog
   3  26  20  90  66  32 661  52   9  41 | 6 = frog
  24  38  27  86  72  69 107 494  18  65 | 7 = horse
 122  92  12  25   6  21  23  26 546 127 | 8 = ship
```

After training on almost the entire training set, you got a 0.41 F1 score after almost 3 hours (on a normal laptop). You can't yet be satisfied with the accuracy of the model: it would make errors 59% of the time.

In this case, it's useful to look at the loss curve, shown in figure 9.4. The curve is decreasing and might keep doing so if you had more data. Unfortunately, for this case you don't, unless you use a smaller test set.

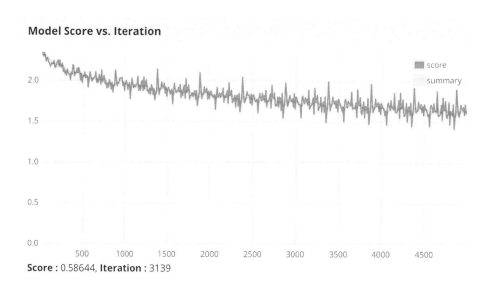

Figure 9.4   CNN full training loss graph

ADJUSTING BATCH SIZE

One thing you can look into when you have such curves is whether you're using the wrong size for the batch parameter. A *batch* or *mini-batch* is a collection of training examples that are put together and fed to the neural network as a single batched input. For example, instead of feeding one image at a time, and thus an input volume (a set of stacked matrixes) at a time, you can squash a number of input volumes together. Doing so usually has two consequences:

- Training is faster.
- Training is less prone to overfitting.

If the mini-batch parameter is set to 1, you'll see a curve that, especially in the first iterations, increases and decreases significantly. On the other hand, if you have a mini-batch that's too big, the network may not be able to learn about specific patterns and features that rarely occur in inputs.

It's possible that a flat loss curve is related to a batch size (100, in this case) that's too large for the data. To see whether something like this will make a difference, it's useful to perform quick tests on small portions of the dataset. The changes in settings can be proven later with full-dataset training if you get encouraging results. So let's set the batch parameter to 48, train on 5,000 examples, and perform evaluation on 1,000 images. You expect a less smooth curve, along with lower loss, and hope for better accuracy:

```
========================Evaluation Metrics========================
# of classes:     10
Accuracy:         0.3274
Precision:        0.3403
Recall:           0.3324
F1 Score:         0.3218
```

As you can see in these results and in figure 9.5, reducing the batch size helped: a loss close to the minimum was reached much faster than with the batch size set to 100. But training took more time: 9 minutes instead of the previous time of 7 minutes. A difference of 2 minutes might be noticed on a larger scale, but it's acceptable if the training time pays off with a significantly better F1 score.

The F1 score improved from 0.30 to 0.32. So reducing the batch size seems to be a good idea that you need to prove with a full training. We won't compare the F1 score of a small training set like this with the F1 score reached when training over 50,000 images, because that wouldn't be fair and might mislead (and frustrate) our efforts. But can you do better with an even smaller batch size? Let's set the batch size to 24 and see:

```
========================Evaluation Metrics========================
# of classes:     10
Accuracy:         0.3601
Precision:        0.3512
Recall:           0.3551
F1 Score:         0.3340
```

Model Score vs. Iteration

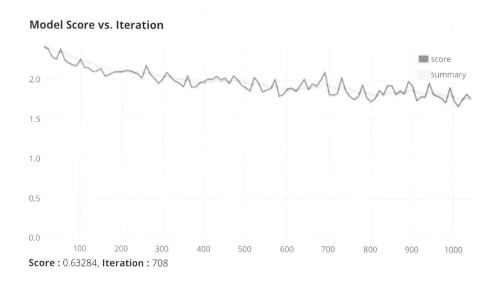

Score : 0.63284, **Iteration :** 708

Figure 9.5   Training with a batch size of 48

As you can see in figure 9.6, the curve is much sharper, and the loss is close to that with `batch` set to 48. The F1 score is higher (0.33), but training took 13 minutes instead of 9.

Model Score vs. Iteration

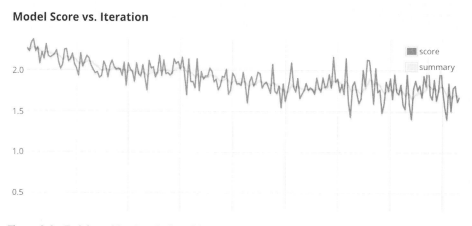

Figure 9.6   Training with a batch size of 24

EVALUATE AND ITERATE

At this point, you have to make a decision: can you afford more costly training in terms of time and computational resources (which may mean more money—for example, if you're running training in production over cloud services) to get better numbers? A good practice is to save the different models you generate together with their evaluation metrics and training times so that you can pick them up in a later stage when you need to make decisions.

With a smaller batch size, the neural network should be able to better handle more-diverse inputs, but the curve is sharper. Training the latest model with 50,000 examples gave the following evaluation results after 5 hours of training on a laptop:

```
=======================Evaluation Metrics=======================
# of classes:    10
Accuracy:        0.5301
Precision:       0.5213
Recall:          0.5095
F1 Score:        0.5153
```

The F1 score of 0.41 improved by 10% to reach a not-bad 0.51. But this still isn't something you'd ship to end users. With such a number, if users looked for images of a deer, they might get only five deer—the remaining images would show cats, dogs, or even trucks and ships!

You tried using more deep convolutional layers, but it didn't help. You've seen that accuracy improves with the amount of data used. Batch size has proved to be an important parameter to get right even during the prototyping phase, to get better results, but changes in batch size have an effect on the training time.

But there are still a number of factors to consider:

- Train for more epochs.
- Check the weights and bias initialization.
- Look into *regularization* options.
- Change the way the neural network updates its weights during backpropagation (the *updater* algorithm).
- Determine whether adding layers would help in this case.

Let's look at all of these options.

EPOCHS

The example currently uses 10 epochs, so the neural network sees the same input batches 10 times. The rationale is that the network should be able to get the right weights for those inputs with a higher probability if it "sees" them multiple times. Low numbers like 5, 10, and 30 are common during the development phase when the network is being designed, but you may change this value when training your final model. If you increase the number of epochs but don't see any significant improvement, the network probably can't do more with the current setup for that data; in that case, you need to change something else.

Changing the number of epochs from 10 to 20 in this case gives the following results:

```
=======================Evaluation Metrics=======================
# of classes:    10
Accuracy:        0.3700
Precision:       0.3710
Recall:          0.3646
F1 Score:        0.3565
```

Training took 28 minutes; see figure 9.7.

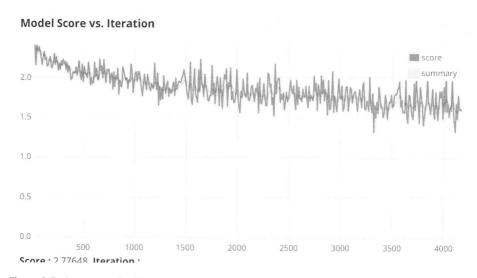

Model Score vs. Iteration

Figure 9.7   Loss curve for 20 epochs

WEIGHT INITIALIZATION

Think about the neural network before it receives any input. All the neurons have activation functions and connections. As the network begins to receive inputs and backpropagates output error, it starts to change the weights attached to each connection. A surprisingly effective change you can make to your neural network is the way those weights are initialized. A lot of research has shown that weight initialization has a significant impact on the effectiveness of training.[2]

Simple things you can do to initialize weights are to set them all to zero or set them to random numbers. A few chapters back, you saw how the learning algorithm

2   See Xavier Glorot and Yoshua Bengio, "Understanding the Difficulty of Training Deep Feedforward Neural Networks," in *Proceedings of the 13th International Conference on Artificial Intelligence and Statistics (AISTATS)* (2010, Chia Laguna Resort, Sardinia, Italy), http://mng.bz/vNZM; and Kaiming He et al., "Delving Deep into Rectifiers: Surpassing Human-Level Performance on ImageNet Classification," https://arxiv.org/abs/1502.01852.

(backpropagation) makes the network weights change: you can think of this visually as moving a point on an error surface (see figure 9.8). A point on such a surface represents a set of weights, and the minimum-height point represents the point where the weights make the network commit the least possible error.

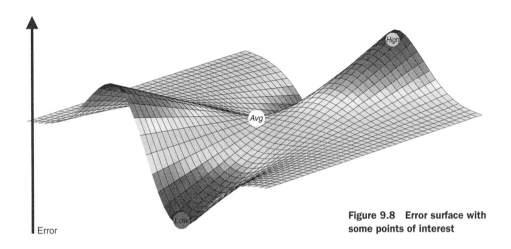

Figure 9.8 Error surface with some points of interest

The highest point in the image represents a set of weights with a high error, the point in the middle represents a set of weights with an average error, and the lowest point represents the point with the lowest possible error. The backpropagation algorithm will hopefully make the network weights move from their starting position to the point marked at the bottom. Now think about the weight initialization: it will be responsible for setting the starting point for the algorithm when looking for the best set of weights. With a weight initialization of 0, the network weights may be at the white point in the center: not bad, and not good. With a random initialization, you may get lucky and place the weights near the bottom point (but it's unlikely) or set the weights somewhere far from there, such as the point marked at the top. This starting position influences the ability of backpropagation to ever reach the bottom point or may at least make the process longer and more difficult. Thus, good initialization for the neural network's weights is crucial for successful training.

A good, commonly used weight initialization is called *Xavier initialization*. Basically, it initializes the weights of the neural network by drawing them from a distribution with zero mean and a specific variance for each neuron. The initial weight depends on the number of neurons with outgoing connections to that specific neuron. You can set this in DL4J in a specific layer with the following code:

```
.layer(2, new ConvolutionLayer.Builder(new int[]{5,5}, new int[] {1,1}, new
    int[] {0,0})
  .convolutionMode(ConvolutionMode.Same)
  .nOut(10)
  .weightInit(WeightInit.XAVIER_UNIFORM)     ⟵   Initializes the weights of the given
  .activation(Activation.RELU)                    layer using Xavier distribution
```

REGULARIZATION

Earlier, when the number of inputs in a single batch was reduced, we noticed the loss curve becoming less smooth. This is because, with fewer batches, the learning algorithm is more prone to overfitting (see figure 9.9).

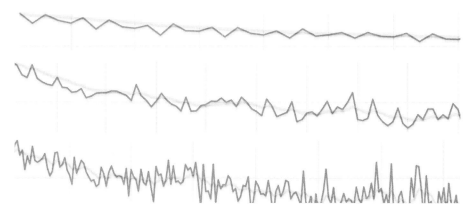

Figure 9.9 Sharpening loss curve with smaller batch sizes

It's often useful to introduce regularization methods in your neural network training algorithm. This helps because of the small batch size, but that's a good practice in general. The amount of regularization to use depends on the use case:

```
MultiLayerConfiguration conf = new NeuralNetConfiguration.Builder()
    .gradientNormalization(GradientNormalization.RenormalizeL2PerLayer)
    .l1(1.0e-4d).l2(5.0e-4d)
```

With regularization and weight initializations in place, let's perform another round of training for 10 epochs on 5,000 images. Here are the final results:

```
=======================Evaluation Metrics=======================
# of classes:    10
Accuracy:        0.4454
Precision:       0.4602
Recall:          0.4417
F1 Score:        0.4438
```

Training took 16 minutes, but as you can see in figure 9.10, the loss is decreasing much more quickly and to a lower value than with previous settings. As expected, the F1 score is high with relatively few training examples.

Having noticed improvements with a greater number of epochs, let's increase it to 20, as we did earlier:

```
=======================Evaluation Metrics=======================
# of classes:    10
Accuracy:        0.4435
Precision:       0.4624
Recall:          0.4395
F1 Score:        0.4411
```

Model Score vs. Iteration

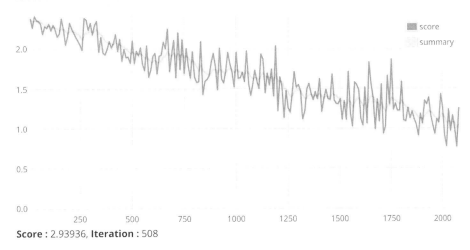

Score : 2.93936, **Iteration** : 508

Figure 9.10 Optimum tuning

Although training time increases to 19 minutes, the curve looks more or less similar, and, surprisingly, the F1 score remains unchanged (see figure 9.11). There are a few possible reasons for that: the first is that you may need more data.

Model Score vs. Iteration

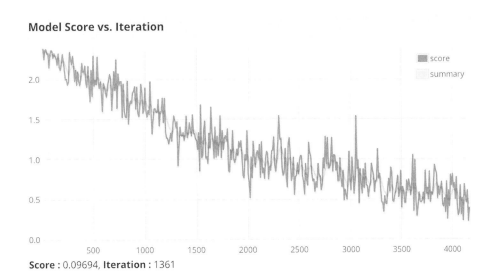

Score : 0.09694, **Iteration** : 1361

Figure 9.11 Optimum tuning for 20 epochs

Let's evaluate the accuracy of the last settings using the entire dataset of 50,000 images (see figure 9.12):

```
========================Evaluation Metrics========================
# of classes:    10
Accuracy:        0.5998
Precision:       0.6213
Recall:          0.5998
F1 Score:        0.5933
```

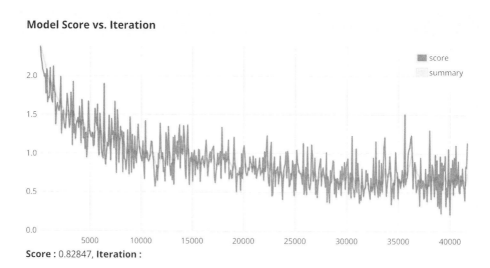

Score : 0.82847, Iteration :

Figure 9.12   Training loss curve for the entire dataset

Reaching good numbers isn't always easy and may require several iterations of the process just described. Looking at recent research is always a good idea to find out whether better solutions exist for various aspects of neural networks. To some extent, tuning a neural network can seem like an art; experience helps, but getting to know the math and dynamics of learning is key for coming up with effective models and settings.

9.2   *Indexes and neurons working together*

We just went through an end-to-end process to set up and tweak a deep neural network to achieve the best results in terms of accuracy. We also briefly noted the time required to train the entire network. With that set, only half the problem is solved. The goal is to use DL models in the context of search to provide more-meaningful search results to end users. Now, the question is how to use and update those DL models together with search engines.

Assume for a moment that you have a pretrained model that perfectly fits the data to be indexed. You index text documents and want to use, for example, a pretrained seq2seq model to extract thought vectors to be used in the ranking function by the search engine. A straightforward solution is to establish a document-indexing pipeline where the document text is first sent to the seq2seq model, and then the corresponding thought vector is extracted and indexed together with the document text into the search engine. You can see in figure 9.13 that the actions and responsibilities of the neural network and the search engine are heavily interleaved.

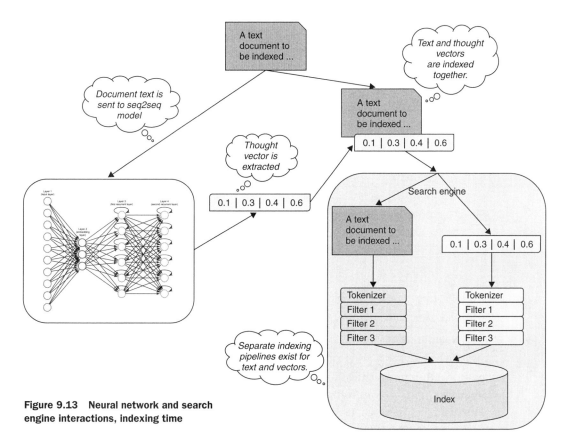

Figure 9.13   Neural network and search engine interactions, indexing time

At search time, the seq2seq model is again used to extract thought vectors from the query (see figure 9.14). The ranking function then performs scoring using the query and document thought vectors (previously stored in the index).

Looking at these graphs, you may think everything seems reasonable. But the neural network may introduce overhead for both indexing and search:

- *Neural network prediction time*—How long does the neural network take to extract thought vectors for documents at indexing time? How long does the neural network take to extract thought vectors for queries at search time?
- *Search engine index size*—How much space do generated embeddings take in addition to storage space used by text documents?

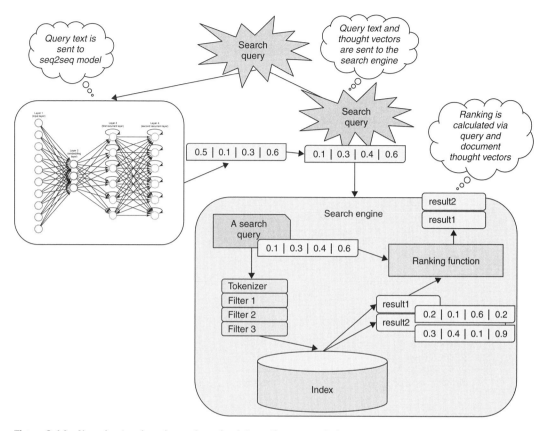

Figure 9.14   Neural network and search engine interactions, search time

In general, the most critical aspect for performance is the query/search phase. You can't expect users to wait for seconds just because your ranking function returns better results. In most cases, users won't ever know what's behind the search box—they just expect it to be fast and reliable, and to give good results.

The previous section addressed the accuracy of results while noting the training times. You also need to track the time taken by the network to compute a full feed-forward pass from the input to the layer from which you get the network output.

In the case of an encoder-decoder network, the feed-forward pass of the encoder side of the network only needs to extract thought vectors. The decoder side of the network is only used if you also want to use the input text to perform training using a target output (if you have one).

The overhead in indexing must also be taken into account. In a "static" scenario where you ingest a set of documents, even if it's huge, that may not be important, because you can accept an aggregate overhead of 1 or 2 hours if it only happens once. But re-indexing or high-volume concurrent indexing may be problematic. *Re-indexing* means indexing the entire corpus of documents in the search engine again from scratch. This is usually done due to a change in the configuration of text analysis pipelines or because a document processor is added to extract more metadata.

For example, let's take a simple search engine based on Lucene with no query-expansion capability. To use the word2vec model to expand synonyms at indexing time, you need to take all the existing documents and re-index them so the resulting inverted index also contains the words/synonyms extracted by word2vec. The bigger the index, the greater the impact of re-indexing will be.

Concurrency is another aspect: can the neural network deal with concurrent inputs? This is an implementation detail and may depend on the specific technology used to implement your model, but it must be taken into account both at indexing time (multiple parallel indexing processes) and at search time (multiple users searching at the same time).

Embeddings, and dense vectors in general, can have many dimensions. Efficiently storing them is an open problem. In the real world, the choices may be limited by the capabilities of the search engine technology used. In Lucene, for example, dense vectors can be indexed as any of the following:

- *Binaries*—Every vector is stored like an unqualified binary, and all embedding processing is done when the binary is fetched.
- *n-dimensional points*—Every vector is stored as a point with many dimensions (one for each vector dimension). Basic geometric and nearest-neighbor queries can be performed. At the moment, Lucene can index up to 8-dimensional vectors, so you'll have to reduce higher-dimensional vectors (for example, 100-dimensional word vectors) to at most 8-dimensional vectors to index them in Lucene (like we did in chapter 8 with PCA for image feature vectors).
- *Text*—It may sound weird at first, but with an appropriate design, vectors can be indexed and searched over like text units.[3]

Other libraries like Vespa (http://vespa.ai) and search platforms like Apache Solr (https://lucene.apache.org/solr) and Elasticsearch (www.elastic.co/products/elasticsearch) may offer more or different options.

9.3 Working with streams of data

All the examples in this book use static datasets. Static datasets are great for illustrative purposes, because they make it easier to focus on a particular set of data. Also, when building a search engine, it's common to start with a set of documents (text and/or images) that you want to index. But as a search engine goes into production and begins to be used, new documents will probably need to be ingested.

Consider an application that allows users to search for popular posts from social networks on various different topics. You might start with a set of downloaded or purchased posts, but because the focus is on popular posts, you need to keep ingesting

---

[3] See Jan Rygl et al., "Semantic Vector Encoding and Similarity Search Using Fulltext Search Engines," https://arxiv.org/pdf/1706.00957.pdf.

data as trends change over time. A similar application might work on news rather than on social network posts. You can download a news corpus like the NYT Annotated Corpus (https://catalog.ldc.upenn.edu/LDC2008T19), but every day, the application must ingest many new articles so that users can search for them.

These days, it's common to use a *streaming architecture* to address incoming flows of data. In a streaming architecture, data flows in continuously from one or more sources and is transformed by functions stacked in a pipeline. Data can be transformed, aggregated, or dropped at any time and finally reaches a *sink*: the final stage of the pipeline, such as a persistence system like a database or a search engine index.

In the previous example, a streaming architecture can continuously ingest posts from social networks and index them into the search engine. Another application working with the indexed data can read the index and expose search features to end users. But you're working with neural networks, so you need to train the neural network models you want to use.

As an example scenario, let's build an application to continuously find the most relevant posts for each of a set of predefined topics; see figure 9.15. To do so, you'll use a streaming architecture to continuously do the following:

- Ingest posts from social networks (Twitter, in this case).
- Train different neural network models to extract document embeddings.
- Index text and embeddings in Lucene.
- For each ranking model and for each topic, write out the most relevant posts.

Finally, you'll quickly evaluate which of the different ranking models (neural or not) is more promising. Such an application could be used, for example, in a preproduction phase to help choose the ranking model that works best for a production application.

To set up the streaming architecture, let's use Apache Flink (http://flink.apache.org), a framework and distributed processing engine for computations over data streams. The Flink streaming pipeline will do the following:

- Stream posts from the Twitter social network (http://twitter.com) that contain certain keywords.
- Extract each tweet's text, language, user, and so on.
- Extract document embeddings using two separate models: paragraph vectors and word2vec averaged word embeddings.
- Index each tweet with its text, language, user, and document embeddings in Lucene.
- Run predefined queries on all of the indexed data using different ranking models (classic and neural).
- Write the output in a CSV file that can be analyzed at a later stage to assess the quality of the search results.

The output file will tell you how the different ranking models reacted to changing data with respect to a set of fixed queries for certain topics. This will provide valuable

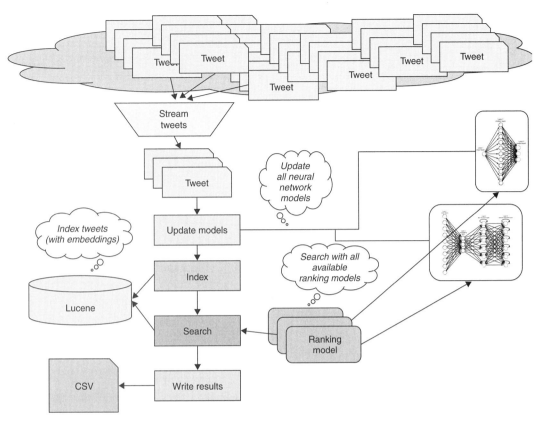

Figure 9.15 Streaming application for continuous training, indexing, and search for social media posts

information about how well the ranking models adapt to new posts. If a ranking model keeps giving the same results despite changing data, it probably isn't the best option for an application that aims to capture trending data.

First, let's define a stream of data coming from Twitter.

Listing 9.5 Defining a stream of Twitter data with Flink

Defines a Flink execution environment

Loads security credentials for accessing Twitter

```
final StreamExecutionEnvironment env =
    StreamExecutionEnvironment.getExecutionEnvironment();

Properties props = new Properties();
props.load(StreamingTweetIngestAndLearnApp.class.getResourceAsStream(
    "/twitter.properties"));
TwitterSource twitterSource = new TwitterSource(props);
```

Creates a new Flink source for Twitter data

```
String[] tags = {"neural search", "natural language processing", "lucene",
    "deep learning", "word embeddings", "manning"};
twitterSource.setCustomEndpointInitializer(new FilterEndpoint(tags));

DataStream<Tweet> twitterStream = env.addSource(twitterSource)
    .flatMap(new TweetJsonConverter());
```

Adds the per-topic filter to the Twitter source

Creates a stream over the Twitter data

Defines the topics to be used to fetch posts from Twitter (only tweets containing those keywords will be ingested)

Starts by converting raw text into a JSON format for tweets

This listing performs the required configuration to start ingesting tweets that contain the keywords/topics "neural search," "natural language processing," "lucene," "deep learning," "word embeddings," and "manning."

You'll next define a series of functions to work on the tweets. We'll also focus on implementation details regarding performance. For example, does it make sense to run the predefined queries every time a new tweet comes in? Perhaps it's better to do this when you have more data (such as 20 tweets) that can influence scoring. For this reason, you'll define a *count window* function that will pass the data to the next function only when it has received 20 tweets. In addition, updating a neural network model with just one sample usually isn't a good idea: using a larger training batch is less prone to fluctuating training error (leading to a smoother learning curve).

Listing 9.6   Manipulating the streaming data

```
Path outputPath = new Path("/path/to/data.csv");
OutputFormat<Tuple2<String, String>> format = new
    CsvOutputFormat<>(outputPath);          Output CSV file

DataStreamSink<Tuple2<String, String>> tweetSearchStream =
    twitterStream
        .countWindowAll(batchSize)
        .apply(new ModelAndIndexUpdateFunction())
        .map(new MultiRetrieverFunction())
        .map(new ResultTransformer()).countWindowAll(1)
        .apply(new TupleEvictorFunction())
        .writeUsingOutputFormat(format);
env.execute();
```

Defines a count window over the streaming data

Updates models, extracts features, and updates the index

Runs predefined queries

Transforms the output in a way that's suitable for composing a CSV file

`ModelAndIndexUpdateFunction` is responsible for updating the neural network models and for indexing the documents in Lucene. In theory, you can split it into many tiny functions; but for the sake of readability, it's easier to split the ingesting and searching processes into only two functions. You can theoretically use as many neural ranking models as you want; this example uses the ones defined in chapters 5 and 6, using word2vec and paragraph vectors, respectively, to influence ranking.

After ingesting each tweet, both paragraph vectors and word2vec models are used to generate two separate embeddings. The vectors are indexed together with the tweet text and used by the `ParagraphVectorsSimilarity` and `WordEmbeddingsSimilarity` classes at retrieval time.

Listing 9.7 Function for updating the model and indexing

```
public class ModelAndIndexUpdateFunction implements AllWindowFunction<Tweet,
    Long, GlobalWindow> {

  @Override
  public void apply(GlobalWindow globalWindow, Iterable<Tweet> iterable,
    Collector<Long> collector) throws Exception {
    ParagraphVectors paragraphVectors = Utils.fetchVectors();
    CustomWriter writer = new CustomWriter();
    for (Tweet tweet : iterable) {              ⊲──── Iterates over the
      Document document = new Document();              current batch of tweets
      document.add(new TextField("text", tweet.getText(),
        Field.Store.YES));          ⊲──── Creates a Lucene
                                           document for the
                                           current tweet's text
      INDArray paragraphVector =
        paragraphVectors.inferVector(tweet.getText());   ⊲──── Infers the paragraph
      document.add(new BinaryDocValuesField(                   vector, and updates
        "pv", new BytesRef(paragraphVector.data().asBytes())));   the model
                                                         ◁ Indexes the
      INDArray averageWordVectors =                        paragraph
        averageWordVectors(word2Vec.getTokenizerFactory()   vector
        .create(tweet.getText()).getTokens(), word2Vec.lookupTable());  ⊲
      document.add(new BinaryDocValuesField(
        "wv", new BytesRef(averageWordVectors.data().asBytes())));
                                                         ◁ Indexes the
      ...                                                  averaged
                                                           word
      writer.addDocument(document);   ⊲── Indexes the document   vector

    }
    long commit = writer.commit();   ⊲── Commits all the
                                          tweets to Lucene
    writer.close();   ⊲── Closes the IndexWriter
                           (releasing resources)
    collector.collect(commit);   ⊲──
  }                                    Passes the commit identifier to the
}                                      next function (this can be used to
                                       track changes to the index over time)
```

Annotations:
- Infers the paragraph vector, and updates the model
- Infers a document vector from word2vec, and updates the model

`MultiRetrieverFunction` contains some basic Lucene search code to run the fixed queries (such as "deep learning search") over the entire index with different ranking functions. First, it sets up `IndexSearchers`, each of which uses a different Lucene `Similarity`.

IndexSearchers with different Similarities are kept in this Map.

Creates an IndexSearcher for the ClassicSimilarity (TF-IDF)

Sets the ClassicSimilarity in the IndexSearcher

```
Map<String, IndexSearcher> searchers = new HashMap<>();

IndexSearcher classic = new IndexSearcher(...);
classic.setSimilarity(new ClassicSimilarity());
searchers.put("classic", classic);

IndexSearcher bm25 = new IndexSearcher(...);
searchers.put("bm25", bm25);

IndexSearcher pv = new IndexSearcher(...);
pv.setSimilarity(new ParagraphVectorsSimilarity(
   paragraphVectors, fieldName));
searchers.put("document embedding ranking", pv);

IndexSearcher lmd = new IndexSearcher(...);
lmd.setSimilarity(new LMDirichletSimilarity());
searchers.put("language model dirichlet", lmd);

IndexSearcher wv = new IndexSearcher(...);
pv.setSimilarity(new WordEmbeddingsSimilarity(
   word2Vec, fieldName, WordEmbeddingsSimilarity.Smoothing.TF_IDF));
searchers.put("average word embedding ranking", wv);
```

Puts the IndexSearcher in the Map

Creates an IndexSearcher for BM25Similarity (Lucene's default)

Creates an IndexSearcher for ParagraphVectorsSimilarity

Creates an IndexSearcher for LMDirichletSimilarity

Creates an IndexSearcher for WordEmbeddingsSimilarity

You can add as many ranking models as you want. Next, you iterate over the available `IndexSearchers` and execute the same query for each of them. Finally, the results are written into a CSV file.

The output aggregated in the CSV file during an execution of `MultiRetriever-Function` contains a line for each ranking model. Each line contains the name of the model first (`classic`, `bm25`, `average wv ranking`, `paragraph vectors ranking`, and so on), followed by a comma and the text of the first search result returned with that ranking model. Over time, you'll get a huge CSV file containing the output of the same query for all the different ranking models.

Let's look at the results of two consecutive executions (manually tagged with `<iteration-1>` and `<iteration-2>` for the sake of better readability):

```
...
...<iteration-1>
...
classic,Amazing what neural networks can do.
// Computational Protein Design with Deep Learning Neural Networks
language model dirichlet,Amazing what neural networks can do.
// Computational Protein Design with Deep Learning Neural Networks
bm25,Amazing what neural networks can do.
// Computational Protein Design with Deep Learning Neural Networks
average wv ranking,Amazing what neural networks can do.
// Computational Protein Design with Deep Learning Neural Networks
```

```
paragraph vectors ranking,Amazing what neural networks can do.
// Computational Protein Design with Deep Learning Neural Networks
...
...<iteration-2>
...
classic,Amazing what neural networks can do.
// Computational Protein Design with Deep Learning Neural Networks
language model dirichlet,Amazing what neural networks can do.
// Computational Protein Design with Deep Learning Neural Networks
bm25,Amazing what neural networks can do.
// Computational Protein Design with Deep Learning Neural Networks
average wv ranking,The Connection Between Text Mining and Deep Learning
paragraph vectors ranking,All-optical machine learning using diffractive
deep neural networks:
...
```

Notice that the non-neural ranking models didn't change their top search result, whereas those relying on embeddings adapted immediately to the new data: this is the kind of capability for which neural ranking models can be useful. Streaming architectures can keep up with high loads of data to be indexed into a search engine, evaluate best models, and carefully orchestrate how neural networks and search engines can best work together.

Summary

- Training deep learning models isn't always straightforward; tuning and adjustments for real-world scenarios are often needed.
- Search engines and neural networks are often two different systems that interact both at indexing and search time. It's essential to monitor their performance in order to keep the overall user experience good in terms of response times.
- Real-world deployments, like the common streaming scenario, must account for load and concurrency and evaluate quality, to achieve the best possible search solution.

Looking forward

We started this book by wondering whether it's possible to use deep neural networks as smart assistants to help provide better search tools. Over the course of the chapters, we've touched on several aspects of common search engines where DL has significant potential to help users find what they're looking for.

I hope you've become more and more interested in this topic as we've looked at increasingly complex subjects and algorithms. This book has given you some tools and practical advice that you can use immediately; hopefully, it has also inspired you to see what can be done better and what issues remain unsolved, and to want to dive in. While I was writing this book, many new DL papers were published, including some related to search. New activation functions have been determined to be useful, and new models have been proposed with promising results. I encourage you not to stop here and to keep thinking about what you and your users need and how to get there creatively.

We're just beginning to scratch the surface of applying DL to information retrieval. You've learned about the foundations of neural search and are now ready to learn and do more by yourself. Have fun!

index

RELATED MANNING TITLES

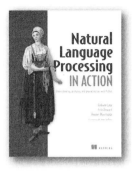

Natural Language Processing in Action
Understanding, analyzing, and generating text
with Python

by Hobson Lane, Cole Howard, Hannes Hapke

> ISBN: 9781617294631
> 544 pages, $49.99
> March 2019

Deep Learning with Python

by François Chollet

> ISBN: 9781617294433
> 384 pages, $49.99
> November 2017

Relevant Search
With applications for Solr and Elasticsearch

by Doug Turnbull and John Berryman

> ISBN: 9781617292774
> 360 pages, $44.99
> June 2016

Solr in Action

by Trey Grainger and Timothy Potter

> ISBN: 9781617291029
> 664 pages, $49.99
> March 2014

For ordering information go to www.manning.com